Lest we forget

Beckenham & the Great War.

Pat Manning and Ian Muir

The annual fair at the memorial 1923

Authors
online

An Authors OnLine Book

Pat Manning pickpatspage@gmail.com
Ian Muir www.beckenhamhistory.co.uk

British Library Cataloguing Publication Data.
A catalogue record for this book is available from the British Library

ISBN 978-0-7552-0746-6

Authors OnLine Ltd
19 The Cinques
Gamlingay, Sandy
Bedfordshire SG19 3NU
England

This book is also available in e-book format, details of which are available at
www.authorsonline.co.uk

Acknowledgements

Cover painted by Beckenham artist Tim Feltham www.timfelthamart.com/Galleries.html

Sincere thanks for help and advice from Arthur Holden and other staff of the Local Studies Dept Bromley Library, the Rev Vince and Mrs Short of St Paul's Church, Beckenham, Ellen Barbet, Roy Hanscombe, Irene Palmer, Cliff Watkins.

Our special thanks for the meticulous proofreading by Andrea Billen.

Pictures provided by the following:
Beckenham Journal BJ
Gerald and the late Phyllis Crease GC
Leon DeGrote's grandson LD
Michele Deporter MD
Florence Neville Eden and Peter Wiseman who owns her album FE
Mary Feltham MF
Vernon Finch VF
Roy Hanscombe RH
Mary Hardcastle MH
Denis Manger DM
Ian Muir IM
Colin Watts CW
Cliff Watkins CWk

References

Extensive use of the Beckenham Journal from 1914 to 1921, the Beckenham Street Directories and the Bromley archives.
The local memorial records compiled by Paul Rason.

Introduction

As a child born in the shadows of WW2 in the 50s who woke up in the 60s I never came to terms with the human tragedy of war. There was physical evidence of war all around, what with bomb sites, prefabs and even air-raid shelters in back gardens being utilised as garden sheds. War was about loud bangs and heroes that were depicted in old black and white TV films because in those days tragedy would never sell a film.

At junior school we were taught the basics of WW1 and WW2 but seemed to concentrate more on the Battle of Hastings back in 1066. I was never to realise the full horror of war till much later. At senior school some of our teachers were war veterans and I can recall one maths teacher who seemed to delight in telling us about the war so we used to start off the topic to avoid the entire maths lesson. Fellow classmates would use old gas mask bags to carry around their schoolbooks and many a pupil would wear a long blue greatcoat that had previously been worn by a member of the RAF. Ex-military uniforms were all the rage with us kids. Never once did anyone think about those families who lost lives in the wars.

I can recall many a time being told off by an adult who would inform me that he had fought for me in the war; that statement never registered, after all he was just an old fogey to us kids. I had uncles who had been in active service during WW2; they did not talk about the war nor did I ask them about it.

Then all of a sudden we were witnessing war coming into the living room via our colour TV sets and films at the cinema had taken their gloves off, it was becoming real. The 'if Hitler had won the war' questions were asked.

In more recent years Britain has been involved in yet more wars and I have seen innocent people killed and maimed. We see, and our children see, the march pasts and the repatriation of soldiers with the families of those that have fallen and I have grown to understand the human tragedy of war.

I am now by my childhood ideals approaching old fogey status and many of those who fought for me in the war sadly are no longer with us, so I cannot thank them. All I can do is remember them. Lest I forget.

Ian Muir

Without the information gained from the Beckenham Journal (BJ) between 1914 and 1921, this book would not exist. A comment in the BJ of 14/10/1916 reads as follows:

'No charge is made for inserting information about men on service killed, wounded, promoted or in receipt of merits. All the BJ is interested in, is that when the war is over, the roll we have been trying to keep since its outbreak, will remain an historical record for the use of generations to come.'

We offer our sincere thanks to the writers and publishers of the BJ and hope that our readers will find this account deserves a place in history.

Contents

German guns captured by the RWKents on show at Thornton's Corner (James Crease at centre)

Chapter One: Travelling in Europe in 1914

The Rev T T Norgate, curate of St George's Church, was a frequent traveller in Europe knowing more about the countries involved in the war than most local inhabitants knew about the country round Beckenham. His illustrated talk at the Public Hall at the beginning of October 1914 entitled, 'The War Drama up to date' was much appreciated with so many photographs from the towns and villages overseas.

The Rev asked the question, 'Why were we at War?' and gave three reasons. The first was that we had given our word to support Belgium and we would not go back on that. The second was similar in that GB had always championed lesser states but the third was that we were drawn in because we were fighting for our lives. Germany's plan of campaign was to assimilate Belgium, overcome France and to establish a great line of guns along the north coast against us and we had to stop this at stage one.

At the time of the murder in Sarajevo on 28 June, Annie Hanscomb from St James's Rd, Croydon, was spending a few weeks holiday just over the border in Austria with a German friend. It was a most peaceful spot among the mountains but most of the guests staying at their pension belonged to Austrian military circles. As an army doctor left he wished, 'Auf Wiedersehen then in London'. 'Are you coming to London then?' asked Annie. 'Of course,' he replied, 'I shall have to be with the army when the Germans take London.' The ladies from military families said that war with England had been expected since the previous summer.

'We were not as anxious as we might have been because we believed that the Kaiser wanted peace but on Saturday 1st August we heard that Germany and Russia were at war although England was still neutral. The excitement and even joy in the town was intense. Every boy who was too young to serve offered himself for training and crowds marched up and down the streets shouting 'Deutschland uber Alles' until we felt sick with apprehension.

The next morning a letter from England warned me to get back to England as soon as possible. I found the station guarded by soldiers but managed to catch a train to Plauen where I had friends, taking

4/5 hours instead of one but the next few weeks were a nightmare. I spent the time with an English friend watching mobilisation, conscious that these men would be going against our own countrymen. When France declared war on 3 August, a wave of hatred swept the place but nothing to the terrible wave when England declared herself the next day. I truly believe that the German people had been thinking that England would join with them! Then they luridly and picturesquely cursed England. It was forbidden to speak English in the street. We heard that London was in a panic and covered with a network of bombproof wire. Craven fear prevailed all over England and leading government men had resigned.

At the end of August we hoped to get away as the railways cleared of troops. The consulates were closed and we haunted the American embassy until they gave us American passports at the beginning of September. We took French leave on 10th September and managed to reach Berlin where the proprietor of the hotel discovered we were English and summoned the police who fortunately could not read English and believed our American passports. After endless visits to the embassy, our passports were stamped by the Prussian police and we left by the first boat on 21 September for Holland where Dutch soldiers told us the English news.

In Germany, if a man is seen on the street in any guise but that of the military he is immediately asked what is the matter with him and so it was a great relief to hear that England was alive and that our men are freely offering themselves for the country's service. When one has seen the mobilisation in Germany and realised the power of the great machine-like militarism there, one cannot feel its overthrow is a light task. The Austrian & Servian war time military strength was 2,451,000 armed with 7mm Mauser rifles and quick firing field guns. On the other hand, the spirit here seems nobler and the ideals higher with a united people fighting with a true British spirit for righteousness and against military despotism.'

Mr John Holley, printer from Venner Rd, Beckenham, left England on 21 July 1914 for a Printing and Arts Exhibition in Bremen, intending to stay with German friends for two or three weeks. They were spending Friday evening of 31 July at the riverside village of Vegesack when they noticed an official handing out papers calling for immediate mobilisation. Back in Bremen on Saturday morning at the consulate John was advised to return home immediately as all foreigners were ordered to report to the police. They found that prices were rocketing and that the cost of potatoes for example had risen by four overnight. He caught the train for Flushing early on Sunday morning struggling to squeeze on board. Fortunately being able to speak German he heard a porter at Osmabruck saying that the train was going no further so that he was able to catch a crowded train coming into the station from Berlin. He managed to get aboard after a lot of pushing and shoving to find barely enough room to stand for the next nine hours. At Goch, he had a fright as all their papers were examined and many were unceremoniously ejected, at least making slightly more room for the rest but there was nothing to eat or drink for the whole way. On boarding the Prinz Hendrik at Flushing, it was too rough to eat on the way over but when landing along the Medway, the passengers were welcomed home with no customs at all and he arrived back home at nearly midnight after the most uncomfortable journey he had ever endured.

Conscription, whereby the state requires all men and sometimes women to serve a period of time in the armed forces began in Prussia in the 18th century, was developed by Napoleon and spread throughout Europe. It never became a British tradition. When GB declared war on Germany in 1914, simple patriotism and the appeal of a regular wage were enough for over a million men to enlist by January 1915 but more were needed if we were to win the war. After attempts by Lord Derby to encourage men to step up in Pals groups did not bring about a sufficient increase in enlistment, the Cabinet thought that compulsory active service was the only answer. An Act passed on 27 January 1916 imposed conscription on all single men aged 18 to 41 with exemption for the medically unfit, religious ministers and conscientious objectors who were dealt with on a case-by-case basis. Of some 16,000, 7,000 worked as stretcher-bearers in the front line where there was a high casualty rate and 73 died when kept cruelly in prison. Conscription extended to married men by May 1916 and to age 51 by the end of the war.

In 1913 France introduced a law to extend the term of French military service to match the size of the Kaiser's army. France's population was only two thirds that of Germany in 1913 so France required all fit males of the appropriate age group to undertake full-time military service for three years from the age of 20. The 2.9 million men mobilised in August 1914 consisted of men in the middle of their three years of obligatory service with reservists aged 24 to 30 and territorials from older men up to 45, not intended for the front line. Conscription in Germany was similar, lasting three years in the cavalry and artillery but only two years in the infantry, then passing into the reserve for four or five years.

Chapter Two: Voluntary Aid Detachments (VADs)

No nation in the world has the capacity to improvise and the will to compromise so thoroughly as Great Britain. The instinct of every British man is to think for himself, act according to conscience, fear God and honour the King. Some far-seeing souls, who realised a great European war might come, arranged a nucleus of purposed effort by establishing VADs in connection with the Territorial Force. At first there were the usual sneers by people who forgot that amateur assistance comes from those most intelligent and responsible in the community.

From Sir Gilbert Parker MP's preface to Kent's Care for the Wounded by Creswick, Pond and Ashton published 1915

There were nearly 100 detachments formed in Kent by the Territorial Force, St John's Ambulance and Red Cross workers attending lectures, drills and camps, getting ready since 1910 in case they were needed. Their hospitals would be village halls, empty houses, public buildings, school or church rooms that could be instantly converted into wards overseen by a commandant, medical officer, quartermaster and 40 to 50 other personnel. Their memorable day came on **Tuesday, 13 October 1914**. The telegram came from Colonel Wilson soon after 10.00pm:

'Mobilise all your hospitals at once. Notify names of places, stations and number of beds available at each to transport officers, Folkstone. Large number of wounded arrive tonight. Authority Director-General, AMS.'

The VAD Chief of Staff, Dr Horace Yolland from 53 Bromley Common, phoned the original Commandant, Dr Ramsbottom, to warn him to expect the first contingent from some 2,000 wounded soldiers at Christ Church in three hours. The acting Commandant, Mrs Ada Neame, had helpers immediately to clear the old and new schoolrooms of the chairs where there had been meetings only the evening before. Beds were collected from all

4

over Beckenham by owners of motor cars and the Red Cross nurses fitted them all in the schoolrooms now converted to wards. Stretcher-bearers and night orderlies, under a former St John's Ambulance member, Quartermaster George Baxter, Commandant G G Fiddes and MO Dr Giddings, were at the ready.

They waited and waited but by the end of Wednesday the wounded had not appeared. Eventually, the next day, their share of the 2,000 turned out to be 25 utterly exhausted soldiers who were suffering from exposure but on the whole not seriously wounded. They were brought by private cars from Bickley station. With their beds separated by curtains, they were made very comfortable and mostly soon recovered.

The MO of the Christ Church hospital was Dr H F Strickland and he was ably supported by a trained staff with Nurses Challenger, Dillon, Buckell, Greig and Gilbey.

Commandant Mrs Ada Grace Neame of Kent district 86 had Nurse Savory as superintendent and Miss Stenning as quartermaster.

The assistant nurses were Mrs Furze and Misses Oakes, Sharpe, Thornton, Manger, Price, Jones, Wilson, Cardross, Grant, Paterson, Morley and Litchfield.

Miss Trimmer was the electrician and carpenter and the supers were Misses Inglis, Young and Cree.

Commandant Miss Sharpe of Kent district 96 had Miss Lewer as her quartermaster.

Her assistant nurses were Mrs Fisher and Misses Fiddes, Conway, Whittington, Brown, Tremel, Reynolds, Elliot, White, Wedekind, Cooper and Wright.

Supers were Mrs Petley and Misses Bayne, Moses, Mather and Roberts.

Cooks were Mrs Butcher and Misses Hochs, Nicholson, Tremel and Hudson with kitchen maids, Misses Clark and Marjorie Neame.

The Neame family of Woodfield, 18 Southend Rd, previously Park Rd, occurs frequently in the Beckenham Journal. Ada Neame's husband, Laurence Harding Neame, was the treasurer for collections such as the £120 needed for a motor ambulance for Beckenham. Their daughter, Marjorie, was a kitchen maid in the hospital and their five sons, Laurence Vincent, Bernard, Eric, Philip Leslie and C M served in the army. Capt L V Neame and Lt C M Neame appear in the photograph of the officers of the RWKent 5th Bn taken in Jhansi, India in 1915.

Commandant Ada Neame, Dr Strickland and Quartermaster Stenning are in this
photo from the album of VAD Florence Neville Eden at
Christ Church Red Cross Hospital FE

As well as the 50 patients in Christ Church Red Cross Hospital, Kelsey
Cottage was used as a convalescent annexe for another 50 patients at first
rented from Mr Preston for as long as his lease lasted and then from Mr
Strickland.

The Beckenham & Penge Medical Society formed a mobile detachment

Kelsey Cottage Convalescent Hospital from Florence Neville Eden FE

with Dr G R Stilwell as commandant, Dr F Trapnell quartermaster, Dr Randell MO, Dr Curtis pharmacist and numbering six other medics, Drs Bennett, Bolus, Colyer, Leathem, Penn and Todd. Being a men's group they received an odd number, Kent 41, like the odd number Kent 39 for the drivers, stretcher-bearers and orderlies of Christ Church. The women's groups received even numbers. A supply depot for bandages, linen, shirts, slippers etc. was made possible at Elmleigh, 15, Hayne Rd by the courtesy of the owner, Frank Hooper.

Kelsey Cottage was built in 1832 by John Woolley near the top of Kelsey Lane where Uplands and Forest Ridge are today.

Four other VAD hospitals were made ready at West Wickham based on Kent 82 at The Warren at Coney Hall donated by the wealthy businessman Sir Robert Laidlaw. It had space for 55 beds and he provided five servants and £25 weekly. The nearby house, Coney Hill, owned by American banker, Herman Hoskier, could accommodate 20 patients and Hayes Grove in Preston's Rd, Hayes for a further 20 patients was made available for a year by Sir Everard Hambro. The fourth, Wood Lodge from James Baker, was never used. When Balgowan School became available in 1916, the West Wickham hospitals all closed after treating 630 patients. Their MO, Dr William Blake, became the medical officer at the German POW camp at Langley Court.

One of the most impressive sights seen in Beckenham at this time

The Military Funeral of Albert Debucquoy IM

was the funeral with military honours of the Belgian soldier, Albert Debucquoy, of the 3rd Chassi Pieds. Wounded in the head by a bayonet, he was one of the first of the wounded from Antwerp sent to Beckenham when the Christ Church Red Cross Hospital was mobilised. His home was in Moocrous where his wife had a baby he had never seen. Dr Strickland and all the staff tried so hard to save him and his friend, Leon DeGroote of 11th de Ligne, was his constant companion. General Falize of the Belgian army and the Rev Father Dans from Belgium attended the funeral with Dr Strickland, nurses, attendants and Belgian refugees. The procession was led by Commandant A L Carpenter and the Shirley Boys Band with the Belgian-flag-covered hearse bearing many wreaths. At the Elmers End cemetery, the firing party lined the gates and fired several volleys after the service.

A ward at Christ Church Hospital. The orderly on the right is Leon DeGroote IM

Leon DeGroote was born in Bruges, Belgium, in 1889. In 1909 he joined the army and served with the 11th Line Regiment. For the next five years he would spend most of his time garrisoned in his home city.

Belgium was considered to be a neutral country. However in 1914 war was looming. Germany, using self-defence as an excuse, demanded that Belgium allow the passage of its armies through its territory. Belgium flatly refused and Germany invaded on 4 August 1914. This act of aggression brought Britain into the war. The Belgian army was small and ill-prepared. They were quickly overrun and retreated to a line along the River Ijzer just a few miles east of the French border. To hamper the Germans the Belgians flooded the low-lying lands around Diksmuide with seawater. Now entrenched, under fire and living in a swamp, the Belgians suffered thousands of casualties with as many succumbing to sickness as to enemy fire.

Gravestone CWk

So Leon contracted erysipelas, a life-threatening and infectious condition. He was evacuated from the line along with one of his officers to whom he may have been a batman.

The pair reached one of the Channel ports where the officer was taken aboard a Red Cross mercy ship. It seemed as though Leon would be left for the next crossing but the officer intervened and demanded that Leon accompany him. So the pair were taken to England and to the Christ Church emergency hospital in Beckenham where Leon was one of the 802 British and 33 Belgian soldiers who were treated. Leon is the soldier on the right in the picture sent to Ian's website by Leon DeGroote's grandson. LG

The birth declaration of Albert Debucquoy born 20/6/1886 in France of Belgian parents was sent to Ian by Michel Depoorter who resides in the same village of Neuville en Ferrain. MD

Past patients of the Christ Church hospital were quick to show their appreciation of their treatment such as the letter from Frank Gould of the

Mediterranean Expeditionary Force who wrote in October 1915 from the YMCA as follows:

'To the Matron of Christ Church:

I am constantly thinking of the jolly time I had at Christ Church. The skill of the doctors, matron, sisters and nurses cannot be praised too highly. The food and cooking was most excellent and it helped them go on to be comfortable and jolly. I only wish I could go for a nice drive this afternoon, motor, side car or carriage. I shall never forget the nice trip to Box Hill. If I get wounded I shall ask to be sent to Christ Church, Beckenham. That's the place for wounded soldiers. I shall tell all the boys to say Christ Church, Beckenham.'

In September 1915, the hospital had been thoroughly cleaned and distempered, a partition built to screen the top ward from the kitchen and a bathroom built. As more patients arrived, those leaving gave a concert and a dozen others, headed by Westminster Rifleman G J Cooke, presented a testimonial to the management and nurses. To celebrate twelve months since Christ Church received its first wounded soldiers, they had a concert at the hospital and Mrs Thorn, one of its kindest friends, had covered all the beds of the lower ward with new red blankets.

Nevertheless, the VADs were looking to take over the newly built elementary school in Balgowan Rd for the duration of the war and this came about over Christmas 1915. The hospital train from Dover arrived at Bromley South station with 60 patients who were taken by private cars to Balgowan where there was also another ward waiting to be filled. The original £1,600 needed before the new hospital could be opened was increased when X-ray apparatus and a motor ambulance were added but such was the generosity of the Beckenham residents that the fund closed on 9.12.1915 at £2,044 17s.

Local schools collected all kinds of gifts for the newly opened Balgowan. China included over 200 cups and saucers and egg cups, plates, tumblers, jugs, teapots, basins, shaving mugs, ashtrays (and cigarettes), handkerchiefs and hot-water bottles. Individuals had contributed far more such as floor coverings for the entire hospital, an operating table and medical bags for the doctors, bedding of all kinds, a bread cutting machine, monthly tea supplies and daily milk, bedside tables and lockers, books, china, dozens of hot-water bottles and anything else requested like shaving equipment, clocks and groceries.

During the next year, about 800 patients had passed through the staff's hands and Balgowan had become a truly magnificent hospital of spotless cleanliness and cheerful, thankful men. They celebrated on the afternoon of Saturday 16 December 1916 with a party, tea and entertainment, remembering the splendid generosity of the Beckenham people without which the hospital could not succeed. With the extension of two large marquees, Balgowan could accommodate 240 patients. By the time Balgowan was returned to the education committee in 1919, it had accommodated 5,257 patients.

The VAD at Balgowan School with Dr Strickland in the centre FE

By the August 1916, Commandant Ada Neame had informed the system that VAD Kent 86 was giving up Christ Church and Kelsey Hospitals as soon as the new girls' school in Lennard Rd was ready for takeover as a new hospital. She thanked the Rev Harrington Lees and churchwardens for the use of Christ Church for the past two years. The land for the new girls' school had been donated by Mr Cator and the building would provide well over another 100 beds to continue the work of Christ Church.

Although built to be a school with classrooms opening off either side of central corridors, these rooms made excellent wards that looked especially attractive with the beds covered in red or blue blankets. The large art room was equipped for recreation with a piano, bagatelle, billiard and card tables. There were already 70 patients in occupation when the director of the Kent VAD, Viscount Chilston, performed the official opening ceremony on Tuesday 24 October 1916. In her vote of thanks, Commandant Mrs Neame admitted that she was afraid to ask for any future help because the Beckenham people were so willing and always gave more. On the previous Saturday, they had held a Pound (weight) Day when over 900 visitors donated gifts of over 1,000 lbs. The sum of £46 13s 6d was donated, some of which collected by Hector, the Great Dane, who was a helper at the hospital.

Helena Harrison, Christ Church VAD (from Joyce Walker's West Wickham and the Great War)

Helena lived with her parents and younger sister, Catherine, at 56 Oakwood Avenue from where she would cycle to the hospital, a distance of about two miles when it transferred to the future Girls' County School in Lennard Rd. Her father was a retired army officer, Lt Francis Sladen Harrison of the 4th Kings Own, and Helena at the age of 18 was destined to stay at home to help her mother while doing a little social work. With the voluntary hospitals opening close by, Helena could live at home and feel she was really helping in the war effort as she describes here.

'I thought myself lucky to be taken on as an orderly, to wait on the nurses, black grates and light fires. When promoted to junior nurse, I was completely happy and would have been terribly disappointed if the war had suddenly stopped. When batches of wounded arrived, dirty and exhausted, straight from the Front, there would be a hectic hour getting them clean and to bed. As septic wounds and frostbites were uncovered and the men winced under the doctor's gentle probing, if you felt queer, you slipped out of the ward and pulled yourself together. Our patients much preferred our homely little hospitals to the big military ones. When they were convalescing, we used to help them get up evening concerts, hurrying through our duties so as to join them in the popular choruses like "Which switch is the right switch for Ipswich?" The first time I was left alone in charge of a ward I felt like Atlas shouldering the world but before the war was in its fourth year, VAD nursing was my ordinary everyday job. We were free to make what we could of a new world.'

Florence Neville Eden worked as a VAD from August 1915 in Beckenham and Bromley. She left a neighbour a bulging album of photos, letters, articles and poems, which was passed on to Peter Wiseman and so to us with grateful thanks.

Florence (1886-1963) was born in Woolwich, the youngest of three children of Charles and Daisy Eden. Charles held a senior position in the Post Office and they always employed servants such as cook and housemaid. Florence had no occupation and the family lived in Bromley in 1891, Lambeth in 1901 and Staines in 1911 but she came to work for the VAD Kent 86 Christ Church in Beckenham in August 1915 and transferred

Cooks in the kitchen at Christ Church include Florence Eden at the sink,
Wedekind and Boyer. FE

to Kent 168 in Bromley August 1916 until April 1925. In WWII she joined
the Beckenham Mobile First Aid Unit of the Civil Defence for the duration.

Mr G G Fiddes of Kent VAD 39 had been the commandant responsible
for equipping Christ Church hospital as you see below but at the beginning
of 1916 he joined the Royal Flying Corps.

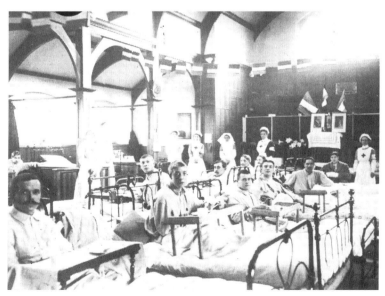
Christ Church Hall as a Military Hospital FE

Chapter Three: The British Army and its Volunteers

At the start of 1914 there were about 975,000 men in the British infantry comprising six divisions with about 18,000 men in a division. This compared with 62 French, 87 German and 114 Russian divisions (extract from 'Forgotten Voices'). Lord Kitchener believed that those in the Territorial Army were useless and unready for war, a sham army to hoodwink a pleasure loving nation! Beckenham had a Territorial Force in the 5th Battalion of the Royal West Kents who had met regularly at Elm Cottage in Beckenham High St which was opposite where the new Pavilion cinema was built in 1914, but they had moved to a new drill hall on 6 June 1914 in Parish Lane. They set off with great enthusiasm on Thursday 6 August 1914 to march to Bromley to join the army for service in France but were soon rejected and returned home penniless.

This was reported in the BJ of 29 August 1914 as follows:

'Territorial Veterans from Beckenham, Bromley and District were called up in the first week of the war and went away full of enthusiasm for duty. Their experiences have not been pleasant and many of them have since returned to their homes. It seems that they should never have been sent away at all, for when they arrived at their destination, they were not expected, no one knew anything about them and there was difficulty finding them food and lodging. After some delay they were found an instructor and told that they were to be enlisted as privates and split up among the various detachments. The NCOs declined as it was contrary to the conditions under which they were called up. No money was paid out and as some men were at the end of their resources, a sum was raised and loaned out to them as required. They hung about and then were told that unless they became privates they must return at their own expense and without the £5 bounty or separation allowance promised at Bromley. Some of them had no jobs to go back to and had wives who had run up bills on the strength of the promised bounty.'

Lord Richard Burdon Haldane recognised the need for the British army to have a regular expeditionary force specifically trained for continental intervention and ready for action as soon as the men reached the foreign shores. He settled on six infantry divisions and one cavalry division with two mounted reconnaissance brigades. They were professional soldiers composed of regulars and reserves who had fought in the Boer War. Led by Sir John French, they crossed into the Continent on 14 August to encounter the German forces of General Von Kluck. The British were so skilled at firing their Lee Enfield rifles from their entrenched positions at Mons that the Germans thought they were firing machine guns. They were trained to hit the target 15 times per minute at 300yds that appeared to be a rate of 28 machine guns per battalion. Haldane's Second Line consisted of a new force of 14 divisions formed between 1906 and 1912 from the old Militia that became the Special Reserve, the Volunteer Force and the Yeomanry. After the battles of Mons, Le Cateau, Aisne and the first battle of Ypres on 18 October, the British army had managed to stop the German advance and trench warfare was starting. What was left of the British army in December was divided into two armies needing support from the men who were enlisting.

Forty per cent of the 85,000 men in the BEF who left for France from 5 August were expected to be lost in the first six months of the war. Following Parliament's sanction on 6 August, Lord Kitchener made an appeal for 100,000 volunteers between the ages of 19 and 30, at least 5'3" tall with a 34" chest measurement, but two fifths were unsuitable on health grounds due to poor diet, housing and medicine. In the first week of the war, Sir Henry Rawlinson appealed to London City workers to enlist with a result that 1,600 men joined the 10th battalion of the Royal Fusiliers, thereafter the Stockbrokers Battalion. Recruiting boomed in the last week of August after the battle of Mons and the suggestion by Lord Derby, Edward George Villiers Stanley, in Liverpool for Pals groups from the same factory, bank, school, football team etc. to join up together. This was encouraged by a desire to help plucky little neutral Belgium, which had been invaded by the German army, and the belief that the war would be over by Christmas. There were the Hull Commercials, Glasgow Tramways, East Grinstead Sports, London Footballers, Grimsby Chums and Sheffield City. Many joined as a release from grinding poverty with the provision of living accommodation and the promise of regular pay of 1/- per day and for a time this worked. Then after almost a year's training they were sent to the Somme where the generals (donkeys) instructed the men (lions) to walk in formation towards the heavily armed German lines, a slaughterhouse for 20,000 men on the first day. Of the 720 Accrington Pals, 584 were killed and from 900 Leeds Pals, 750 were lost.

The situation was different in Beckenham where the majority of the working class were not at work in industry but as domestic and support for the wealthy in their rich houses but there were still many examples of friends enlisting together. The Beckenham Journal of 5 September 1914 stated that 20 council dustmen enlisted after work on the Thursday, driven to the centre in East St, Bromley in three of the council dustcarts. This same paper had reported the loss in Belgium on 23 August of Lt C K Anderson of the Royal West Kents, brother of the Rev S K Anderson, curate of St James's church. Many of the old boys from the Beckenham & Penge Grammar School for Boys were listed in the BJ of 19 Sept, and hundreds of local men were joining up from their city companies. Out of 60 members of the Beckenham Cricket Club who were listed as serving in the forces on 10 October 1914, 25 appear on the memorial plaque. CW

Capt Edgar Westcott MC was one of the first to volunteer from Alleyn's School and after marrying Edith Mabel Roberts in 1918, he survived almost to the end of the war when he was killed on 4 November 1918 in the Prince of Wales Own, aged 25. He was buried in the Artres Communal Cemetery and his wife was left widowed in 3 Cedars Rd, Beckenham.

The honours list of Abbey School collected by Mr G J Gulliver, a master since 1879, consisted of 180 names, 156 army and 24 navy. Of these, 25 had been killed, 12 wounded and 2 were POWs. There were 2 VCs and 1 DCM. They are named on p3 of the Beckenham Journal of 13/11/1915. The headmaster of Churchfields Rd School collected the names and regiments of 451 relatives of 260 boys at his school in 1914. There were 94 brothers, 1 aunt, 21 fathers, 8 brothers-in-law, 225 uncles and 101 cousins from 28 services from Australian Navy to the Kent Cyclists and Welsh Fusiliers.

The boys from Christ Church were among the local lads fired with enthusiasm to fight for their country. They included Mary Feltham's father, Bill Moreland, and several of his friends who tried to join up one Saturday in the public hall where the local West Kents were waiting to encourage enlistment. Now Bill Moreland from Balgowan Rd, Beckenham was born at the Croydon Rd maternity home on 28 September 1897 and so at the beginning of September 1914 was not quite 17. He declared that he would be 17 in three week's time but the other boys, apart from Fred Bunting, were all too young. Bill, as William Graham Moreland, 240474, was sent to India on 30 October with the 5th Battalion of the Royal West Kents with whom he remained for the duration of WWI. He became an acting warrant officer, class 2, and served in the Jhansi, Rawalpindi and Jubbulpore Brigades of the Indian army until Dec 1918 when he joined the 18th Indian Division in Mesopotamia. They were the last battalion in the British army to return home from abroad after 5 years 84 days!

Pte Stanley Smith wrote home from India about their jungle camp and training in fieldwork and musketry and how surprising it was how in the blackness of the night you could not help imagining things. From time to time men were drafted to reinforce the 2nd Bn of the RWKents on active service in Mesopotamia. Alfred and Frank Rule and Ernest Knight wrote of their journey to the land of the original 'Garden of Eden' by rail, boat and barge towed by paddle steamer.

They eventually became stuck in the mud and had to strip off to pull the steamer and barge off. Using the native sailboats called ballums to take the stores, they punted their barge to deeper water, were pulled by steamer across the rapids and eventually reached their camp by the Euphrates where living was made so uncomfortable by the flies, prickly heat and mosquitoes that they would not be sorry to hear that the war had come to a successful conclusion! Alfred died age 29 on 13 January 1916 and was buried in the Kut War Cemetery.

On 13 May 1916, all the 5th Bn left Jhansi to the regret of the local people, especially the chaplain, Norman Bennett, who was a personal friend of the Rev Harrington C Lees of Christ Church, Beckenham. He said that the regiment had won the golden opinions of them all as athletic, clean-living men, many with a business background. The church had now lost the band and the best choir they had ever had which had produced Maunder's 'Oliver to Calvary' on Good Friday with soloists in Sgt Hunt, Lt Smithers, Cpl Hanmore and Stanley Smith. Bill Moreland was able to rescue a fellow from drowning when they were bathing in a large dam with thanks to the training received from Mr H R Austin, Beckenham School's swimming instructor in life saving and artificial respiration. The soldier recovered sufficiently to be able to walk back to camp!

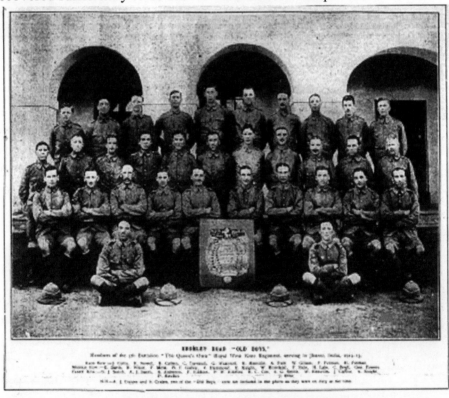

Back row J Collis, R Newell, R Collett, C Turnbull, G Wakenell, R Henville, A Rule, W Gibson, F Putnam, H Putnam.
Middle row E Davis, N White, F Moss, W F Galley, V Hammond, E Knight, W Moreland, F Rule, H Lake, C Brett, Geo Powers.
Front row S J Smith, A F Smith, A Anderson, P Ribbins, P W Ribbins, R C Cox, S G Smith, W Henville, J Callow, A Knight with seated on ground P Hawkes and J Ellis. A J Copper and S Craker were on duty.

The Beckenham greengrocer and local councillor, James Crease, had five sons between 1885 and 1893, four of whom joined the cavalry unit of West Kent Yeomanry in 1908 centred at Bromley and trained at summer camps. The youngest, Sidney Herbert born 1893, was still at school but some time possibly in 1915, they met at the Railway Hotel in Beckenham where the photograph was taken. The four in the West Kent Yeomanry are wearing an Invicta hat badge of the West Kent Yeomanry and a bandolier but Sidney in the centre has no bandolier and has a different hat badge.

From L to R starting back row, Gilbert 1891-1971, Sidney Herbert 1893-1985, John Stanley 1889-1960, Edwin Hugh 1885-1976, Percy Vivian 1887-1966. GC

Percy's son, Gerald, has his father's documents as follows. 'Percy Vivian Crease of No 39 Territorial Force Embodiment 5.8.1914 Corporal WKY230 is required to attend at the Drill Hall, Bromley at 10.00 that day.' This is reported in the BJ 8.8.1914 when they were under the control of Major Sir Samuel Scott. There were five officers and 124 men practically all present. The BJ of 15.8.1914 reported Percy's promotion to sergeant.

A year later in September 1915, the Crease boys were still waiting to be sent on active duty. It was reported in the BJ of the 25th that they enrolled at the beginning of the war and have been 'doing their bit against their will in England ever since. Three of the brothers left England for a nameless destination yesterday where we hope they will meet with victory and success and yet return home safe and sound.' This nameless destination was Gallipoli where Edwin, Gilbert and Percy, all of the 1/1st West Kent Yeomanry, were posted. Gerald has correspondence indicating that they sailed on Titanic's sister ship SS Olympic from Liverpool to Gallipoli on 25 September 1915. They arrived at Lemnos on 1 October, then Helles on 8th eventually at the front line on 26th from where they were eventually evacuated on the night of the 8 January 1916.

According to John's medal records at Kew, he was not sent overseas and was probably in the second line regiment of the 2/1st West Kent Yeomanry under the orders of the South Eastern Mounted Brigade. In July 1916, he applied to join the RE Signals as a motor cyclist, a despatch rider.

Trench warfare reduced the need for cavalry and in April 1917 the units of the Territorial Force were regrouped and used for various tasks while the men were renumbered. John became 194723 and a Corporal in the RE. The 1/1st West Kent Yeomanry with the East Kents became part of the Corps of Hussars, Percy 245007 and Gilbert 270522 as sergeants and Edwin 270507 rising through quartermaster sergeant to 2nd Lt. Since Gallipoli the 1/1st had served in Egypt and finished the war on the Western Front but Percy at least was no longer with them. He had received injuries that caused him to transfer to the second line regiment as acting regimental sergeant major in part of the East Coast Defence Scheme based in Suffolk on bicycles until April 1918 when they were transferred to Dublin.

Percy's demob certificate reads 'Soldiers' demobilisation account Regtl 245007 Arms Corps/Regt – Cavalry 25.1.1919 £49 10s 9d.'

Sidney had been too young to join his brothers in the Yeomanry and the following news cutting from the Beckenham & Penge Advertiser of 6 Aug 1914 neatly sums up what he was doing at the beginning of the war. 'Presentation to Mr S H Crease. The closing of the summer term at the Beckenham County School was marked by a presentation on Wednesday 29 July 1914 by a presentation of a silver watch to Mr S H Crease. He entered the school as a pupil in September 1905, leaving in July 1911 when he was appointed a member of staff. He secured Oxford Junior Local in 1908, Oxford Senior Local in 1909, London Matric in 1910 and London Inter Science in 1912. It was his intention to become a day student at Kings College, London where he was reading for an Hons degree in Physics.' The

B&P Advertiser of 9 July 1914 reported John Crease as one of the lighting engineers at the county school's al fresco concert and Gilbert Crease as one of the stewards. They were also old boys of the school.

Sidney took his degree in physics and after the war returned to the Beckenham Boys Grammar School as head of physics until 1958. His son James says that his father enlisted with the Artist's Rifles otherwise the 28th London Rifles. This is confirmed on Sidney's medal card where it says that he served in France in March 1916. By 27.3.1917, Sidney was a 2nd Lt in the Loyal North Lancashire Regiment and he completed his service as a Lt in the Royal Engineers.

The National Archives medal card of Sidney Herbert Crease GC

A few of the many large Beckenham families who served are shown below:

The seven sons of Mrs Emily Coppard in August 1914 were all members of the Royal West Kent D Territorials: Frederick 34, Herbert 32, Leonard 24, Jack 21, Percy 20, Harold 18 and Wilfred 17.

Among the extensive lists in the Beckenham Journal of young men enlisting in Kitchener's army were four brothers Creswell and three each of the brothers Byron and Uzzell. W F Creswell in Army Ordnance Corps has two brothers in the same and another in the Royal West Kent Regiment. Second Lt S H Byron HAC in France, Capt Lewis Byron in the Natal Mounted Rifles in S Africa and Pte C J Byron in the HAC. L/Cpl J Uzzell of the 3rd Queen's West Surreys is in France, W E Uzzell 6th Bn Queens and Sidney Uzzell Coldstream Guards.

Widower James Bunting Housden was a retired tea merchant who lived at Brooklyn, 31 Cator Rd, Beckenham. He had at least one daughter and six sons in time for them to be bullet fodder for WWI. One of the army brothers Housden in the Royal Artillery wrote of sleeping as they force-marched 30 miles in the pouring rain at night and that their two divisions of 40,000 men held and forced the retirement of 350,000 German Army Corps in October 1914, blocking their route to Paris. In September 1918, James wrote to the Beckenham Journal with news of his family's progress in the war. One of his sons, Arthur Thomas of the Artists Rifles B Coy 1st/28th Bn, had been killed on 30.10.1917, aged 28 in Belgium where he was buried, leaving his wife, Mary Ann Eliza Rosina Housden. His eldest son, Major Edwin Housden of the Field Artillery, was suffering from a shell wound in the head and his fifth son, Leslie G Housden, was recovering from serious wounds. His nephew, Signaller P Housden, had been injured in the thigh by a shell and his son-in-law, Lt E S Ferrott, had been severely wounded by bullets through the neck, lung and shoulder.

William Henry Mantle of 128 Parish Lane, bandmaster of Alexandra Troop, Beckenham, Boy Scouts, received a king's letter in appreciation of the service of five of his sons in the forces: Pte Arthur Royal Scots Fusiliers, Gunner Philip Henry RFA, Pte John Loyal N Lancs, in the army before the war but disabled at Ypres, Musician Charles, Royal Marines on HMS Queen in Dardanelles, Pte Joseph 3rd Bn East Lancs.

Of the seven serving Libretto boys from Hawthorn Grove by September 1917, three had been killed, Charles, Thomas on the Indomitable and Pte Edward James. The youngest son who had been called up underage was returned home after Edward's death on 25/9/1917.

Chapter Four: The Contemptible Little Army

Pte Harry Roberts, son of Bromley Rd headmaster, Benjamin Roberts, wrote home in May 1915 from the trenches where they were ankle deep in mud to say that none of them had taken their boots off since last Sunday week but that 'our 'contemptible little army' had been giving the enemy hell lately. Our hats are all squashed as we had to take the wire out of them and we are very much in need of a wash and a shave. Things have been very lively here during the last 3 days as we saw a bayonet charge the day before yesterday and we were able to get a pot at the Germans as they ran past huge gaps made by our artillery in their trenches.'

BEF is correctly used to refer to the British Expeditionary Force in France prior to the end of the first battle of Ypres 22/11/1914 by which time it had stopped the German advance although had lost most of its fighting strength. Kaiser Wilhelm II reportedly issued an order on 19/8/1914 to exterminate General French's contemptible little army. After the war its survivors proudly formed the Old Contemptibles Association with dates on its badge from Aug 5 to Nov 22 1914.

Corporal Strange, a postman from the Beckenham post office who lived at 26 Burnhill Rd, rejoined the Army off the Reserve and described his experiences from Beckenham to Mons, Marne, Cambria, Aisne and Ypres in the BJ of 9/1/1915, p8. Called to the colours on 4 August 1914 and sent to the depot to be equipped, he was soon in contact with his old comrades of the Oxford & Bucks Light Infantry. There were something like 1,400 men rejoined off the Reserve, a battalion of trained men ready for the Germans. Most were drafted to Aldershot, including Corporal Strange, to form part of the 2nd Division, 5th Brigade of the BEF. After a few stiff marches to improve fitness, they left for Boulogne where the people were very friendly and keen to exchange souvenirs for the army badges.

After a day's train ride, they spent several days marching in very hot weather until they could hear the rumble of guns from the Belgian frontier. There were 2,000 armed Germans in the woods, firing recklessly from the hip, looking like ants with no end to them but although they outnumbered the guns of the BEF 30 or 40 to one, at Mons there were only about 50 casualties in Corporal Strange's brigade. They were in close contact with the enemy near the River Marne and compelled the Germans to retire with heavy losses, followed by a big fight at Cambria where the Germans retreated across the River Aisne. Then began the battle of the trenches between 600 and 800 yds apart. Big damage occurred if a shell dropped in a trench and in three weeks shells accounted for 30 killed and 50 wounded with trenches blown apart by the German Black Maria or coal box shells so called because they emitted dense black fumes on exploding.

They entrained for Ypres in Belgium where lots of abandoned animals followed them, dogs, cats, sheep, goats and two donkeys until action began. Six thousand men of the BEM were attacking 80,000 Germans over ground with little or no cover but they drove them off at whatever cost. When Corporal Strange was shot in the arm he was evacuated to Boulogne where he developed pneumonia while waiting for a ship for England. He kept the bullet from his wound and had it mounted on his watch chain.

Lt L Chalk, second son of Vernon R Chalk of Aberdeen House also owner of several shops in Beckenham High St wrote home.

'I have just come out of the worst place in our line. It was an impressive time when I came up to the trenches at midnight with my old gun limbers rolling over the cobbles of a city of desolation where one brick hardly remains on another. I absolutely lost the hearing of my left ear for about a week, but it now seems practically all right. I was going from one gun to another when an 8-inch shell landed close by. I fell like a shot rabbit into another shell hole close by and did not get touched, but the terrific din went right through me.

I had a narrow shave last Sunday. A 'whiz bang' (6 inch explosive shrapnel) burst over one of my gun emplacements, and fortunately only caught one man. It was an absolute miracle we were not all washed out! I also had a terrible experience in the last trench I was in. The Germans had mined us. And after heavy shelling us they blew our trenches up and charged. Several poor fellows were buried alive, but we had them all out of our trenches in half an hour of it taking place, but it was a pretty unhealthy evening.

I wonder what sort of picture you have in mind of the 'trenches' under fire? The incessant roaring of heavy artillery and explosions, together with all sorts of conditions of small fire arms, from the primitive mortars we use here, to the up-to-date Vickers Light Machine Gun. Heaps and heaps of sandbags; men toiling and sweating filling them and getting them into position. The mud, always present, pools of blood, these trenches were captured only a week ago. Clouds of filthy blue bottle flies, the most intolerable smell, the moans of dying men and the awful sight of the stricken.

This gives you some idea, but no description is adequate. Being so near home, one would hardly credit what we have to put up with in the trenches. The Germans were seen to be building a very strong redoubt last Sunday behind their first line, and about 10.20pm I got two machine guns on it then sent up some 'Very Lights'. By Jove they dropped their spades and scuttled like blazes back, but they were back in about an hours time, hard at it. They've indomitable pluck, so I loosed off again. I had got together quite a collection of German trophies, but had to abandon them when I last came out as was too done up to take them further. Still there are plenty of Germans left yet! So I still have a chance of getting you something.'

German officers praised the soldiers in action against them according to an article by an American reporter, Herbert Corey, in The Times in May 1915. Herbert was a reporter with the German army at the battle of Neuve Chapelle in France. The Germans were led to believe that the new English troops were raw, undisciplined guttersnipes and slum sweepers but their officers realised that they were the best blood in England. They saw their foes in fight, as prisoners and as they lay dead, as lean, full-templed, long-jawed men, sons of good fathers, city clerks or boys who had played in the open air. When the West Kent Regiment charged across the open fields, they were cheering and waving their rifles in the stream of bullets played against them, closing the gaps as men stumbled and fell. Having gained the last possible inch and were ordered to fall back, they did not crawl but rose and walked, picking up their wounded and lighting cigarettes.

Chapter Five: The Effect of War on Beckenham

The immediate result was panic! The wealthy rushed to buy food to stock up against shortage but then the newspapers issued an appeal to patriots to consider the poor who as a result would not be able to afford raised prices. The price of sugar had already risen since it was not available from Europe.

Lord Kitchener's appeal for young men to enlist was followed by requests for blankets, flannel shirts and socks. Mrs Horace Smith of Ivy Bank, The Avenue received blankets, some 368 of which were taken by Mr Philip Neame to the ordnance officer at Chatham. One thousand large size flannel shirts and one thousand pairs of socks were wanted for those enlisting. Mrs Bell of The Cottage, Oakhill Rd or Capt Nott of the 10th battalion York & Lancaster Regiment, Frensham, Farnham would receive them. The store of Walter Cobb Ltd Sydenham was advertising all the materials for home crafts to help the army and navy; flannel, wool, calico and knitting wool, all at special prices. The Red Cross had begun to meet at 1 Kemerton Rd on Thursdays from the beginning of September.

As food became scarcer, Mrs Hannah Susan (Deacock) Greig, wife of the grocer giant David Greig, had the lawns of the Red House dug up to grow potatoes and other vegetables, keeping chickens as well. Soldiers billeted locally were invited every Wednesday to a meal of beefsteak pudding and a sing-song in the billiard room. The Greigs had moved to the Red House in Southend Rd to accommodate their handicapped daughter, Violet, and had scarcely settled in when WWI began.

Belgian refugees were arriving in Beckenham where Mr E R Stilwell was the Hon Secretary of the War Committee. There was a desperate need for accommodation of families of three or more and there were eventually three hostels in the town at 11 Shortlands Rd, 2 The Avenue and 32 Foxgrove Rd. Five orphaned Belgian boys were attending Bromley Rd School where they were being taught in French. The boys had lost their parents and all adult relatives in the fighting. A concert given by Mrs Drughorn at Banavie on Saturday afternoon 17 October raised £68 8s for the refugees.

Then the newly built schools of Balgowan by 1915 and Beckenham County in Lennard Rd by October 1916 replaced Christ Church. Dr George

Robert Stilwell, grandson of Dr Ratheram Stilwell, was the commandant of the Kent VAD 41 medical group. The Greig's daughters, Cissie and Rosa, worked as kitchen maids in the cottage hospital, riding down there from the Red House on a terrible old motorbike they called 'Red Indian'. Elizabeth Florence Greig was summoned for riding a motorbike without a rear light in the High St and having no licence because she had forgotten to renew it. The worst of the war was what was happening to friends and family at the front where, for the last year of the war, Cissie served as a nurse. Both Cissie's and Rosa's future husbands were badly injured but survived the war, Captain Val Kempson, Cissie's husband, recovering to be capped several times for England football but nephews and cousins were not so lucky. Ernest James Rapp enlisted as a Territorial in 1913 and served until 1917 before receiving a fatal injury at Arras on the morning that he rescued a badly injured Yorkshireman who survived the war.

Although the air-raid sirens would go and they had to black out the windows, no bombs ever fell on Beckenham, the nearest falling on Brixton, but people were warned to take shelter from the shrapnel from the shells.

Every week, the roll of honour was published in the Beckenham Journal. There were so many stories of bravery. Private George Raven from Shortlands was only 15 when he enlisted in 1915 and was killed a year later in France after service in Gallipoli and Egypt. Captain Philip Collins, captain of the Beckenham first XI hockey, was killed in Flanders in June 1915, his brother Lt Commander Hugh Collins having been lost at the sinking of HMS Monmouth the previous November. Two local men died when HMS Formidable was sunk in January 1915; they were Harry Marcham of Hawthorne Grove, aged 21 and Albert Spencer of Burnhill Rd, fireman, who joined the ship at the outbreak of war and left a widow and five children, the youngest he had never seen. L/Corp Albert Roberts, eldest son of the headmaster of Bromley Rd School, was last seen advancing and firing on the enemy as the Germans entered the trenches. Alfred Ellis from Anerley and Corp Bernard Ronald Druitt from 172 Birkbeck Rd were the last to be killed in the long drawn-out battle of the Somme out of eight friends who had joined up together 18 months previously.

Bernard's father, George Druitt, did not survive long after his only son's death, leaving his mother, Emily Druitt, alone.

BECKENHAM ROAD PENGE

Appeals for enlistment took place all over Beckenham and Penge, particularly in the commodious building of the new cinema, the Pavilion, once it had opened in early October in Beckenham and at The Triangle by the Crooked Billet in Penge.

Mr Bryce Grant of the department store would preside over the meeting at The Triangle while various speakers begged the young men to serve their 'King and Country', asking their sweethearts to do all in their power to urge their boyfriends to enlist in Kitchener's Army. At present we had only about 900,000 regular and reservist soldiers which we must build up to equal the strength of the French and German armies so that when the end came, we would have a voice in the future of Europe and our men would have jobs to go back to.

The volunteer movement came into operation for the defence of London where about 70,000 men had enrolled to assist the London Fire Brigade and for defence against air attacks. They were described by some as shirkers in finding the VTC a convenient refuge from enlistment in the armed forces but recruits were those under 18, over 41 or those with poor health or business reasons. Being nearest to the seat of war, Kent became popular with the volunteers with eight battalions: four in West Kent and one each in Mid Kent, East Kent, St Augustines and the Cinque Ports. The Beckenham Volunteer Training Corps (BVTC) became known officially as the A (Beckenham) Company of the 3rd Bn of the West Kent Volunteer Fencibles with 313 men, while Bromley were B Company with 256 men and Orpington were C Company with 120 men. They attended camp, church parades and inspections, dug trenches, performed drill and route marches, practised rifle shooting and formed a cyclists and signallers group under the command of C A Elgood (still remembered today by old girls of the Beckenham Girls County School as the chairman of the governors up to WWII). The cost was borne by the men themselves and local people, not the War Office or local council, including purchase of uniform and rifles.

Beckenham's VTC began in the week of 14/11/1914. Its commandant was Alfred L Carpenter and its four platoon commanders were C R Glanville, C D Hills, H E Beall and H D Mackenzie. They had drill grounds at Foxgrove cricket ground, an orderly room at 6 Bromley Rd where they would accept recruits and a band. The bandmaster was J Doe of 109 High St. The Invicta

3rd Vol. Batt. Royal West Kent Regt.

ORDERS.—"A" COMPANY.

Duty.—Orderly Officer.—Lieut. H. D. Mackenzie. Monday, June 10th.—L.-Cpl. Nimmo; Pte. Collins. Tues.—Cpl. Preston; Pte. Gibb. Wed.—Pte. White; Pte. Woodhams. Thurs.—Pte. Pullen; Pte. Watts. Fri.—Pte. Gentry; Pte. Blinks. Sat.—Sergt. Oakley; Pte. Browne.

Parades.— Sunday, June 9th.— Company Parade, Foxgrove-road, 9.45 a.m.: Dress, Drill Order, No. 1. Tues.—Nos. 1 and 2 Platoons, Foxgrove-road, 8.30; Nos. 3 and 4 Platoons, Technical I'tute, 8.30. Wed.—All men, who have not fired Part 2 Musketry Course, Foxgrove-road, 8.30. Thurs.—Same as Tuesday.

badge of Kent was to be on their caps and they had two cups, the Clapham Cup for Shooting and the Hill's Cup for Efficiency. It was called the 3rd Volunteer Battalion A (Beckenham) Company. A memorial in St George's Church in Beckenham is to 14 of the 3rd Volunteer Battalion who died in the fighting of WWI. They were in the London Rifle Brigade, Kings Royal Rifle Corps, Army Service Corps, South Wales Borderers, Royal Fusiliers, Middlesex Regiment and Royal Engineers with a tendency to being older than the normal man enlisting. Most would be at work during the week with large drafts at the weekends and evenings at 8.15pm. Under their Commandant Alfred Carpenter of 46 Manor Rd, Beckenham, they would parade as a company in Bromley Rd, form trench-digging parties, attend drill, battalion training and musketry sessions with the object of producing a well trained force.

In October 1915, they had a recruiting drive, a march through Beckenham and Penge headed by their band and brought up at the rear by their cyclists and signallers. Their aim was to increase their numbers so that they could be a battalion in their own right. On Sunday 23 July 1916, they were sworn in to take the oath to serve the king and from 23 September 1916 they became the **7th Bn Kent Volunteer Regiment** under **MAJOR** Alfred L Carpenter.

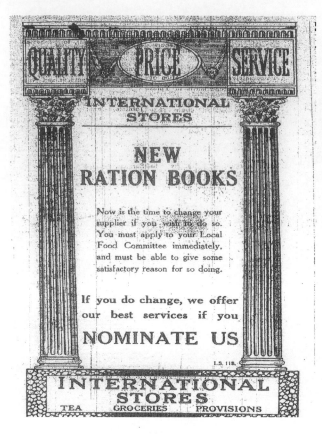

QUALITY PRICE SERVICE

INTERNATIONAL STORES

NEW RATION BOOKS

Now is the time to change your supplier if you wish to do so. You must apply to your Local Food Committee immediately, and must be able to give some satisfactory reason for so doing.

If you do change, we offer our best services if you

NOMINATE US

I.S. 118.

INTERNATIONAL STORES
TEA   GROCERIES   PROVISIONS

Food was not a problem before the end of 1916 apart from the panic buying by the wealthy in the first days of the war which emptied the shops. Later, wheat and other food imported from USA and Canada was increasingly lost because of the unrestricted submarine warfare of the German U-boats. What with the battle of the Somme, shortage of coal and loss of imported wheat, the war was beginning to affect people at home. In February 1917, the German navy sank 230 merchant ships. The government appropriated 2.5 million acres of farmland to be worked by the Women's Land Army who had taken over from the men at war but the nation was becoming anxious.

Panic buying returned at the end of 1917 and, in order to even out distribution and guarantee supplies, rationing was introduced. Everyone was asked to register with a butcher for meat and a grocer for sugar, butter, cheese and margarine, starting with sugar in January 1918 and the other commodities in April. This rationing corrected signs of malnutrition that had begun to appear in poorer communities since it prevented the wealthy buying up all the stocks. The meat ration covered not only the usual 'butcher's meat' but also bones, suet, sausages, bacon, venison, horse, poultry, rabbits, hares and game. The grocers advertised corned beef as being 'off the ration'. On 19.1.1920 the sugar ration was reduced from 8oz to 6oz temporarily to defeat the producers who had raised prices seven times since 1914.

The theoretical daily rations for the British soldier were as follows:

20oz bread, 3oz cheese, 4oz jam, 4oz butter/margarine, 8oz fresh vegetables and 2oz dried, 8oz tea, salt, pepper, mustard, ¼oz chocolate, ½ gill rum, 20oz tobacco. Hot food was impossible when battle was imminent or in progress.

The sinking of the Cunard passenger liner, Lusitania, in the first year of the war, turned public opinion against Germany and contributed to USA's entry into WWI. The ship left New York for Liverpool on 1 May and went down 11 miles off Ireland on 7 May 1915 at 14.28.

James Baker, of Sherbrook 16 Brackley Rd, Beckenham, was packing in his cabin on B deck when the ship was torpedoed twice and began to list to starboard. He went up to the boat deck, found a lifebelt and joined the men who were pushing a boat full of women and children away from the side of the ship. The davits gave way and the lifeboat swung inwards, knocking the men over. When the same happened with another boat, James began cutting a raft clear but water began to pour over the side of the ship. He ran for the stern and dived off to swim away from the sinking ship. After he had swum a few strokes, the ship's stern rose high in the air and sank. After half and hour he found a spar to rest on near to a friend who was holding on to a box lid. Then they were picked up on to a raft with 17 survivors, eventually about 25 and the trawler, Indian Empire, rescued them along with about 120 from other boats. In all there were 761 survivors and 1,198 who died as the ship took only 18 minutes to sink.

Two women with relatives in Beckenham were among the lost, Mrs Rosina Thomas Leverich, widow of William Leverich from New Orleans, with her daughter, Rosina Philips Leverich age 24. They were American citizens of private means but they owned a house in Mackenzie Rd, Beckenham and Mrs Leverich's sister, Elizabeth Cole, lived at Abbotsleigh, Albemarle Rd, Beckenham. Elizabeth was married to an overseas dealer in heavy machinery and had children about the same age as their cousin Rosina, including a medical student Thomas Philips of 26, a prep school teacher Arthur Philips of 23 and a daughter Marjorie Philips age 14. Philips had been the sisters' maiden name.

The new manager of the Pavilion cinema, Mr Edward Hardiman, lost his American friend, who was aboard.

Before the war, Ronald Graham worked at the Bridge Pharmacy at the top of Beckenham but on enlistment he was stationed at the Crystal Palace in the Naval Division. In September 1916 he won the DSC as flight sub lieutenant in the Royal Naval Service when he beat off four enemy seaplanes off the Belgian coast. Other striking air exploits were those of Capt Gilbert Muflis Green from 18 Hayne Rd, Beckenham. He had already brought down four enemy planes single-handed and another shared with a brother airman. Then he flew into a squadron of six bombers and brought two down in flames. The next day he engaged an Albatros that dived out of control. He already held the French Croix-de-Guerre and the MC with bar but now he had been awarded the DSO and the Serbian Order of Karageorge and these while flying in the roughest of conditions in the Balkan Mountains.

 Tom William Thornton, proprietor and editor of the Beckenham Journal, and his wife Clara had four sons born between 1883 and 1902, Hedley Thomas, Frank, Stanley and Victor who was just 16 by 1918. Only Frank of the other three survived the war.

Their father, known as TW, spent his long life working for Beckenham and there was no project involving Beckenham that did not receive his support. Without the history of the war recorded in his local paper, this book could not have been written and there would have been no Kelsey Park where the townspeople could have celebrated the peace but less well known is that we owe the spring flowers of St George's churchyard to him and that the precious resource of the Bromley library street directories, recording who lived where, were his production.

When Hedley Thomas Thornton died on 25 January 1916 age 33 at the family house in the High St, he had just been granted commission as 2nd Lt in 5th RWK regiment, sixteen years after joining the volunteers. As a diabetic, he could not serve overseas, but he served the regiment in Beckenham to the very best of his ability. His military funeral is described in the Beckenham Journal of 5/2/1916, p5, col 4-6 with societies, businesses, military, Freemasons, churches and residents all represented and the wreaths forming a cross in St George's churchyard covering 10yd by 7yd.

In common with so many of the losses recorded in the paper, the

The Christ Church War memorial

JAMES P. KYDD	WILLIAM J.G.TAYLOR
WALTER WARREN	CHARLES HALL
ALFRED SPENCER	JOHN A.BALLANTYNE
FRANCIS R. EMSON	STANLEY THORNTON
WALTER BRAND	NORMAN A.AERTS
H. OLIVER BEER	CECIL A. SPEYER
ALFRED J. PICKUP	WILLIAM CUNNINGTON
ALFRED J. BOWMAN	ARCHIBALD LANGFORD
HEDLEY T.THORNTON	HAROLD L.READING
R.MAUND D'OMBRAIN	F. MACLEAN ABBOTT
HARRY A.YOUELS	LESLIE C.JOHNSON
ERNEST S.PROVIS	HENRY T. GRANT
GERALD D. BROOKE	DAVID DE.B. STOCKS
KENNETH C. JONES	HAROLD STANDRICK
ERIC H.L.CLARK	H. CHARLES BUNTING
CLAUDE S.COOMBS	IVAN C.MACLEAN
GEORGE F.T. OAKES	ALEC C. MACLEAN
JOHN POTTER	DOUGLAS AITCHISON
JOHN W. SALES	THOMAS H.BUTCHERS
ALBERT C.TAYLOR	KENNETH G. OLIVER
LEONARD P.MILES	SYDNEY HALL
HENRY W. LOVELOCK	HARRY COLLIS
PERCIVAL EDWARDS	SYDNEY E. BOOTH
THOMAS H. ORAM	HECTOR F.MACLEAN
A HENRY R. OAKES	FRANCIS R. AERTS
J.BERNARD P.ADAMS	THOMAS F.BOWMAN
PERCY SANDERCOMBE	GORDON FAULKNER

Thorntons suffered for several weeks while waiting for the death of their son Stanley Thornton to be confirmed towards the end of June 1917, killed in action 3/5/1917.

In addition to the plaque in Kelsey Park near the main gates to TW Thornton, unveiled by his granddaughter Valerie Sheldon, on 31/5/2000 there is a plaque above the one-time site of the business in the High St unveiled in November 2002. CWk

New signpost erected at Thornton's corner in June 2013; Valerie Sheldon, granddaughter to editor TW Thornton, is 3rd from left, front row. CWk

Chapter Six: Beckenham's Large Houses Serve the Country

At the end of October 1914, 3,000 troops were expected in Beckenham, the first thousand from the 7th City of London Territorials billeted at Kelsey Manor and the Old Squire's House, Village Place. They came marching smartly down Church Hill from the station on Friday 30 October with firm swinging steps, singing as they passed, presenting a great advertisement to young men considering enlisting in Kitchener's Army. A second thousand would be billeted at Mr Moore's property, Oakwood, in Bromley Rd and in Mr Lutwyche's Craven College at Elmers End.

Soldiers parading at Kelsey Manor in 1917 IM

Khaki became a feature of our streets but Beckenham's residents were asked not to treat the troops in the local pubs where they would get drunk but to donate games, magazines, papers, billiards, table tennis, bagatelle etc. to the clubs that were set up by the churches like the Baptist church in Elm Rd, Crescent Rd and Bevington Rd. Ladies worked hard to provide refreshment, free on Sundays and most evenings concerts were arranged. Another problem would be to supply hot water for baths/showers for two thousand or more men but the first of the troops departed with Capt Mansfield Jones in charge after only three weeks on 18 November to everyone's disappointment.

Later on in 1915, more troops arrived. The City of London Royal Fusiliers were here for some time followed by some of the Guards. Christ Church became the 'garrison' church with the vicar the Rev Harrington C Lees conducting the service, after which the troops would march back to their barracks with the band of fifes and drums.

Military Quarters, Village Place, Beckenham.

Yet another of Beckenham's large houses, Eden Cottage, became a recuperative home for mentally disabled ex-servicemen. It was one of two houses built in 1837 in woodland either side of the River Beck near where it flows into Kelsey Park. Today its site is occupied by four luxury houses in South Eden Park Rd behind the Chinese garage. Among Eden Cottage's well known residents in the 1870s was Charles Arthur Hoare (1847-1908), son of Peter Hoare of Kelsey Manor, who ran a horse-drawn coach from Beckenham to Sevenoaks himself for enjoyment, storing the high coach in a special coach house in the grounds that survived until the new houses were

MILITARY HOSPITAL. CHRIST CHURCH SCHOOLS. BECKENHAM. W. J. Steed, Beckenham.

built. His son, Capt Reginald Arthur Hoare of the Pembroke Yeomanry, was killed in France September 1918.

An appeal for support by Sir Frederick Milner in October 1924 was entirely successful and, renamed as Eden Manor, the property continued to

Langley Court

house ex-servicemen until WWII, eventually being pulled down in 1963. The other house, Eden Lodge, was also adopted by Sir Frederick Milner, the pair making an ideal peaceful home for the wounded soldiers.

Eden Manor at the rear between the wars. IM

Towards the end of 1918, Langley Court was being used as a camp for up to 100 Polish POWs under the guard of 30 British soldiers. Appeals were made for old magazines and games for our men being posted here as they returned from active service.

Chapter Seven: The Dardanelles

Site of the Gallipoli campaign to reach Constantinople (Istanbul) 25.4.15 to 9.1.16

EIGHT MONTHS, TWO WEEKS, ONE DAY

By late 1914, trench warfare in France had reached a stalemate and Winston Churchill, who was First Lord of the Admiralty, proposed a naval attack on the Gallipoli Peninsula with the aim of the Allies advancing through the Sea of Marmara to reach the Ottoman capital of Constantinople. Unfortunately the decision was based on erroneous reports of the Ottoman strength, poor planning, insufficient artillery, inaccurate maps, overconfidence, lack of support and use of inexperienced troops. The Allies consisted of Australia, New Zealand, Newfoundland, UK, France and French West Africa set against the Ottomans, Germany, Austria and Hungary. The Allies had hoped that Greece and Bulgaria would fight for them but the opposite happened. The plan was to land and secure the territory on the northern shore, to capture the Ottoman forts and artillery there leaving a clear way for the navy to proceed through to the Sea of Marmara. It fell to an army of 17,000 Australian and New Zealand troops as the 3rd Infantry Brigade to spearhead the attack on Anzac Cove on 25th April, thereafter celebrated as Anzac Day when they emerged as independent fighting nations. Anzac Day commemorates their landing on 25 April and loss of 8,709 Australians.

As winter approached, the Allied troops died from over exposure in the cold and many drowned in the flooded trenches. They planned to withdraw to Egypt and it can be said that the evacuation was probably the best planned of any action of the campaign. William Scurry's self-firing rifle was rigged to fire by water dripping into a pan attached to the trigger. It deceived the Ottoman troops into thinking the trenches were still occupied and the Allies were withdrawn to Egypt although many were left as POWs.

Many of the lessons learnt by this fiasco of a campaign were used when planning the landings in Normandy in 1944 and those on the Falkland Islands.

As Major Churchill, he volunteered for death or glory in the trenches and was trusted by his fusiliers due to his air of invincibility, supported by his wife Clemmie's belief in him. Lloyd George summoned him back to government in 1917 to forge the weapons of war and to energize the munition factories so that with Russia out of the war and Germany ready to annihilate Britain in March 1918, Churchill was ready. The goal of Germany's spring offensive, called Operation Michael, was to break through the Allied lines to seize the Channel ports and to drive the BEF into the sea. They were fighting over the wilderness of the 1916 spring offensive of the Somme but whereas the Allies replaced their casualties with the US soldiers, the German army failed to recover. The war machine delivered a massive tank fleet of 10,000 that won the non-stop 40-day battle for Britain. The 100-day 2nd Battle of the Somme offensive reversed the German advance and the war was won for the Allies by the 3rd September.

C F Chandler of 11th battalion Australian Infantry, killed 1.8.15, only son of Mr and Mrs Arthur Chandler of 9 Barnmead Rd, left Beckenham five years before to practise pearl fishing in Australia.

Fred Semark third son of Mr and Mrs H Semark of Seward Rd, Beckenham, was only 17 when killed by a sniper at the battle of the Dardanelles 14.8.15. Enlisted at The Triangle.

Mr Harding, scoutmaster of 1st Sydenham Scout Troop, husband of Florence of 26 Clifton Terrace, Beckenham killed 7.8.15, buried Shrapnel Valley Cemetery.

2nd Lt G K Colbourne MC awarded for conspicuous gallantry at Cuichy, son Dr L Colbourne of Llanfair, Beckenham died 11.9.15.

Gunner T Harry Dedman wrote to his wife at 133 Parish Lane enclosing his bullet-ridden tobacco pouch, after the Battle of Hill Ache Baba on the August bank holiday, hoping to be home by Christmas, saying we are all torn and tattered from the Turks' barbed wire designed to keep us off the hills. He died 2.10.15. Harry's mother lived 59 Durban Rd, Beckenham.

Rupert Brooke, the war poet, died from sepsis from an infected mosquito bite 23.4.15 on a French hospital ship off the island of Skyros in the Aegean where he is buried.

His brother, 2nd Lt William Alfred Cotterill Brooke of the Post Office Rifles, youngest of three sons, was killed on 14.6.15 at the Pas de Calais having enlisted only on 15 May.

The Soldier

If I should die, think only this of me
That there's some corner of a foreign field
That is forever England. There shall be
In that rich earth a richer dust concealed;
A dust whom England bore, shaped, made aware,
Gave, once, her flowers to love, her ways to roam,
A body of England's, breathing English air
Washed by rivers, blest by suns of home.
And think, this heart, all evil shed away,
A pulse in the eternal mind, no less
Gives somewhere back the thoughts by England given;
Her sights and sounds; dreams happy as her day;
And laughter; learnt of friends; and gentleness,
In hearts at peace, under an English heaven.

Chapter Eight: WWI Air Raids

An attack by Britain, dropping 11 bombs on the Zeppelin sheds at Friederichshafen at Lake Constance in November 1914 caused much damage. The raid, diving through heavy fire, was carried out by Wing Commander Edward Briggs, Flight Commander Babbington and Commander Sydney Sippe from Westgate Rd, Beckenham. (Beckenham Journal 19.5.1917 p3.) However early in 1915, the Kaiser sanctioned an air campaign against Britain's military bases and ammunition dumps although excluding royal palaces and residential areas.

One of the deadliest raids of the war by the Germans took place on 13 October 1915 when 71 were killed and 128 injured. Five Zeppelins from Hage and Nordholzunder the overall command of Mathy set out to bomb London but only L15 commanded by Breithaupt reached the City, dropping all his bombs near the Bank of England. The other four lost their way. L13 was looking for the Chilworth Gunpowder Mills and aircraft factories at Vickers and Brooklands but found Woolwich instead. L11 found Coltisham and L16 bombed Hertford instead of East London.

Alois Bocker on L14 steered a course for Woolwich, veered off left at the Isle of Sheppey and reaching the sea at Hythe thought it was the mouth of the Thames. He dropped 9 bombs on an army camp, killing 15 soldiers and wounding 11. Eventually he found his way to Selsdon and dropped the rest of his bombs on private houses in Edridge Rd, Beech House Rd, Oval Rd where the school was hit, Chatsworth Rd, Moreland Rd and Stretton Rd. If you examine today's map, the area is one with railway junctions and storage yards that would have appeared a suitable target but also provides a reason why Beckenham with its open fields and farms escaped the bombs that fell all round. A bomb that fell on the corner of Sydenham Rd and Fairlawn Park killed 18. Beckenham Iron Foundry was concealed in Ravenscroft Rd and produced unnoticed the magnetos for the first planes to bomb Germany. Later it moved between New Beckenham and Lower Sydenham stations.

William Cunningham Sims, butcher, was married to Ellen Mary Walter, whose mother, Eliza Harriet Walter, lived at 73 Stretton Rd with Ellen's sister, Daisy Alice and brother Sydney Amor, all three being killed when the bomb fell on their house. Daisy and Sidney died immediately but Ellen's mother Eliza was terribly injured and lingered on for three more days. Thomas, Bronwen's great-grandfather, served for 22 years in the Royal Engineers but re-enlisted in 1914 although aged 60. He was away when the bomb fell.

Daisy Alice and Eliza Harriet are seated on either side of Thomas with Sidney Amor on Eliza's left BL

45

William the butcher sold up his business and signed on for service as part of the British force in Istanbul, leaving his wife Ellen with their three children, Fred, Eric and Beryl but Ellen had lost her own family to the raid. She is extreme back right in the picture, next to her brother Frederick.

William and his two brothers survived the Western Front and Ellen had three more children after the war, Daphne, Jean and Brenda. Jean Florence Walter Sims was born 12 June 1924 and became a much loved teacher at Highfield School, Beckenham, Mrs Jean Lewis. Jean became my friend in her final years through her daughter Bronwen Howells, one of my artistically gifted biologists at Langley Park School, who had lost her great-grandmother to the Zeppelin raiders. BH

As the war went on, the Zeppelins became targets for the British fighter pilots and the anti-aircraft guns and the German Gotha G V replaced them as a long-range night bomber. A daylight attack on 13 June 1917 killed 162 civilians and is recorded in The History of Bromley Rd School p 33. In 1917, a number of children were recorded as permanently absent from the school because they had been evacuated to the country. Air attacks were being launched by Germany although the damage inflicted was minimal compared with WWII. On the morning of 13 June 1917, an assistant in charge of an open-air class, Miss Kilbourne, saw a German plane. The class was brought in, the children were brought away from the windows and all were detained until 12.25 in school. Air raids continued through 1917 and 1918 although there were no bombs on Beckenham. After night raids, the children were not expected at school until 9.45, to give them more sleep.

The boys of the Beckenham Grammar School, whose school was on the baths' site, first experienced an air raid on a Saturday morning during break when they watched the sky full of planes over Clock House Station, 'looking and sounding like a swarm of angry bees'. The Churchfields Rd anti-aircraft gun suddenly went off and the staff called the boys in to assemble in the basement. Afterwards the boys would collect the shrapnel.

By the summer of 1918, the Royal Insurance Company was offering cover for a premium of £1 a year to insure against bodily injury caused by enemy raids with TW Thornton the agent.

Chapter Nine: Prisoners of War

On Thursday, 27 March 1919 a welcome back dinner was given at the Beckenham Public Hall in honour of the officers and men who had spent much of the war as POWs of the enemy. Friends and relatives worried constantly about their menfolk held prisoner but the majority survived and were repatriated. The War Office requested that it was notified immediately when relatives received postcards from British POWs with names and addresses since the men were entirely dependent on food and supplies from England. Their first cards were sent via Limburg forwarded to Copenhagen and a reserve of 12,000 parcels of food was kept at Rotterdam to meet emergencies. To the considerable number of soldiers who fell into enemy hands at Cambrai, the Central Prisoners of War Committee had sent 4,000 set of clothes, socks, vests, pants and cardigans as well as food.

Personal parcels weighing between 3-11 pounds could be despatched through the post office every three months using a coupon from the man's regimental care committee. It could contain any of the following: pipe, sponge, pencils, tooth powder, pomade, shaving stick, razor, bootlaces, handkerchief, health salts, insecticide, comb, toothbrush, buttons, chess, draughts, dominoes, dubbin, hobnails, sweets, brass polish, mitts and a muffler. Money could be sent as a postal order.

In the Schneidemuhl camp in Germany at the end of the war, about 40 men died from pneumonia in a fortnight and the death rate in Turkish hands was considerable because of brutal treatment. Six of our Beckenham men died in captivity.

Lance Corporal George J Harrod, 240520 5th RW Kent, died in Tarsus, Iraq after the surrender of Kut 16.10.16 and is buried in the cemetery at Bagdad.

Pte George Edward Wakenell, 240157 RW Kent, died in Turkish hands 29.10.16. Buried in Bagdad cemetery. Parents Arthur and Priscilla Wakenell of Beckenham.

Cpl William Beasley RW Kent died of wounds 18.8.16 in hospital at Minden, Westphalia in Germany having written to his parents in 9 Somerville Rd, Penge.

Capt Ivan Clarkson Maclean DSO, MC and bar, Royal Army Medical Corps, son of Major General Maclean, died of wounds 4.4.18 aged 36, buried Premont British cemetery.

Major Percy Garrad, London Reg and Kings African Rifles, died of pneumonia at Mivembe in Portuguese East Africa, 18.9.18.

L Cpl William J Norris, 20548, son of William and Ellen Norris of 238 Blandford Rd, died in hospital aged 19 from pneumonia and heart failure 23.11.18, buried Malone communal cemetery.

Relatives passed on the news to the Beckenham Journal when they heard from their POW husbands and sons.

Pte Ernest W Barton, son of Mr and Mrs E M Barton of 21 Park Rd was taken prisoner in Dulmer, Germany 30.11.17. He had attended Bromley Rd School and St George's choir for four years before becoming a telegraph boy, then a postman. He had already been wounded and in a French hospital for three weeks last September.

Pte Norman J Richardson had been in France with the Norfolk Reg before being wounded on 14.10.17 and kept a prisoner in Germany. He had attended Elmers End School and worked for about seven years for the greengrocer Mr Goddard at 90 High St.

Capt Frank Neville Hudson, airman, had been reported missing for six weeks before his parents, Mr and Mrs Frank Hudson of Camelot, Beckenham, heard that he was a POW in Germany.

At their celebratory dinner, the honoured guests were waited on by a squad of boy scouts while they enjoyed the meal of oxtail soup, roast beef supplied by Hagger the Beckenham butcher, vegetables, plum pudding, cheese and dessert. It was rounded off with ale and tobacco. The entertainment included songs and humorous verses and they were toasted with the 'Heartiest Welcome Home'. They each received a souvenir booklet decorated with WELCOME HOME and the Allied flags with the names of all the Beckenham POWs that the organisers had managed to contact. At least one was absent because Pte Henry Harrod, R W Kent, a POW in Kut, had been exchanged for a Turkish POW and was at present a staff sergeant in India.

Beckenham soldiers as POWs	Regiment
Lt F Allerton	Rifle Brigade
Lt H Bush	3rd Kings Reg
Lt J A Cains	Argyle & Sutherland Highlanders
Lt V Coombs	RAF
Capt Noel Cranswick MC	12th Kings Royal Rifles
Lt Arthur Finch	London Rifle Brigade
Lt K Hooper	3rd East Lancs
Capt F N Hudson MC	Buffs & RAF
Lt Hughes	Essex Reg
Lt T Kent	R F C
2nd Lt F O Lane MC	Machine Gun Corps
Lt R Petley	London Rifle Brigade
Capt R W W Parker	Shropshire Yeomanry
2nd Lt Stockwell	
Lt S J Wilmott	Northumberland Fusiliers
Lt W Wilson	RAF
Capt S Wimble	London Rifle Brigade
J E Adams	Middx Reg
Pte J Adnams	Middx Reg
Sgt T Andoyer	R Inniskilling Fusiliers
Sgt F R Andrews	RAMC
Cpl C L Arnold	East Surrey
Cpl G L Baldwin	Leister Reg
Pte E Barton	RWK
Pt E A Bennett	RWK
S Bourne AB	R N V R
Pte J B Bradley	Middx Reg
Rfn H Brett	London Rifle Brigade
Pte R Buist	Sherwood Forresters
Rfn E Byfield	London Rifle Brigade
Gnr F W Carter	Machine Gun Battalion
Pte H Carter	Bedford Reg
Cpl W L Clark	RWK
Pte E Coles	RWK
Pte A H Collins	RWK
Pte H Collis	RWK
Pte G Cooper	RWK
Pte P Cooper	RWK
Pte P Cotman	East Surrey
Pte L Davis	Essex Reg
Pte R Dealing	R F
Pte E Dickinson	City of London Reg
Pte T Dow	RWK
C Duddey	R N D
Pte S Eagle	London Rgt
Pte J W Ellis	Royal Sussex
Pte J Filby	East Kent
Pte F Foster	Suffolk Reg
Pte H Francis	Royal Fusiliers
Pte W George	East Surrey
Pte E Gooch	Royal Fusiliers
Rfn C Goswell	K R R
Sgt G Gregory	
Pte G E Hanscombe	East Kent
AB G S Hawley	RNVR
Pte W Hobbs	RWK
Pte Honey	East Kent
Pte F Hollis	RWK

49

Pte F Holton	Innisking Fusiliers
Sapper L Howckam	Royal Engineers
Rfn E Humphries	Cambs Rifles
Pte W Ianes	East Surrey
Sgt R Jackson	RB
AB F W Jefferey	RNVR
Cpl A E Jennings	RWK
G Jones	RWK
Pte G Lane	Queens Royal West Surrey
Pte G H Latter	Middx Regiment
Pte C Larby	Essex Regiment
Pte A Lewis	Royal Fusiliers
Pte A S Morphew	Essex Reg
Sgt J Morris	RWK
Cpl B J Nash	RB
Pte E Parker	Royal Fusiliers
Rfn E Parker	W Yorks
Pte J Parnell	Royal Fusiliers
Pte W Perrey	RWK
Pte E Pettitt	Middx Reg
Pte A Peters	RWK
Rfn F W Player	C S Rifles
Cpl W H Pyne	South Wales Bords
Pte H Richards	RWK
Pte N J Richardson	Norfolk Reg
L Ripley AB	RNVR
Rfn C Rippengal	LRB
Pte Russell	
Pte F Sarson	QWR
Pte R Saxton	Middx Reg
Pte B Saunders	East Kent
Cpl F L Scott	Royal Irish Rifles
Cpl L Semark	Lanc Fusiliers
Pte W Skinner	RDC
Pte E H Smith	London Reg
Pte W Smith	Canadian R
Pte J Smith	London Reg
Pte H R Songer	East Surrey
Pte E Speller	Middx Reg
Rfn W Springhall	RB
Pte A E Stone	RWK
Cpl H Stokes	RMLI
Pte W Thatcher	W Yorks
Spr G Telley	Royal Engineers
Rfn B Tomblin	LR
Pte F Tyler	
Pte J Verrall	RWK
Rfn H Warman	RB
Rfn R J Watson	LR
Pte W C Weatherill	RWK
Gnr E West	MGC
Pte M D Whincop	RWS
G Whibley	RGA
Sgt T Whitehead	East Surrey
Pte J Wilson	RWK
Rfn A Wright	16th London Reg

There were of course German POWs taken and Langley Court was used to house German officer POWs.

A story in the paper 1 September 1917 related to two German flying officers who had escaped from the Holyport camp at Maidenhead, a straight 35 miles away. They were Lt Josef Flink and Lt Orbun Alevander von Schultz aiming to find an airfield to fly a plane home. PC Cleever from Beckenham Police Station was cycling with his dog, a collie cross foxhound, in Kent Lane, West Wickham at 1.45am when his dog suddenly ran on ahead barking and growling. It was very dark and pouring with rain but the dog had seen the two men crouching under a hedge. The escaped prisoners realised the game was up and admitted they were Germans. Both men were tall powerful fellows dressed in semi-military uniform but were wet through, covered with mud and had been sleeping in the woods for several days so they went quietly to Beckenham Police Station escorted by the dog!

Beckenham Police Station before WWI IM

51

Chapter Ten: End of war

How was the news of peace received in Beckenham? People were shy in the early hours of Monday morning 11 November 1918 of celebrating too soon. Then as residents collected by the journal offices, lorries from the aerodrome began arriving, decked with flags and with the men sitting on the bonnets and mudguards. Soldiers billeted in the big houses were given leave to rejoice and when the two Beckenham maroons sounded off at 11.00am the children in Bromley Rd School cheered in the playground and were given the rest of the day off. Everyone found some red, white and blue to wear, including a satisfied cat in a shop window. By the evening, the dingy lights in the Beckenham Council Electricity Department had been exchanged for much brighter ones, the bells had been sounding at the parish church and an impromptu band from the Balgowan Red Cross Hospital of tin whistles, spoons and tin trays had been playing round a lamp in the High St raising a goodly show of pennies for the cottage hospital. The boys of Chancery Lane had a bonfire and fireworks had been found hidden away to celebrate. A thanksgiving service at St George's church saw the choir singing from the Hallelujah Chorus and the Baptist

Crowds gather at Thornton's corner IM

church at Elm Rd was full, unlike the evening classes at the technical school that were deserted!

Beckenham celebrated peace on Saturday 26 July 1919 by concentrating mainly on the children. Large crowds in their brightest clothes lined the route from the council offices to Kelsey Park to watch the procession led by a shining fire engine and the band. Demobbed soldiers and sailors, Boy Scouts and Girl Guides led the children from Bromley Rd wearing red sashes, Churchfields with white and Alexandra and Elmers End in blue. The theme of the service held in the park was that it was for the future of these 10 to 15 year-olds that our brave men had fought the war often at the cost of their lives. The great audience sang the hymn 'Through the night of doubt and sorrow' and after the address by the rector the Rev Plowden-Wardlaw the massed choirs of children sang Land of Hope and Glory, Hearts of Oak and Rule Britannia.

The children marched to the Kelsey mansion, over 2,300 of them, to each receive a bag of cakes and a ticket for lemonade before taking part in their sports which included a blindfold horse race to give everyone a chance. There were plenty of events following each other in quick succession. Meanwhile the firemen had arranged a display of fountains in the lake, Mr Hill's Living Marionettes performed on the little stage and the Scouts and Guides attracted an audience with their cockfighting where two participants sat astride a rail and belaboured each other with bags of hay until one fell off.

Music was provided by the Upper Norwood Prize Band and the Beckenham Orchestral Society and the teas provided by the Kelsey mansion were in heavy demand although brought to a close by some heavy showers that sent thousands running for home. As it dried up in the evening, people came out again to admire the canopies of Allied flags at Thornton's corner, the trees at the council offices with their display of Japanese lanterns, the windows outlined with twinkling fairy lights and the Three Tuns which was outlined with red, white and blue electric lamps. The honour of flying the biggest flag went to Mr J Smith in the High St for his red ensign. At 10.00pm surplus naval flares were set alight among the trees around Kelsey Park that produced a wonderful sight, a fairyland of green tints and light reflected from the windows of the mansion.

The Daily News of Bouverie St, London announced a competition 22 March 1919 to find the British family with the largest number of male members in the fighting forces, army, navy, air force and Royal Army Medical Corps but the end of the war brought problems as men suffered from unemployment and widows needed support. The Beckenham & Penge Branch of Discharged and Demobbed Soldiers and Sailors had about 150 members increasing by 15 to 20 members per week in June 1918. An out-of-work national donation scheme ran for 26 weeks from December 1918 to October 1919 for two periods of 13 weeks, the second paying less than the first. Working women had to cede their jobs to returning soldiers and sailors. They asked the civilian population not to forget the members of the merchant navy who may have been torpedoed many times and fired upon while struggling in the water. If disabled, they needed a living pension too. Twenty widows on their books by October 1919 had no pensions because their husbands had died since leaving the service even though their deaths had been accelerated by their wartime experiences and aggravated by it. They felt that the state should provide a pension. By 1920 there were 158 unemployed in Beckenham of whom 124 were ex-servicemen.

The discussion began in the Beckenham Council about a war memorial and in January 1919 it was suggested it take the form of an improved cottage hospital with a tablet recording the fallen and those who had earned special distinction. As we know, this idea was supplanted by the construction of our Beckenham war memorial. Sir Philip Armand Hamilton Giggs, one of five official British reporters during the Great War for the Daily Telegraph and Daily Chronicle, wrote convincingly for a specific war memorial, summarised as follows.

'After months of discussion, a confusion of ideas about the character of a memorial hopelessly divides committees. Where is the shrine to which future generations will come with bared heads remembering the sacrifices made? Not in a pleasure garden, a new church organ or set of bells. Hospital extensions will better accommodate the sick but what if a future government at last makes itself responsible for the health of the nation and rebuilds its hospitals? Lord Leconfield has presented England's highest summit, Scafell Pike, to the nation as a war memorial, but it is to have no monument to the suffering of the men who kept England safe on the hills. Today's widows and orphans are giving their shillings so that soldiers who were theirs will always be remembered by a visible sign, a shrine to the courage and patience of those who died to save us when we were threatened with destruction. It should arrest the mind of the passer-by to remember the tragedy as well as the valour, a warning that war brings slaughter, ruin and broken hearts. Its essential spirit is for Remembrance. Remember first.'

Chapter Eleven: The Beckenham War Memorial

It was nearly two years after the armistice and still Beckenham had no war memorial, likewise Bromley and Penge. How could it be that our towns, where large numbers of young men had sacrificed their lives, were so apathetic about subscribing towards a memorial? A small village near Boston in Lincolnshire had raised a considerable sum towards a war memorial before it was realised that no lives had been lost and many country villages had had their wayside crosses in place for the past 12 months. By the beginning of August 1920 West Wickham's 1,301 inhabitants had organised the cross that would be in place within four months and subscribed £177 to cover easily the expected £158.

Perhaps the cost of the Beckenham memorial was part of the trouble, also the fact that we had decided to both collect to rejuvenate the Beckenham Cottage Hospital as well as erect a stone monument. For at least six months the collection was divided between the two and a list of subscribers was published regularly in the Journal. The total at the end of August 1920 was £2,727 19s 10d of which the monument was to receive £1,468 19s 4d and the cottage hospital £1,259 0s 6d. This would have been a generous sum compared with that collected by West Wickham had not the estimate for the intended design come to £3,500! Beckenham's population of 33,345 found

it much more difficult to come to an agreement over the form and kind of its war memorial than a small village.

The fund was closed by the end of November when it was decided to donate all the subscribed money to the monument, a total of £2,198 12s 10d.

By eliminating the two allegorical figures, sinister with snake and sword to represent barbarism and discord and benign with laurel wreath and flowers for peace and plenty, this sum was sufficient.

A correspondent to the Journal, 'Gadfly'

asked why now that all contributions were going to the monument were people not subscribing more, so that we only have enough funding for a rather 'mousy' structure (and not the one shown here in the picture)? BJ

It was asked if the chairman of the UDC remembered promising at the beginning of the war that the services of the men who went to enlist would not be forgotten. There were requests to be able to donate small sums without having to have one's name in print. Then there was considerable disagreement as to the site of the war memorial. Suggestions included the west side of St George's churchyard, Kelsey Park, the quiet open corner opposite Thornton's and the junction of Croydon and Rectory Roads. Many thought there were bound to be accidents saying, 'The mad way that motorists rush from Croydon Rd into Rectory Rd, oblivious of traffic from Beckenham Rd, makes people hold their breath. One of these days the monument will be toppled over.'

Of the 7,700 households in Beckenham, only 500 contributed to the public memorial, perhaps because the multiplication of monuments through the district did not fit in with the tragedy of homeless and workless ex-servicemen. Others thought it would be wrong to undertake too large a venture that would leave subsequent generations having to pay for it.

Penge was also torn between providing 'Homes of Rest' for disabled men and the conventional memorial, settling on the latter, a cross to be erected in a semicircular space set back from the recreation ground in Croydon Rd at a cost of between £300 and £400.

John Hanscombe born 3/1/1842 in Norwood, South London, married Sarah Ann in North Ormsby, Yorkshire 6/10/1872. She was born in 1853 at Ecclesfield near Sheffield as were two of her sons but most of their children were born in Beckenham. Their only daughter, Mary Elizabeth, was born in Beckenham, their second child, on 15 February 1879 and she stayed there all her life. The name Hanscombe was to become very well known with nine sons taking part in WWI as soldiers. George Edward, with 21 years service in the East Kents, was badly wounded at Cambrai and became a POW of the Germans on 30.11.17. He was one of the ex-POWs made welcome home at the public hall dinner for POWs on Thursday 27 March 1919. Bert and Joe were also in the East Kents and it delighted their mother in that all three, with their families, were able to spend Christmas 1918 with her at Kimberley Rd. Frank and Richard Arthur were members of the West Kents but were both out of the country with Frank travelling back from abroad. Of the others, James, who was married with six children, was invalided out and living in Wales, Frederick John was posted with his regiment and David was convalescing at Rotherhithe. Stephen, the youngest, was at Darlington with the RFA and he had only just married in armistice week. Most of the others were married with families.

Unveiling of Beckenham War Memorial
Thornton's Series.

Of all the sons, it is Bert DCM, MM, who has become the most famous, because on him was bestowed the honour of unveiling the Beckenham War Memorial on 24 July 1921 in the absence of Lord Haig. Born in Ecclesfield, Yorks, in 1887, Bert became a municipal dustman for Beckenham marrying Ellen Cromwell at the parish church on 25 April 1909 when he was 22 years old. In October 1915, Bert was serving in France in the 7th Bn East Surrey Regiment at the Hulluch Quarries close to the Hollenzollern Redoubt leading a bombing party. They captured a German trench and held it for 22 hrs to retain their position and join up with their officer, Lt Findlay. On 1 January 1916 Bert was mentioned in dispatches and promoted to sergeant and awarded an MM at a special parade at Kingston on Thursday 4 January 1917 by Lt Col H P Treeby. Both he and his brother Richard Arthur were awarded the DCM, Distinguished Conduct Medal, which is second in importance only to the VC. In Bert's case it was awarded when at Cambrai at the end of 1917, most of Bert's battalion was captured and made POWs but Bert was one of only seven men who evaded capture and reached their own lines. To compare, 2nd Lt Alfred James Terence Fleming-Sandes from

Queens Rd, Beckenham, of the 2nd Bn of the East Surreys was awarded the VC at the Hollenzollern Redoubt on 20 September 1915 when he rallied his men by seizing some bombs, jumping on the parapet and throwing them at the enemy only 20 yards away. The local committee chose Mr Hanscombe for the unveiling for both his war records and those of his eight brothers who served in the forces and suffered 21 wounds.

The memorial, which was designed by Mr Newbury A Trent, bore 711 names of the Beckenham fallen on 12 tablets. It is approximately 7.5 metres high, and is a rectangular white Portland stone column.

At the summit is a broad Celtic cross, enriched on one side in high relief with an equestrian figure of St. George slaying the legendary dragon (symbolic of the destruction of evil) and on the reverse side the phoenix rising from its own ashes (symbolic of immortality).

The Rev R Stewart Fleming from the Beckenham Baptist Church in Elm Rd was responsible for the sermon at the unveiling service. He spoke as follows: 'We are met to honour the memory of the 711 of our town who laid down their lives in the Great War whose names are inscribed on this monument. They were called to surrender their lives at a time when life was instinct with sweetness and hope. They were yearning for the large excitement that the coming years would yield. Life was calling to them with an eager voice. They saw the future aglow with happiness both for themselves and for those they loved. Then with startling suddenness came the call to arms. They who had known nothing more fierce than the friendly rivalry of healthy sport were called upon almost without warning to face death in a hundred terrible forms. They did not flinch. They loved life, they loved righteousness and freedom more. They hated death and war but they hated injustice and tyranny more. They fell fighting for

SERGT. HANSCOMBE, D.C.M., M.M.
Photo: London News Agency.

58

home, for England, for God. Many fond hopes lie buried beneath the monument which you have erected in their memory and honour.'

The flag slowly fell as Sgt Bert Hanscombe stood silent and still as though overcome with the thought of the number of men that the one monument represented. Then came half a minute's silence as part of the service. Mr C A Elgood said that the memorial which had just been unveiled was the outward and visible sign that the memorial owed to the men who had left Beckenham to fight in the Great War and it was most appropriate and fitting that it should have been unveiled by Sgt Hanscombe who was an employee of the Beckenham District Council. He joined the forces on September 4th, one month after the declaration of war and served until the end. He was one of nine brothers who served and he himself was covered with distinction.

The Rev R Stewart Fleming's own son, John Allister Fleming, RWK Regiment, died of wounds age 23 in July 1916.

Prince George, The Duke of Kent laid a wreath at the memorial on Thursday 20 October 1932 when amongst others he was introduced to Mr Hanscombe, then secretary of the Beckenham British Legion Branch. The Prince, later that same day, forsaking his chauffeur-driven vehicle, walked part of the way to the High Street to open the new town hall and unveiled a plaque to record this second event.

Bert and Ellen had two children. Their daughter Winifred died in infancy but their son Harold Stanley born 1916 emigrated to New Zealand where he became a house painter and raised a family of four.

Bert moved away from Beckenham to the Midlands where he died from heart failure age 65 on 30 April 1952 in the presence of his stepdaughter-in-law. He had been working as a lorry driver for wholesale butchers and lived in Penn, Wolverhampton at 42 East Croft Rd.

James Hanscombe, born at his maternal grandparent's house in Ecclesfield 1880, married Lucy Edith Maud in Beckenham in 1905. She was born in Beckenham 1883. Their first son, Walter James, was born in Beckenham in 1906 but then they moved to 10 Harrison St, Penydarren in Merthyr Tydfil where they had John William in 1908 and Roy Hanscombe's father, Robert Osborne, in 1910 and three more. Robert married Mildred Griffiths in 1937 and Roy was born in Walthamstow, Essex 1 April 1940. Roy has been the source of much of the information given here about the family.

Roy's grandfather James moved to Wales to become a stoker at the ironworks. He had joined the 3rd Bn East Surrey Regiment 4 May 1915

as Pte 9195 James Hanscombe, joining the army in France until October 1916 when he was shipped home because he had suffered shrapnel splinter wounds to his head with loss of teeth. He was discharged as unfit for service by August 1917, awarded a silver war wound badge and a pension of 8s/3d per week. He eventually moved to Walthamstow but he died while visiting in Wales in 1944.

George Edward was born at his paternal grandparent's house in Norwood, Surrey in January 1878. After a time as a gas worker, he joined the Duke of York's Military School in Canterbury when he was 20 and went on to serve as Pte 203565 with the East Kent Regiment (The Buffs) in India and Aden where he contracted malaria. He served back home until July 1910 when he discharged to the Army Reserve only to re-enlist with The Buffs in November 1914. Wounded in the arm in 1916, posted as a Lewis Gunner in France in 1917, he was badly injured in the hip in November and captured, becoming a POW in the Julich Military Hospital in Germany. He suffered greatly during his time as a prisoner as can be seen in his before and after WWI pictures below. He survived and died in Beckenham in 1951 in his seventies.

George Edward Hanscombe
1878 1951

Frank was another of the boys to have been born in Yorkshire but this time it was Middlesbrough in 1882. A boy, Samuel, had died in infancy after being born 6/10/1881 and it is likely that John had looked for work in the North. Frank joined the 9th East Surrey Regiment (The Gallants) at Aldershot in June 1915 and after training for a short time at Chobham and Blackdown Camp, they embarked at Southampton docks for Boulogne on 31st August.

Like his brothers, he was in time for the Battle of Loos after long forced marches across France. For the rest of the war, he miraculously survived numerous battles, ending with the Battle of Sambre in 1918, 4-11 November.

After another baby boy, Alfred, dying in infancy in 1885 after his birth on 10 October 1884, Frederick John was born at Sultan St, Beckenham, 26 January 1886. He enlisted in May 1915 in the 1st/22nd (Queens) London Regiment as Pte G/8170 but he was not sufficiently fit to be sent overseas although he served faithfully in this country throughout the war being seriously injured by a falling gun when loading ammunition. When he was demobbed in 1919, he was sent to a hospital in Wiltshire leaving his wife, Louisa Annie, to manage on her own while they waited for a place nearer home.

Richard Arthur was born in 1888 in Beckenham and attended Churchfields School. He worked as a brick builder's labourer before enlisting in the 1st Bn (Beckenham) Royal West Kents in April 1915. Landing in France in September 1915, the idea was to strengthen inexperienced divisions with regular army troops although many like Richard were new recruits. While he was on transport duty, he was kicked in the neck by a mule, but until January 1916, the division spent its time repairing and deepening trenches before taking part in the many battles of 1917 like Vimy, La Courcelette, Scarpe and Passchendaele.

At the end of December 1917, they had a wonderful relief from the trenches when they travelled by train to Italy via Marseille and Nice. They were needed to hold the line of the River Piave on the Venetian Plain but by the end of March 1918 were recalled to France to help stave off the German advance round Amiens. Again the journey by train was a pleasant interlude along the Riviera but in France the Forest of Nieppe had to be held against constant attack by mustard gas. This is where Richard earned his DCM for continuous gallant conduct covering a long period of service in France. This soldier has on every occasion showed exceptional gallantry, a very high sense of duty and has taken part in many actions.

Born in Beckenham on 18/7/1890, Joseph (Joe) was a plumber's assistant  and railway porter before joining the East Surrey Regiment 3rd Bn when nearly 18 on 26/1/1908 where he remained for five years until the end of March 1913. At the start of the war, he embarked as a Reservist at Dover on 9 August for Salonika but there the extreme temperature and malaria were affecting thousands of troops, 63,398 out of 100,000 in 1917 alone. Joseph was repatriated at the beginning of November 1918 and treated for malaria at a special camp at Chelmsford, Essex and the Bridge of Allan in Scotland.

David was born in Beckenham in 1892 but at the age of 16 in March  1908 he became yet another regular soldier in the Hanscombe family. He enlisted at Kingston on Thames as Pte 9480 in the 8th Bn East Surrey Regiment to train at the Duke of York Military School at Dover. For July and August, the regiment spent time at the Wilsworthy training camp under canvas in Devon but discipline was very strict. David absconded with a friend, Alfred Boosey, on 6th August and they were charged at the petty sessions with desertion. Posted to the 2nd Bn of the East Surreys, David served in India, Rangoon and the Andaman Islands in the Indian Ocean where it is likely that he was a guard in the very large prison at St Blair. The battalion returned to England at the end of 1914 to be posted to France on 19 January 1915. Several campaigns later after a serious chest wound and gunshot to the knee he was discharged as unfit for service with a silver war wound badge and a pension of 12/6d per week on 10/11/1916.

Living with his brother Fred John at Rotherhithe and separated from his wife Winifred, David eventually recovered enough to re-enlist on 24/4/1919 in the 1st Bn Royal Welsh Fusiliers. He was promoted to Sgt 4179891 in Ladha, Waziristan, Afghanistan but while superintending a woodcutting party at Prospect Piquet in 1922, David was killed by a sniper and was buried locally. He was awarded the Waziristan medal and his name appears on the memorial plaque in St Giles church, Wrexham, Clwyd in Wales.

Stephen, the youngest of the family born 15 October 1895, was 19 when he left his landscape gardening and enlisted as Gunner 29917 in the Royal Artillery. Sent to France in July 1915 he started a long and courageous service in France on the huge, heavy calibre guns that would become stuck fast in the awful sticky mud. When he was demobbed in March 1919, it was in the class Z which meant that he could be recalled if needed. This was abolished 31/3/19.

And what of Mary Elizabeth, only sister of all these brave men? She grew up in Beckenham with her brothers and married William John Cousins from the Royal Navy in 1900 when they were both 21. John served from September 1898 to July 1919 when discharged medically unfit. They had five children, Emily Florence, Mary Elizabeth, William John who died as a baby, Ellen and Robert. Mary died 24/1/1941 and her husband died 9/5/1945.

In 2012 the new MP for Beckenham, Colonel Bob Stewart, former

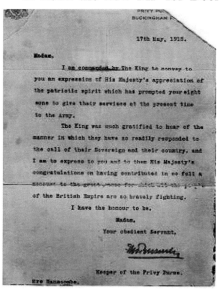

The letter from the King to Mrs Hanscombe

commander in Bosnia and one-time guard of Rudolf Hess in Spandau prison, supported the idea that the Beckenham War Memorial should be moved away from where it had always been in full view of the town's visitors. Beckenham Green was thought to be a suitable alternative, a site where it would be exposed to vandalism as well as where the ground beneath is pockmarked with cellars and former building works. We hope that future historians will appreciate the respect that was shown to our brave Beckenham WWI fighters by the residents of the 21st century who chose to leave the memorial in its original position.

We realise today that the names on the memorial are just some of the total number of the fallen. Many who died from wounds, disease or Spanish

flu, perhaps months after discharge from the forces, were buried at the Elmers End cemetery, often recognised by a military style funeral, without their names being submitted for the memorial. Other names appear on neighbouring memorials like that at Shortlands where 45 of the names are not also present on the Beckenham memorial.

All pictures and stories related to the Hanscombes are supplied by James's grandson, Roy Hanscombe.

The following poem by John Oxenham can be seen on the back of the Beckenham memorial.

To You Who Have Lost
I know, I know
The ceaseless ache, the emptiness, the woe,
The pang of loss-
The strength that sinks beneath so sore a cross.
Heedless and careless, still the world wags on, And leaves me broken
Oh my son, my son.
Yea think of this
Yea rather think on this,
He died as few men get the chance to die-
Fighting to save a world's morality.
He died the noblest death a man may die,
Fighting for God, and Right, and Liberty-
And such a death is Immorality.

Chapter Twelve: Stories from the names on Beckenham's War Memorial

Two years of gloom our home has past and still we mourn for him we loved so dear. In an unknown grave somewhere in France our dear boy now sleeps, the memory of that last goodbye and of his boyhood days at home we never can or shall forget.

Art Willis died 3/10/1915 age 21.

We have been able to identify close to 600 names out of the 711 lost locally in WWI although this is only a fraction, perhaps a third, of the total killed. Figures released by the South Suburban Gas Company in August 1918 indicate that 10% of the 454 who had enlisted were killed or missing, with five POWs. Figures released in June 1919 from the Royal West Kent Regiment were that from 15 battalions, 6,073 were killed. With 18,000 men in a battalion, this is about 22%.

The primary source has been the Commonwealth War Graves Commission started by Sir Fabian Ware, 1869-1949, commander of a mobile Red Cross unit, that recorded as many war graves as could be found. Recognised by the War Office in 1915 and the Prince of Wales in 1917, by the end of the war in 1918 there were 587,000 graves identified and 559,000 registered but with no known grave. Memorials to the missing include Ypres Menin Gate, Thiepval on the Somme, Helles at Gallipoli and Tyne Cot in Belgium. Today, Google www.cwgc.org to have an excellent chance of identifying a name from the memorial even though the forenames are only represented on it by initials. Occasionally a deceased member of the forces is not recognised by the Commission if it is thought that the war was not the immediate cause of death. Peter Wiseman, Ellen Barbet and Cliff Watkins have found many references in Elmers End Cemetery to those who died from wounds or sickness months after discharge or from the outbreak of Spanish flu. Sometimes the task is impossible without additional information, such as the 53 entries for Field H. The soldier's medals of the National Archives sometimes record names not in the CWGC and just occasionally the spelling may be wrong.

Using findmypast.co.uk or ancestry, the census records for 1911 and 1901 are the next step to confirm that a name found on the CWGC is linked to Beckenham. The BMDs are useful providing forenames and marriages, especially as a widow may have moved away to a family home leaving no apparent Beckenham connection. The list of private residents in Beckenham, Penge and Anerley from Kelly's Directory for 1914 has assisted identification and occasionally Genes Reunited has solved a problem.

Compiled in the War Office, there are 80 volumes of 'Soldiers who died in the Great War 1914-1919,' that commemorate some 635,000 listed alphabetically and we have used part 56 of the Middlesex Regiment supplying rank, birth place, enlistment, date, place and nature of casualty.

The Beckenham Journal recorded as many of the local killed and wounded as were notified, first of all by Frank Thornton, and the weekly accounts have listed many who are not on the Beckenham Memorial at all and others where success has come from a vital snippet of local information. Valuable accounts of shipping lost during the war are found online too.

We have to thank Irene Palmer for passing on her research which greatly assisted completing the following alphabetical list. We apologise if some of our identification is wrong and welcome any corrections.

ABBOTT FRANK MACLEAN of HMS Surprise died 23/12/1917 age 24, son of John Colpoys and Nellie Buchanan Abbott of Travancore, India. Memorial CHATHAM NAVAL MEMORIAL, grave 20. Found by reference in BJ 13/11/1915 when lieutenant on HMS Albion.

ABBOTT, JOHN GURNEY Second Lieutenant Rifle Brigade 6th Bn. attd. 59th Trench Mortar Bty.
Died 21/09/1917 age 27, Panel 145 to 147. TYNE COT MEMORIAL.
Son of Donald Nicoll Abbott and Grace Abbott, of 2, Overbury Avenue, Beckenham.
Elected Underwriter of Lloyds in 1911 and joined Inns of Court O T C in Jan 1916.

ABEL JAMES EDGAR MC 2nd Lieutenant RWK 6th Bn.
Died 22/12/1917 age 37, buried at HONNECHY BRITISH CEMETERY.
Son of James born 1845, manager bookbinding and Hannah Ruth born 1856 of 14 Shortlands Rd.

ABURROW WILLIAM Pioneer 124824 Royal Engineers 13th Labour Bn. Died 23/01/1916 age 47 Grave Pink's. 8. 20. PORTSMOUTH (KINGSTON) CEMETERY.
Husband of Ellen Aburrow, of 7, Stanmere Terrace, Beckenham.

ADAMS JOHN BERNARD PYE Lieutenant Royal Welsh Fusiliers died 27/2/1917 age 26 buried COUIN NEW BRITISH CEMETERY. Son of Harold John and Georgina Adams of St Johns, Oakwood Ave, Beckenham. See BJ 10/3/1917.

ADAMS P L
Two possibilities Lieutenant Adams of Machine Gun Corps died 3/10/1916 buried Doingt Communal Cemetery East.
Or Private Adams of the York and Lancaster 6th Bn. died 1/10/1918 buried Sucrerie Cemetery, Epinoy.

ADCOCK JOSEPH BENJAMIN sapper Royal Engineers, L Signal Bn., died 21/4/1918 buried HARINGHE BANDAGHEM MILITARY CEMETERY.
Born abt 1886 Wandsworth, married Lilian Baker of Bromley 1915.

AERTS, NORMAN ARTHUR Rifleman 303096 London Regiment (London Rifle Brigade) 5th Bn.
Died 13/05/1917 age 19 Grave XVIII. M. 18A. ETAPLES MILITARY CEMETERY.
Son of Emily Clara and the late John Emile Aerts, of 3, Wickham Rd., Beckenham.
Born at Highbury, London. His brother Francis Robert Aerts also fell.

AERTS, FRANCIS ROBERT MC Second Lieutenant Welsh Regiment 13th Bn.
Died 26/12/1919 age 26 Grave P7. 8097. BECKENHAM CREMATORIUM AND CEMETERY.

AITCHISON DOUGLAS JAMES RAF and Royal Field Artillery died 17/4/1918 of septicaemia at the RFC hospital, Hampstead, age 21, buried CAMBERWELL OLD CEMETERY grave 69.22704, son of the late optician James born 1861 and Kate Sarah born 1863 of 11 Westgate Rd.

ALISON, LAUGHTON HASSARD Second Lieutenant Royal Berkshire Regiment 1st Bn.
Died 15/05/1915, Panel 30. Memorial LE TOURET MEMORIAL.
Visitor to 27 Southend Rd., Beckenham as a Cambridge student in 1911, born abt 1891.

ALLFREY N L not in CWGC or among 90 in National Archives but could it be Captain Hugh Lionel Allfrey son of Edward Richmond Allfrey of Eden Park Beckenham born abt 1882 died The Buffs 18/9/1918 in Vendhulle?

AMNER GEORGE CECIL 29087 Private Duke of Cornwall's Light Infantry 6th Bn. formerly 1218, City of London R. Fusiliers.
Born Brixton, lived Bermondsey.
Killed in action 23 Aug 1917 Panel 80 to 82 & 163A. TYNE COT MEMORIAL.
Although no obvious connection with Beckenham he is the only Amner G C in the National Archives or CWGC.

ANDERSON ERNEST GEORGE died long after the echo of guns died away. He enlisted in the Bucks Hussars and transferred to the Fusiliers. Twice gassed, he returned to his service with the Post Office but died in Beckenham Cottage Hospital on 20 March 1920. A keen cricketer, he was the youngest son of Charles Anderson of Burnhill Rd. and husband of Manda Annie Anderson. Reported in the Beckenham Journal on 27/3/1920.

ANDERSON, HENRY LAWRENCE Lieutenant Colonel 9th Bhopal Infantry.
Died 29/10/1914 age 47 Grave VI. F. 2. PONT-DU-HEM MILITARY CEMETERY, LA GORGUE.
Son of Major General Robert Patrick Anderson and Mary Anderson; husband of Ethel A. A. Anderson. 1911, 22 Southend Road Beckenham.

ARCHER WILLIAM GEORGE 33892 Private Alexandra, Princess of Wales's Own (Yorkshire Regiment) 13th Bn., formerly 043735, R.A.S.C.
Killed in action 21/12/1917 Grave II. A. 14. CROISILLES BRITISH CEMETERY.
Born Uxbridge, lived Beckenham, enlisted Bromley.

ARNOLD CHARLES S/1118 Private Queen's Own (Royal West Kent

Regiment) 1st Bn. Died of wounds 25/4/1915 in the Canadian Dressing Station at St Julien as reported by the captain commanding A company of the Royal West Kents in BJ 13/11/1915. Enlisted Bromley, born Elmers End, Beckenham, 1911 18 Upper Elmers End Road.

ASHBY A J. There are 12 in the National Archives with these initials.

ASHDOWN ALBERT Sergeant G/378 Queen's Own (Royal West Kent Regiment)"A" Coy. 8th Bn.
Died 5/10/1918 age 30 Panel 7. VIS-EN-ARTOIS MEMORIAL.
Son of John and Jemina Ashdown, of 7, Blakeney Rd., Beckenham, Kent.

ASTE NORMAN HENRY 2nd Lieutenant Royal Garrison Artillery 23rd Heavy Bty.
Died 04/08/1916 age 27 Grave I. M. 22. ALBERT COMMUNAL CEMETERY EXTENSION.
Son of John and Margaret Aste. 1911 6 Foxgrove Road, Beckenham.

ASTON DOUGLAS PHILIP Private 43329 Royal Inniskilling Fusiliers1st Bn.
Died 23/04/1917 age 21 Panel 6, ARRAS MEMORIAL.
Son of Christopher Penrhyn Aston and Emma Aston, of 28, St. John's Rd., Penge.

ATKINSON LEWIS De BURGH 1413, Captain Royal Sussex Regiment 2nd Bn. Awards Mentioned in Despatches. Died 16/08/1916 age 35. Pier and Face 7 C THIEPVAL MEMORIAL.
Son of Humphrey Alexander Atkinson and Harriet Atkinson, of "Stoneville", King's Rd., Cheltenham, husband of Louise Christine Atkinson, of 9, Langley Rd., Elmers End, Beckenham, Kent.

AUDOYER JOHN
Killed in action on or about 21/8/1915.
Son of Mrs Audoyer 14 Villiers Rd., Beckenham, born abt 1888 Lewisham. BJ 10/8/1918 recorded his brother Thomas as POW in Germany. Not shown in CWGC.

BAKER CHARLES Private 696 Royal West Kent Regiment.
Died 26/4/1916 grave XX.G.2 AMARA CEMETERY.

Born abt 1881 age at enlistment 33, married Ada Emma Taylor of 15 Marlow Rd., Anerley, 24/4/1905.

Or BAKER CECIL DOUGLAS Captain Grenadier Guards 1st Bn., formerly RNVR Anti Aircraft Corps.

Died 29/7/1917 DUHALLOWS A D S CEMETERY.

Son of the late Arthur Henry Baker of Elderslie, Beckenham, wife of Gwendoline Peyman.

BARKER F C C and BARKER W O cannot be found in the CWGC or National Archives. There is Frederick Charles George Barker 246568 born Chelsea and William Clifford Barker 18949 with a wife in Bromley but there is no reason for doubting the given initials.

BARNES, JOHN WALDEGRAVE PERCY Private 30133 Northamptonshire Regiment 2nd Garrison Bn.

Died 01/10/1917 age 26 Grave P6. 7438. BECKENHAM CREMATORIUM AND CEMETERY.

Son of the late John George Waldegrave Barnes and May Barnes, of 136, Elmers End Rd., Beckenham.

In 1911 census May was widowed and her five daughters and one son all bore the name Percy and were born in Queensland, Australia.

BARTHOLOMEW, BENJAMIN JAMES Second Lieutenant Cameron Highlanders 4th Bn.

Killed in action 18/11/1916 age 20. Grave I. Z. 13. BECOURT MILITARY CEMETERY, BECORDEL-BECOURT.

Son of Mr. M. and Mrs. G. Bartholomew, of 3, Hayne Rd., Beckenham, the youngest of ten children, the last two of whom were born in Beckenham, Elizabeth and Benjamin James.

BARTON WILLIAM DUNN Rifleman R/3219 King's Royal Rifle Corps 12th Bn.

Died of wounds 19/3/1917 France & Flanders, age 25. Enlisted Southwark, born Kensington abt 1887, residence Lambeth.

Spouse Emily Adelaide Sandle married 2/6/1912 St Paul, Westminster Bridge Road, Southwark.

Son of Mr and Mrs T Barton 23 Somerville Rd., Penge. BJ 7/4/1917.

BASKERVILLE, JOHN FRANCIS Private 19398 Coldstream Guards 3rd Bn.

Died 30/11/1917 age 32 Panel 2. CAMBRAI MEMORIAL, LOUVERVAL. Son of John Baskerville; husband of Alice Maud Baskerville, of 60, Ravenscroft Rd., Beckenham.

BEASLEY CHARLES Private Australian Infantry AIF 25th Bn.
Died 5/8/1916 just before his brother William, age 28 VILLERS-BRETONNEUX MEMORIAL.
Reported missing 29/7/1916. BJ 16/9/1916.

BEASLEY, WILLIAM Lance Corporal G/393 Queen's Own (Royal West Kent Regiment) 6th Bn.
Died of wounds as POW 18/08/1916 Grave V. C. 7. HAMBURG CEMETERY.
Enlisted Bromley. Family at 9 Somerville Rd, Penge of Charles, Arthur, Harry, William and George; there were two other sons on active service, two sons-in-law and about 26 nephews.

BEATSON ROGER STEWART MONTRESOR Lieutenant King's Own Yorkshire Light Infantry 6th Bn. attd. 10th Bn.
Killed in action. 01/07/1916 age 25 Mem. B. 6. GORDON DUMP CEMETERY, OVILLERS-LA BOISSELLE.
Son of Mrs. Constance Mary Beatson and the late Mr. Walter William Gordon Beatson, East India merchant, of 3 Scott's Lane, Beckenham.

BEATSON WALTER WILLIAM GORDON Second Lieutenant Royal Flying Corps.
Died in a flying accident at Hounslow on 18/07/1916 age 18 Grave E/4. 84. BEDFORD CEMETERY, BEDFORDSHIRE.
Younger brother of Roger Stewart Montresor Beatson.

BEAUCHAMP WILLIAM EDWARD Private G/37712 The Queen's (Royal West Surrey Regiment) 7th Bn.
Killed in action 21/10/1917. Panel 14 to 17 and 162 to 162A. TYNE COT MEMORIAL.
Born Blackheath 1881, Kent, lived Beckenham, enlisted Bromley, husband of Florence Maud married 1904.

BECKFORD CYRIL EWART Rifleman R/14365 King's Royal Rifle Corps 2nd Bn.

Died of wounds 17/05/1916 age 22 Grave III. L. 7. ST. PATRICK'S CEMETERY, LOOS.
Son of Joshua and Elizabeth Jane Beckford, of 14, Waverley Rd., South Norwood, London. Born Beckenham.

BEER ALBERT Private L/10976 Queen's Own (Royal West Kent Regiment) 8th Bn.
Killed in action 16/4/1917 Bay 7 ARRAS MEMORIAL.
Born Lewisham, residence Penge. Enlisted Bromley.

BEER HENRY OLIVER Second Lieutenant Queen's Own (Royal West Kent Regiment) 8th Bn.
Killed in action 26/09/1915 age 20 Panel 95 to 97. LOOS MEMORIAL.
Son of Henry and Mary A. Beer, of The White House, Oakwood Avenue, Beckenham.

BELCHER, ALBERT EDWARD Private G/11820 Queen's Own (Royal West Kent Regiment) 6th Bn.
Killed in action 07/10/1916 Pier and Face 11 C. THIEPVAL MEMORIAL.
Born abt 1894 Beckenham, enlisted Bromley, son of Albert Edward and Margaret Ann of 30 St Margaret's Rd, Elmers End, Beckenham.

BELCHER E A Gunner 207489 Royal Field Artillery, 4th reserve Bde.
Died 6/3/1917 buried Little Totham All Saints churchyard, Essex. Only one of this name on the CWGC but no obvious Beckenham link.

BELCHER FRANKLIN NARES Lance Corporal 2916 7th London Regiment Born 1881, age at enlistment 37.
Died 9/11/1918, Kent.
1911 The Briars Lessness Park Belvedere Kent. Son of civil servant James Belcher and Elizabeth.
Not found on CWGC because not recognised as dying in service but present on National Archives. He was discharged permanently unfit in July but died from paralysis in September in Bromley.

BELL W 267 records in CWGC.

BENFIELD, FREDERICK WILLIAM Private 2168 Royal Army Medical Corps 16th Sanitary Sect.

Died of wounds 8/06/1916 age 37 Grave I. P. 16. MAILLY WOOD CEMETERY, MAILLY-MAILLET.
Son of George and Harriet Maria Benfield, of 423, Battersea Park Rd., Battersea, London.

BENHAM, WALTER EDWARD Second Lieutenant Royal Field Artillery "A" Bty. 245th Bde.
Died 03/11/1918 age 32 Grave S. V. E. 4. ST. SEVER CEMETERY EXTENSION, ROUEN.
Husband of Jennie F. Benham, of 149, Blandford Rd., Beckenham, Kent.

BENNETT, RISDON MACKENZIE Lieutenant Royal Air Force 204th Sqdn. formerly Royal Naval Air Service.
Died 28/09/1918 age 18 ARRAS FLYING SERVICES MEMORIAL.
Son of Dr. James H. Bennett, of Corner House, Bromley Rd., Beckenham.

BERRY W 115 records in CWGC.

BERTOLLE, GUSTAVE Rifleman A/200135 King's Royal Rifle Corps 17th Bn.
Killed in action 06/10/1916 age 36 Grave I. G. 17. BLIGHTY VALLEY CEMETERY, AUTHUILLE WOOD.
Son of William and Elizabeth Bertolle, of 40, Manor Rd., Beckenham. Gustave was a jeweller.

BEWSHEA, CLAUDIAN ALFRED Lance Corporal G/10069 Queen's Own (Royal West Kent Regiment) 1st Bn.
Killed in action 04/10/1917 Panel 106 to 108 TYNE COT MEMORIAL.
Born abt 1891 Beckenham, enlisted Anerley. Married 1914 Alice E Curtis, Patricia born 1916, lived 28 Lucas Rd, Penge, correspondence clerk. Son of George Bewshea, of 101, Edward Rd., Penge, London, and the late Sarah Bewshea.

BEWSHEA, SIDNEY ROBERT Private 8405 Leicestershire Regiment 2nd Bn.
Killed in action 31/10/1914 age 32 Grave I. D. 6. LE TOURET MILITARY CEMETERY, RICHEBOURG-L'AVOUE.
Son of George Bewshea, of 101, Edward Rd., Penge, London, and the late Sarah Bewshea. Born abt 1883, printer's machine minder.

BIGNELL S G Name not found.

BINSTEAD H G Name not found.

BLACKMAN, JAMES EDWARD Stoker 1st Class K/2972 Royal Navy H.M.S. "Jason". Struck a mine and sank off west coast of Scotland.
Died 03/04/1917 age 25 Grave O. 191. OBAN (PENNYFUIR) CEMETERY.
Son of Edward and Jane Blackman of 51, Churchfields Rd., Beckenham, Kent.

BLAKE HENRY Lance Corporal G/4074 Queen's Own Royal West Kent Regiment 6th Bn.
Reported from a wounded comrade from B Co RWK 6th Bn., in the Lewis Gun section. As they went over the top from shell hole to shell hole, he was killed by a shell on 17/7/1917. Bay 7 ARRAS MEMORIAL.
He lived with his sister, Mrs Hawkes from 18 Chancery Lane.

BLAKE CHARLES EDWIN NORMAN MC Major Royal Horse Artillery and Royal Field Artillery 70th Bde.
Killed in action 30/07/1918 age 32 Grave III. F. 9. BUZANCY MILITARY CEMETERY.
Son of Charles Blake of 11, The Avenue, Beckenham, Kent.

BOAKES WILLIAM Rifleman 3845 2nd Bn. Rifle Brigade.
Died 25/4/15 L29 Y-FARM MILITARY CEMETERY BOIS-GRENIER.
Son John William and Elizabeth Boakes, 40 Chancery Lane, Beckenham, born abt 1894 Poplar.
1901 14 St George's Rd.

BOILING ERIC Private G/2220 The Buffs (East Kent Regiment) 8th Bn.
Killed in action 26/09/1915 Panel 15 to 19. LOOS MEMORIAL.
Born Oxford, lived S Norwood, enlisted London.

BOLTON, HENRY ROBERT ARTHUR Rifleman 472466 London Regiment (The Rangers) "D" Coy. 12th Bn.
Killed in action 09/04/1917 age 19 Grave I. A. 40. LONDON CEMETERY, NEUVILLE-VITASSE.
Husband of Annie Lilian Bolton, of 74, Durban Rd., Beckenham, Kent.

BOND, ALBERT WILLIAM Private 25198 East Surrey Regiment 1st Bn. Died 20/05/1918 age 37. Grave Plot 2. Row D. Grave 5. TANNAY BRITISH CEMETERY, THIENNES.
Son of Richard and Frances Bond, of Beckenham. 1911 164 Blandford Road.
Husband of Mary Jane, daughter Florence Lillian born 1909.

BOND, LESLIE HORACE GEORGE Private 245296 Manchester Reg 2nd Bn. Died 30/08/1918 age 20 Grave I. H. 9. BRIE BRITISH CEMETERY.
Son of Clarence A. and Louisa M. Bond, of Blandford Rd., Beckenham.

BOOTH, SYDNEY EDWIN Second Lieutenant Royal Air Force 20th Sqdn.
Died in flying accident 03/12/1918 Grave N. 1. CHARLEROI COMMUNAL CEMETERY.
Born 1895, served since Sept 1914, husband of Hilda Winifred Booth married Sept last, of 4, Manor Grove, Beckenham. P3 BJ 21/12/1918

BOWDEN, STANLEY Rifleman 650721 London Regiment (First Surrey Rifles) 21st Bn. posted to 2nd/23rd Bn.
Died 25/4/1917 KARASOULI MILITARY CEMETERY.
Son of Harry Charles and Rosa Annie Bowden, of 204, Mackenzie Rd., Beckenham. Volunteered Aug. 1914. Twice wounded in France with 2nd Bn. First Surrey Rifles. Native of Dulwich, London.

BOWEN H C Thomas Bowen lives at 2 Trenholme Rd, Anerley but no connection established and nothing in CWGC.

BOWMAN, ALFRED JAMES Rifleman 2938 London Regiment (First Surrey Rifles) 21st Bn.
Died 01/10/1915 age 24 Panel 134. LOOS MEMORIAL.
Son of Thomas and Rosina Jane Bowman, of Christchurch Cottage, Beckenham.

BOWMAN THOMAS FREDERICK, Private 41733 Royal Fusiliers.
Died 26/3/1920 grave P7 8200 BECKENHAM CEMETERY as reported in the BJ.
Born abt 1878, married 1906 Ellen Freeman, 1911 lived 50 Foxgrove Rd, a plumber.

Brother to Alfred Bowman above.

BRACKLEY HORACE Private G/20227 The Buffs (East Kent Regiment) 8th Bn.
Died of wounds 23/06/1917 age 36 Grave XIV. LIJSSENTHOEK MILITARY CEMETERY.
Husband of Daisy Olive Brackley, of 61, Churchfields Rd., Beckenham.

BRADY GERALD CHARLES Private 14981 Dorsetshire Regiment 5th Bn.
Killed in action 26/09/1916 Pier and Face 7 B. THIEPVAL MEMORIAL.
Born Kensington, Middlesex, lived Beckenham, enlisted London.

BRAND W 16 records in CWGC.

BRAYBROOK ARTHUR CHARLES Private 22943 Essex Regiment.
Died 20/10/1915 IV.B.213 PORTIANOS MILITARY CEMETERY.
Son of Mr C Braybrook 5 Kimberley Rd, Beckenham.

BRAYBROOK HORACE V. 15355 B Co 2nd Middlesex Reg., was buried with full military honours at Elmers End cemetery on 23/10/1919. Enlisted at the beginning of the war and injured in 1915 and August 1917, he was discharged and spent his last ten months under Balgowan hospital where he died 16/10/1919 age 21 from flu and lung haemorrhage. Second son of Mr C and the late Mrs Braybrook, 5 Kimberley Rd.

BRECK ALBERT G Private G/14419 Royal Sussex Regiment 2nd Bn.
Died 18/09/1918 age 31 Grave VI. C. 9. JEANCOURT COMMUNAL CEMETERY EXTENSION.
Son of George and Nancy Breck, of Rotherhithe, London; husband of Lydia E Breck, of 16, Eden Rd., Elmers End, Beckenham.

BROOK, JAMES EDWARD BLYTHE Private 3019 Australian Infantry, A.I.F. 28th Bn.
Died 29/07/1916 age 26 VILLERS-BRETONNEUX MEMORIAL.
Son of Benjamin Blythe Brook and the late Martha Elizabeth Brook, of 4, Cedars Rd., Beckenham. Born Dulwich.

BROOK, NEVILL BENJAMIN BLYTHE Company Quartermaster Sergeant 869 Northumberland Fusiliers "A" Coy. 1st/6th Bn.
Died 27/04/1915 age 25 Panel 8 and 12. YPRES (MENIN GATE) MEMORIAL.
Brother of James Edward Blythe.

Brooke C D There is Brook C D of the Army Service Corps died 5/9/1916 France but not Brooke C D.

BROWN JAMES LAMBERT Private G/19322 Duke of Cambridge's Own (Middlesex Regiment) Bn1/8th (T.F.)
Killed in action 30/11/1917 Panel 9 CAMBRAI MEMORIAL LOUVERAL.
Born Beckenham 1888, lived Chiswick, enlisted Hounslow. 1911 203 Blandford Rd, Beckenham.

BROWN PHILIP ANTHONY Lieutenant 12351 Durham Light Infantry 13th Bn.
Killed in action 04/11/1915 age 29 Grave I. F. 5. RATION FARM MILITARY CEMETERY, LA CHAPELLE-D'ARMENTIERES.
Son of Anthony and Jane Chalmers Brown, of "Broomhill", 29 Southend Rd., Beckenham.

BROWN ROBERT JAMES Private G/320 Queen's Own (Royal West Kent Regiment) 6th Bn.
Killed in action 08/03/1916 age 18, Panel 95 to 97. LOOS MEMORIAL.
Born Brixton, Surrey, lived 43 Birkbeck Rd, Beckenham, enlisted Bromley.

BROWN THEODORE ANTHONY MC Captain The Buffs (East Kent Regiment) "B" Coy. 3rd Bn. attd. 1st Bn.
Died 15/04/1917 age 27 Panel 15 to 19. LOOS MEMORIAL.
Brother of Philip Anthony.

BRYAN JOHN HOLT Private 2675 Surrey Yeomanry (Queen Mary's Regiment).
Died 11/12/1915 age 39. Grave E. 148. ALEXANDRIA (CHATBY) MILITARY AND WAR MEMORIAL CEMETERY.
Son of John and Mary Bryan; husband of Nellie E. Bryan, of 6, Marlow Rd., Anerley, born at Burton-on-Trent. Member Penge Football Club.

BRYANT THOMAS ARTHUR Lance Corporal 56771 Welsh Regiment 14th Bn.
Killed in action 19/04/1918 Grave IV. F. 3. WARLOY-BAILLON COMMUNAL CEMETERY EXTENSION.
Born Beckenham, lived Anerley, enlisted Cardiff.

BULPITT HARRY SIDNEY GEORGE Private 5363 Household Cavalry and Cavalry of the Line (incl. Yeomanry and Imperial Camel Corps) 16th (The Queen's) Lancers.
Died of wounds 21/06/1917 Grave C. 38. VILLERS-FAUCON COMMUNAL CEMETERY.
Born Brighton, Sussex, lived Penge, enlisted Woolwich.

BUNTING HARRY Private 240896 Queen's Own (Royal West Kent Regiment) 7th Bn.
Killed in action 28/03/1918 Panel 58 and 59. POZIERES MEMORIAL.
Born Beckenham, enlisted Bromley.

BUNTING, JOHN HENRY Private 8153 West Yorkshire Regiment (Prince of Wales's Own) 1st Bn.
Died 20/09/1914, age 27 LA FERTE-SOUS-JOUARRE MEMORIAL.
Son of Mr. and Mrs. Bunting, of 32, Chancery Lane, Beckenham.
Also served in the North-west Frontier Campaign, 1908.

BURBRIDGE R W Possibly Burbidge. Louisa Burbidge lived 12 Oak Grove Anerley with son William Herbert b 1892.

BURCH HARRY MM Corporal 16578 Duke of Wellington's (West Riding Regiment) 2nd Bn. Formerly 8000, Dragoons.
Died of wounds 13/10/1916 age 32 Grave I. L. 10. GROVE TOWN CEMETERY, MEAULTE FRANCE.
Son of John and Salome Burch, born Amberley, Glos, enlisted Huddersfield, 1901 at 1 Station Rd, Beckenham when father a carman for dairy farm.

BURGOYNE ALFRED Driver T3/030457 Army Service Corps 211th H.T. Coy.
Died home, 04/03/1915, age 31. Grave Screen Wall. X4. 1. 6829. BECKENHAM CREMATORIUM AND CEMETERY.
Husband of Mrs. M. A. Burgoyne, of 12, Churchfields Rd., Beckenham.

Enlisted Deptford, born Battersea, lived Beckenham.

Private A Burgoyne A S C of 71 Churchfields Rd, d at Bournemouth 12/3/15.

BURLES PHILLIP HENRY Private G/12901 Queens Own (Royal West Kent Regiment) 1st Bn.

Died 28/08/1916 age19 Pier and Face 11 C. THIEPVAL MEMORIAL.

Son of Philip and Harriett Burles, of 17, Tennyson Rd., Penge.

BURTONSHAW JOHN HORACE Lance Corporal G/4829 The Queen's (Royal West Surrey Regiment) 2nd Bn.

Died 14/07/1916 age 36 Grave XVI. X. 3. OVILLERS MILITARY CEMETERY.

Husband of Selina Maud Burtonshaw, of 125, Church Fields Rd., Beckenham.

BURTONSHAW WILLIAM ALBERT G/1673 Private Queen's Own (Royal West Kent Regiment) 7th Bn.

Killed in action 28/8/1915 Pier and Face 11.C THIEPVAL MEMORIAL.

Enlisted Bromley, born Norwood, London, married Caroline Ada Killick 1899.

On the CWGC, William is listed as Burtenshaw. Brother of John Horace.

BUSH JOHN EDWARD Private 228165 London Regiment 1st Bn. (Royal Fusiliers) Formerly 936, Royal Army Medical Corps.

Killed in action 20/11/1917. Grave B.8. LOUVERAL MILITARY CEMETERY DOIGNIES.

Born and lived Beckenham, enlisted Chelsea.

BUTCHER, THOMAS HORELAND Private G/18881 Royal Sussex Regiment 7th Bn.

Died 13/08/1918 age 19 Panel 6. VIS-EN-ARTOIS MEMORIAL.

Son of James Butcher, of 7, Lea Rd., Beckenham.

BUTLER HARRY Private 3545 HAC 2nd Bn.

Died of wounds 1/12/1916 age 26 Grave Green Dump Cemetery Mem 11. ANCRE BRITISH CEMETERY BEAUMONT HAMEL.

Late of Manor Rd, Beckenham.

BUTTERIS JOHN GEORGE Private G/2669 The Queen's (Royal West

Surrey Regiment) 7th Bn.
Died of wounds 02/07/1916 Grave II. B. 30. DAOURS COMMUNAL CEMETERY EXTENSION.
Enlisted Lambeth, born abt 1897, son of Sidney George and Martha Isabel Butteris of 13 Byne Rd, Sydenham.

BYRON CLEMENT JOHN Second Lieutenant Honourable Artillery Company 2nd Bn.
Killed in action 10/01/1917 Grave Reference B. 34. BEAUMONT-HAMEL BRITISH CEMETERY.
Son of John and Clara Byron, of "Wyefield", The Knoll, Beckenham, Kent, from Hackney, London.

CANNINGS ALBERT EDWARD Private 8110 Lancashire Fusiliers 1st Bn.
Killed in action 04/12/1916 age 19 Pier and Face 3 C and 3 D. THIEPVAL MEMORIAL.
Born Chelsea, lived 181 Blandford Rd, Beckenham. One-time porter at New Beckenham Station.

CANNON LEONARD ROBERT Private TR/10/23441 East Surrey Regiment 10th Bn., Training Reserve 30th Bn. Formerly T.R./9/2268 25th Bn.
Died home 28/08/1917 Grave W5. 7421. BECKENHAM CREMATORIUM AND CEMETERY.
Born Dover, enlisted Bromley.

CARMAN LESLIE GUY Second Lieutenant Mentioned in Despatches. The Buffs (East Kent Regiment) 7th Bn. K.
Killed in action 04/10/1916, age 19. Grave XIII. F. 8. SERRE ROAD CEMETERY.
Son of Albert and Kate Carman, of "The Bays", Parklangley, Beckenham.

CARR, BERNARD WILLIAM JAMES Private 515859 London Regiment Bn. 14th (County of London) (London Scottish).
Killed in action 23/08/1918 Grave VIII. N. 26. CABARET-ROUGE BRITISH CEMETERY, SOUCHEZ.
Born Peckham, lived Beckenham, enlisted Bromley.

CARTER FREDERICK W Rifleman 43758 B Co Royal Irish Rifles 2nd Bn.
Died of wounds at 61st Field Ambulance 31/3/1918. SAINS-EN-AMIENOIS COMMUNAL CEMETERY.
Youngest son of Mr and Mrs A Carter of 26 Chancery Lane, Beckenham, choirboy St George's church.
BJ 1/6/1918.
Another F W Carter was killed in action 15/4/1918, second son of Mr and Mrs Carter of Bell Green, Lower Sydenham who had already lost two sons one in November 1915 and another in November 1917, leaving their fourth son serving in Mesopotamia.

CASSIDY ALBERT Private G/12671 British Expeditionary Force Royal Sussex Regiment 7th Bn.
Died of wounds 29/11/1917 III.A.17. TINCOURT NEW BRITISH CEMETERY.
Born 1887, enlisted Bromley. Of 6 Kingswood Rd, Penge.

CASSIDY WILLIAM EWART GLADSTONE Private 39647 Northumberland Fusiliers Bn. 12/13th Formerly T/260844, R.A.S.C.
Killed in action 8/10/1918 Panel 3. VIS-EN-ARTOIS MEMORIAL.
Enlisted Park Royal, London Born abt 1898 Anerley, son of the late James Pestell and Annie Jane Cassidy of 77 St Hugh's Rd. Brother of Albert leaving one surviving son.

CATHIE SIDNEY Private 31776, Northumberland Fusiliers 11th Bn.
Killed Somme Sunday 24/9/1916, age 26 THIEPVAL MEMORIAL. BJ 22/9/1917

CATON, NORMAN NEWTON MC Lieutenant Royal Field Artillery "C" Bty. 124th Bde.
Killed in action 21/04/1918 Royal Field Artillery "C" Bty. 124th Bde. Grave B. 30. COUIN NEW BRITISH CEMETERY.
Son of Mr. Erasmas Stanley and Mrs. K. M. Caton, of "Barncote", Reigate, Surrey, born 1891.
1911 19 Foxgrove Road Beckenham.

CHALK FREDERICK DUDLEY Private Po./15693 Royal Marine Light Infantry Portsmouth Bn. RN div.

Killed 11/5/1915 Panel 2 to 7 HELLES MEMORIAL Ansac Cemetery, Gallipoli, Turkey.
Son of Ellen Chalk 96, Elmers End Road, Beckenham.

CHAMPION J possibly John Arthur Champion from 41 Rowland Grove, Sydenham, husband of Georgina S Champion age 37 of the 8th Bn. Seaforth Highlanders died 22/8/1917, remembered on the Tyne Cot Memorial.

CHANDLER CHARLES FREDERICK Private 1521 Australian Infantry, A.I.F. 11th Bn.
Killed at Dardanelles 01/08/1915 age 26 Grave II. G. 61. SHELL GREEN CEMETERY.
Only son of Mr Arthur and Mrs Louisa Chandler, 9 Barnmead Rd., Beckenham who left Beckenham five years ago to practise pearl fishing in Australia.

CHANNON EDWARD CHARLES Private 42957 Essex Regiment 10th Bn. Formerly 10860, Bedfordshire Regt.
Killed in action 26/04/1918 age 19 Panel 51 and 52. POZIERES MEMORIAL.
Son of Mrs. R. Channon, of 5, Witham Rd., Anerley, London. Born Hammersmith, Middlesex, lived Anerley, enlisted Bromley.

CHANNON JOHN GEORGE Able seaman, J 353 Royal Navy HMS Scott.
Died 3/3/1918 Grave E.30.5 HASLAR ROYAL NAVAL CEMETERY.
Born son of John Channon Dec 1891 - Fulham, London, married Dorothy Winifred Marsh 1914 Bromley living at 8 Oakfield Rd, Penge.
HMS Scott was a destroyer named after Sir Walter Scott launched October 1917 but mined or torpedoed off the Dutch coast on 15/8/1918 by the German U-boat UC 17 with the loss of 22 of the crew. According to the CWGC, AB John George Channon died while serving on HMS Scott on 3/3/1918.

CHARMAN SAMUEL J Sapper WR/253982 Royal Engineers 119th Railway Coy.
Died 01/12/1918 age 27 Grave VIII. G. 9. TINCOURT NEW BRITISH CEMETERY.
Husband of Ethel Charman, of 10, Tennyson Rd., Penge, London.

CHATFIELD SIDNEY Lance Corporal C/42519 Royal Fusiliers (City of London Regiment) 20th Bn.
Died of wounds at Rouen, 25/3/1917 O.VIII.K.7 ST SEVER CEMETERY EXTENSION ROUEN.
Born Beckenham son of Mr and Mrs Chatfield, Blandford Rd, lived Penge husband of Lilian, enlisted Bromley.

CHILLEY, MICHAEL MAYBRICK Private 241719 Middlesex Regiment 4th Bn.
Died 27/04/1917 age 26 Grave II. G. 31. AUBIGNY COMMUNAL CEMETERY EXTENSION.
Son of Charles and Caroline Greig Chilley, of 94, Venner Rd., Sydenham, London.

CHRISTMAS BERNARD LODELL Captain Royal Fusiliers 1st/3rd Bn.
Died 19/5/1916, age 23, grave West side HENU CHURCHYARD Pas de Calais.
Son of Mrs S F Christmas and the late A G Christmas, provision merchants.

CHRISTOPHERS PERCY EDWIN Private 253237 London Regiment (Royal Fusiliers) 3rd Bn.
Killed in action, 09/04/1917 age 20 Panel 5. LONDON CEMETERY, NEUVILLE-VITASSE.
Son of Elizabeth Doe (formerly Christophers), of 150, Blandford Rd and the late Tom.

CHURCHER LEONARD EDWIN Private 50315 King's (Liverpool Regiment) 12th Bn. Formerly T/8/292934, Royal Army Service Corps.
Killed in action, 16/8/1917 age 32, Panel 31 to 34, 162, 163. TYNE COT MEMORIAL.
Born Beckenham, son of Edwin William and Mary Ann, husband of Tabitha Lilian Headington formerly Churcher, enlisted Kilburn.

CLAMP GEORGE Driver 2376 Royal Horse Artillery and Royal Field Artillery 13th Bde.
Died 02/11/1917 Grave XIV. K. 13. BAGHDAD (NORTH GATE) WAR CEMETERY.
Born Beckenham, enlisted Woolwich.

CLANFIELD ROBERT Private 41496 Suffolk Regiment 2nd Bn.
Killed in action 02/08/1918 age 19. Grave Reference III. F. 4. SANDPITS
BRITISH CEMETERY, FOUQUEREUIL.
Born Elmers End, enlisted Bromley.

CLARK C MM Sergeant 357 Royal Engineers 509th (London) Field Coy.
Died 24/12/1916 age 52 Grave VI. A. 73. BETHUNE TOWN CEMETERY.
Son of John and Hannah Clark, of Crockham Heath, Emborne, Newbury;
husband of Daisy Clark, of 37, Churchfield Rd., Beckenham, Kent.
Died as a result of an accident when he rode into the river at night and was
weighed down by his heavy bandolier. His cap was found on the bank and
his horse was saved from the river where it was found.

CLARK C 158 matches in CWGC. 2nd Lieutenant Cyril Clarke of the East
Surrey regiment came from 11 Queens Rd, Beckenham and died of wounds
16/6/1916, buried Corbie Communal Cemetery Extension. BJ 24/6/1916

CLARK C DOUGLAS was responsible for the enlistment of recruits for
5th Bn. RWK. Born 1880, eldest son of Charles Douglas Clark, educated
at The Abbey and Tonbridge where he represented the school as marksman
at Bisley. Joined Volunteer Bn. RWK that later merged with the Territorials
as sub lieutenant 1900, captain 1905, major 1912 according to BJ 29/8/14.
When he was encouraging enlistment in Bromley he was working with
Lieutenant Hedley Thornton but he left for India and Mesopotamia on 14
October. He died as Lieutenant Col Clarke on the transport Melita as it
arrived in Plymouth on 23/1/1920, leaving a widow and two children. He
is buried in St Mary's churchyard Hayes where on the day of his funeral the
masses of flowers included the badge of the RWK worked on a cushion in
white flowers from his regiment. Ref BJ 31/1/1920.

CLARK, ERIC HENRY LLOYD Second Lieutenant Royal Field Artillery
5th Bty.
Died 01/07/1916 age 19 Pier and Face 1 A and 8 A. THIEPVAL MEMORIAL.
Son of Francis John and Lily L. Clark, of "Gulmarg", 12, Albemarle Rd.,
Beckenham.

CLARK HENRY Sig.
Killed in France 25/3/1918.
Brother of E Clark of 20 Blakeney Ave. Front page memorials BJ 27/3/1920.

CLARKE BRYAN LLOYD Lieutenant, 23rd Indian Cavalry (Frontier Force) and Royal Flying Corps.
Died 19/04/1915 age 26 Grave III. A. 44. HAZEBROUCK COMMUNAL CEMETERY.
Son of Lieutenant Col. Sir Marshal Clarke, K.C.M.G., and Lady Clarke, of "The Eyrie", Wadhurst, Sussex, late of 7 Cedars Rd, Beckenham. BJ 24/4/1915 p1.

COBB JAMES CASSELS Lieutenant Queen's Own (Royal West Kent Regiment) 5th Bn.
Died 23/08/1918 age 33 Grave VIII. G. 5. DERNANCOURT COMMUNAL CEMETERY EXTENSION.
Son of Arthur Stanley and Margaret Ritchie Cobb, of The Parsonage, Bitterne, Ringwood, Hants. Born at Pontypridd, Glam.
1911 76 Scotts Lane, Shortlands.

COLBOURNE ERIC KRABBE MC Second Lieutenant Princess Charlotte of Wales's Royal Berkshire Regiment 3rd Bn.
Died of wounds 27/06/1915 Grave I. B. 18. CHOCQUES MILITARY CEMETERY.
Son of Louis Colbourne, of Beckenham, Kent, England, was born in Buenos Ayres on the 25/6/1888. He was educated at Berkhampstead School, and came to Victoria, BC in 1907. He was articled to Mr. Frank Deveraux, B.C.L.S. and obtained his commission as a Land Surveyor in 1912. After the outbreak of war he went to England where he obtained a commission in the 3rd Royal Berkshire Regiment, in January 1915. He died at Chognes, June 27, 1915, of wounds received in action and was buried in the Military Cemetery there. He was awarded the Military Cross for conspicuous gallantry at Cuinchy a few days before his death. Lieutenant Colbourne was married December 31st, 1912, to Florence Marion only daughter of George Gillespie, Victoria BC. Lived Llanfair 16 Park Road Beckenham.

COLE WILLIAM Private 203222 Queen's Own (Royal West Kent Regiment) 2/4th Bn.
Killed in action 19/4/1917 Egypt.
Born Beckenham 1899 lived 21 Eden Road Beckenham. Enlisted Bromley, Kent.

COLEMAN W 79 records in CWGC.

COLLETT FREDERICK JAMES Able Seaman J/46313 Royal Navy H.M.S. Destroyer "Mary Rose".
Died 17/10/1917 age 21 when the two destroyer escorts to a Scandinavian convoy were sunk by two German light cruisers that went on to sink 9 of the 12 merchant ships in the convoy. Panel 21. CHATHAM NAVAL MEMORIAL.
Son of Frederick Arthur and Amy Matilda Collett, of 11, Mackenzie Rd., Beckenham.

COLLETT FREDERICK WILLIAM Private 2670 Middlesex Regiment 16th Bn.
Died 01/07/1916 age 24 Grave II. E. 26. AUCHONVILLERS MILITARY CEMETERY.
Son of Frederick William and Emma Collett, of 26, Durban Rd., Beckenham.

COLLIER RONALD INGLIS Lieutenant Royal Navy H.M.S. "Tipperary".
Sunk in the battle of Jutland with loss of 185 crew.
Died 01/06/1916 Panel 11. PORTSMOUTH NAVAL MEMORIAL.
Gained Masters and Mates Cert just before killed. Born 1890 Norwood, lived Westgate Rd, Beckenham.

COLLINS ARTHUR DUPPA, 2nd Lieutenant RFC 52nd Squ.
Died 1/4/1917, age 22, grave III.A.13, buried Grove Town, Meaulte.
Only son of the late William Pratt and Marie Collins of Beckenham, now of 10 Lingfield Ave, Kingston on Thames. Educated Eastbourne College, joined staff P&O in London and enlisted in Artist's Rifles in Jan 1915. Commissioned in RFC Jan 1916.

COLLINS A J Possibly Albert Collins 23/3/1918 G/1776 Royal West Surrey.

COLLINS ALFRED WILLIAM Private 15882 East Surrey Regiment 7th Bn.
Killed in action 13/08/1916 Pier and Face 6 B and 6 C. THIEPVAL MEMORIAL.
Born abt 1894 Penge, Surrey Enlisted Kingston-on-Thames.
1911 Son of Mr James C and Mrs Annie Collins, 44 Thesiger Rd.

COLLINS HUGH DUPPA Lieutenant Commander Royal Navy H.M.S. "Monmouth".
Died 01/11/1914 age 30 PLYMOUTH NAVAL MEMORIAL.
AND
PHILIP COLLINS the eldest of four children of Philip George Collins (sometimes called Robert George) and Susan Kate Breffit, all born in Beckenham between 1882 and 1888 when their parents were either living at 10 or 21 The Avenue.

HMS Monmouth lost 1 Nov 1914 in the battle of Coronel

His siblings were Hugh Duppa Collins born 22/6/1884, Helen Dorothy born towards the end of 1885 and Geoffrey Abdy born in 1888. By 1911, the family had moved to a 16-roomed house in Beckenham Place Park when Hugh was a lieutenant aboard HMS Glasgow at Portsmouth, having entered the service on 15/5/1899. Both Philip and Geoffrey were educated at Rugby and Oxbridge and became solicitors like their father. They were also devoted to the game of hockey with Philip being vice president of the Hockey Association and secretary of the International Board. At the beginning of WWI, both Philip and Geoffrey enlisted in the Rifle Brigade, a battalion of sharpshooters and scouts armed with accurate Baker rifles. At the same time, their brother, Hugh Duppa Collins, was lost with all hands in the Battle of Coronel off Chile on Sunday 1/11/1914 when serving as lieutenant commander aboard HMS Monmouth. It was the worst British naval defeat of WWI. He is remembered on the Plymouth Naval memorial.

He left a wife, Elspeth Marion Towers-Clark whom he had married at Freshwater, IoW in 1913 and a daughter, Joycelyn Helen born 1915. Philip Collins died later on that year on 30/7/1915 with the rank of captain and Geoffrey survived the whole of the war, leaving with the same rank in 1918 to die in his 99th year. He remained as keen as ever on hockey which is possibly how he came to marry Joan Mary Ratcliffe in 1936, an international hockey player from Cornwall. A member of the Law Society Council from 1931 to 1956 and its president in 1951, he was awarded a knighthood and became Sir Geoffrey Abdy Collins. He was elected president in 1931.

COLLINSON WILLIAM HOLMES 2nd Lieutenant Machine Gun Officer Northumberland Fusiliers 6th Bn.
Died 5/1/1916 grave I.J.19 RAILWAY DUGOUTS BURIAL GROUND.
Born Edmonton 1890, grandson of Harriet Ann Collinson of 5 The Knoll, Beckenham and only son of William Rowley Field Collinson and Sarah Haslewood Holmes. He was the 16th direct male descendant of his line. BJ 15/1/1916 p6.

COLLIS HARRY LEONARD Private 240293 Queen's Own (Royal West Kent Regiment) 1st/5th Bn. Mesopotamian Expeditionary Force.
Died 1/11/1918 Panel 29. BASRA MEMORIAL.
Son of Harry T. Collis and Fanny of The Stables 37 The Avenue, Beckenham when born abt 1899.

COMYNS-LEWER ALEXANDER DAVID Private 2570 London Regiment (London Scottish) 1st/14th Bn.
Died 01/11/1914 age 26 Panel 54. YPRES (MENIN GATE) MEMORIAL. (Served as LEWER). Son of the late Alexander Comyns and Ethel Harriet Comyns-Lewer, of 2, Oakwood Avenue, Beckenham.

COOK WILLIAM RICHARD Gunner 7088 Royal Marine Artillery 3rd R.M. Bn.
Died 08/10/1918 age 41 Grave Prot. 393. MALTA (CAPUCCINI) NAVAL CEMETERY.
Son of Mr and Mrs Susan Ann Cook, of 37, Whateley Rd., Penge, Beckenham, Kent. Born 5/11/1877, Brixton.

COOMBS CLAUDE STUART 2nd Lieutenant Queen's Own (Royal West Kent Regiment) 6th Bn.

Died of wounds 3/07/1916 his 21st birthday, Grave II. A. 43. BOULOGNE EASTERN CEMETERY.
Son of Edward Alfred and the late Edith Coombs, of Longside, Albemarle Rd, Beckenham.

COOPER ALFRED VICTOR Rifleman 473286, formerly 6547, London Regiment (The Rangers) 1st/12th Bn.
Killed in action 07/10/1916 Pier and Face 9 C. THIEPVAL MEMORIAL.
Born Beckenham.

COOPER ROBERT CECIL BERNARD Private 52141 Lincolnshire Regiment 7th Bn.
Died of wounds 24/09/1918 age 19 Grave IV. B. 28. TERLINCTHUN BRITISH CEMETERY, WIMILLE.
Son of Mrs. L. J. Cooper, Beckenham. Born Bermondsey; attended the Royal Masonic School.

COOPER, REGINALD LEOPOLD Rifleman 9335 London Regiment (London Rifle Brigade) 5th Bn.
Died in action in France 02/03/1915 age 20 Grave III. C. 2. LONDON RIFLE BRIGADE CEMETERY.
Son of Mrs. L. Jane Cooper and the late rule maker Mr. Walter H. Cooper, of 48, King's Hall Rd., Beckenham.
Brother of Robert Cecil Bernard Cooper. Cooper family grave in Elmers End Cemetery, Beckenham.

COOPER, RONALD PERCY Private 11091 Duke of Cornwall's Light Infantry 7th Bn.
Died 30/11/1917 age 27 Panel 6. CAMBRAI MEMORIAL, LOUVERVAL.
Son of William Henry Cooper, of 4, Witham Rd., Anerley, London, and the late Rosa Jane Cooper.

COOPER THOMAS ALBERT Private G/68597 Royal Fusiliers (City of London Regiment) 4th Bn., formerly 41445, 4th Res Bn. Suffolk Regt.
Died of wounds 29/5/1918 France & Flanders.
Born Penge, lived Anerley, enlisted Bromley.

COOPER WILLIAM SAMUEL Private 203303 Queen's Own (Royal West Kent Regiment) B Coy 2/4th Bn.

Killed in action 19/9 1918 Egypt, age 24 Grave E.8 RAMLEH WAR CEMETERY.
Son of James Walter Cooper of 24 Blandford Rd, Beckenham; husband of Sarah Ellen Parker formerly Cooper of 9 Seward Rd, Beckenham.

COPELAND WILLIAM HENRY PROCTOR Private 12520 Queen's Own (Royal West Kent Regiment) 8th Bn.
Died 15/07/1916 age 35 Grave I. B. 61. LA NEUVILLE BRITISH CEMETERY, CORBIE.
Son of Henry and Eliza Copeland, of Beckenham; husband of Kate Edith Copeland, of 101A, High St., Beckenham, Kent with four children between 7 and 13.

COPSEY, HAROLD GEORGE Wheeler 93822 Royal Field Artillery 62nd Bde. Ammunition Col.
Died 08/04/1916 age 21 Grave O. 3. SAILLY-LABOURSE COMMUNAL CEMETERY.
Son of George William and Clementina Alice Copsey, of 107, Mackenzie Rd., Beckenham.

CORBIN, CHARLES ROBERT PEEL Lieutenant Worcestershire Regiment 11th Bn.
Died 31/10/1916 age 23 Grave 0.22. SALONIKA (LEMBET ROAD) MILITARY CEMETERY.
Son of Eustace Rhodes St. Clair Corbin, M.B. Lond., M.R.C.S. Eng., and Linda Augusta Jane Corbin (nee Peel), of "Merivale", 7, Beckenham Rd.
2nd Lieutenant Charles Robert Peel Corbin worked for the County & Westminster Bank from Dulwich College and worked his way from corporal in W Kent Yeomanry to sergeant in Gallipoli and 2nd lieutenant in 11th Worcesters but died of wounds incurred 13/10/16 when fighting Bulgarians in Macedonia. The British Army was being called to fight battles of others with pointless loss of life.

CORLEY W R Not found.

CORNISH GEORGE Private 22996 East Surrey Regiment 2nd Bn.
Died 22/09/1918 age 33 Grave A. 141. SARIGOL MILITARY CEMETERY, KRISTON.

Son of Edwin (tailor) and Thirza Cornish; husband of Mrs. C. W. Cornish, of 1, Kent House Rd., Beckenham, Kent.

COULTER AUSTEN JOSEPH Private G/11661 Queen's Own (Royal West Kent Regiment) 7th Bn.
Killed in action 13/7/1916 Pier and Face 11C, THIEPVAL MEMORIAL.
Born Streatham, Surrey, enlisted Bromley.

COURTIER FRANK ALFRED Private 10688 Princess Charlotte of Wales's (Royal Berkshire Regiment) 5th Bn.
Killed in action 03/07/1916 Pier and Face 11 D. THIEPVAL MEMORIAL.
Born Kennington, Surrey. Enlisted London.

COURTNEY LAWRENCE EDWARD Private 74978 Royal Fusiliers (City of London Regiment) 24th Bn.
Killed in action 11/9/1918 Panel 3 VIS-EN-ARTOIS MEMORIAL. Born Chelmsford, lived Beckenham, son of Stanley T and Gertude Courtney, enlisted London.

COUSINS ROBERT EDWARDS Private 8981 Welsh Regiment 2nd Bn.
Killed in action 31/10/1914 Panel 37. YPRES (MENIN GATE) MEMORIAL.
Born London, lived Beckenham, enlisted Merthyr.

COX ARTHUR Private 93216 Durham Light Infantry 2nd Bn. Formerly 3210, Norfolk Regt.
Died 24/09/1918 Grave I. E. 1. CHAPELLE BRITISH CEMETERY, HOLNON.
Son of Mr. W. Cox, of 3, Stanmoor Terrace, Beckenham. Enlisted Maidstone.

CRADDOCK EDWARD JAMES Private 12481 Royal Fusiliers 9th Bn.
Died of wounds 16/10/1915 Grave IV. C. 58. LILLERS COMMUNAL CEMETERY.
Born Walworth, lived King William Fourth Croydon Road Elmer's End Beckenham in 1911. Enlisted Southwark.

CRAIG JOHN MCADAM Lieutenant 57th Wilde's Rifles (Frontier Force) attd. 58th Vaughan's Rifles (Frontier Force). Served on The North-West Frontier of India, 1908.

Died 01/11/1914 age 28 Grave I. A. 8. BETHUNE TOWN CEMETERY. Son of James Craig GP and Mary, Royal Air Force, Uxbridge, Middx. In 1891 and 190 Briscow House, 20 Copers Cope Road, Beckenham.

CREE ARTHUR THOMAS CRAWFORD Lieutenant Durham Light Infantry 7th Bn.
Died 12/05/1915 age 33 Grave No.2 VI. A. 47. BEDFORD HOUSE CEMETERY.
Son of Arthur Walker Cree and Elizabeth Cree; husband of Ivy E. M. Cree, of Anthonys, Chesham Bois, Bucks. Born at Beckenham.

CREE CHARLES EDWARD VICTOR Lieutenant Sherwood Foresters (Notts and Derby Regiment) 6th Bn.
Killed in action 20/07/1916 age 29 Grave I. G. 5. BELLACOURT MILITARY CEMETERY, RIVIERE.
Son of Arthur Walker Cree and Elizabeth Cree (nee Newby), of "Brodsworth", 124, Bromley Rd., Beckenham, brother of Arthur Thomas Crawford Cree.

CRIPPS JOHN HENRY Private G/12879 Royal Sussex Regiment 7th Bn. British Expeditionary Force.
Killed in action 31/03/1917 Grave II. M. 24. FAUBOURG D'AMIENS CEMETERY, ARRAS.
Born Chalfont, Essex. Enlisted Bromley.

CROSS ARTHUR JAMES Private L/10355 Queen's Own (Royal West Kent Regiment) 8th Bn.
Killed in action 21/03/1918 Panel 58 and 59. POZIERES MEMORIAL.
Born 1894 Beckenham, enlisted Woolwich, Kent.

CROSS W Not found.

CROSSLEY CHARLES Private M2/078305 Royal Army Service Corps.
Died 28/10/1918 Grave XVII.D.5 GREVILLERS BRITISH CEMETERY.
Born Sydenham, lived Purley, Surrey. Enlisted London. Married Susan Florence Tester Mar 1910. He is shown on the CWGC as Crossley G.

CROSSLEY JAMES RICHARD Private 1205 Monmouthshire Regiment 3rd Bn.

Killed in action 02/05/1915 Panel 50. YPRES (MENIN GATE) MEMORIAL.
Born Beckenham. Death Enlisted Cwm, Mon.

CROWTHER LESLIE OAKES Captain 2473 Royal Flying Corps 12th Sqdn, 5th Royal West Kent.
Killed in action 06/12/1916 age 25 Grave II. B. 22. AVESNES-LE-COMTE COMMUNAL CEMETERY EXTENSION.
Son of Herbert Oakes Crowther and Nellie Oakes Crowther, of Beckenham. Leslie was educated at St Andrews, Eastbourne and Malvern College, spending two years further in New York and Dresden. With the onset of the war, he joined the Royal West Kents in September 1914 but transferred to the RFC in December 1915. He qualified for his aviator's certificate at the Shoreham Military School flying a Maurice Farman biplane on 15 December. The next year was spent as Captain Leslie Oakes Crowther at the Front flying a de Haviland BE2 where it is said that his time was spent 'in many thrilling air fights and bomb-dropping expeditions'. His death came about not in combat but by a serious defect in the plane's design where the joystick was detachable. He was flying a BE2d, a Bleriot Experimental dual control version with full controls in the front compartment. With Leslie in the front seat and his co-pilot, Fanstone, in the rear, the plane circled the airfield at Avesnes. Leslie pulled back on the joystick to counteract a tendency to nosedive but it came out from the socket and Leslie was killed as the plane went down and hit the ground from 300ft. He is buried at the Avesne-le-Comte Communal Cemetery Extension.
THERE IS A PICTURE OF HIM HERE. Great Britain, Royal Aero Club Aviators=92 Certificates.

CRUICKSHANK KENNETH GEORGE Second Lieutenant Royal Flying Corps 32nd Sqdn.
Died 12/07/1917 age 21 ARRAS FLYING SERVICES MEMORIAL.
Son of James Cruickshank, of "Amberley", 20, The Bridle Rd., Purley, Surrey, and the late Elizabeth Antonia Cruickshank (nee Hallamore).

CRUCKSHANK JAMES GEORGE Private G/711 Queen's Own (Royal West Kent Regiment) 6th Bn.
Died 30/11/1917 Panel 8. CAMBRAI MEMORIAL, LOUVERVAL.
Lived 102 Arpley Road Beckenham Road, Penge.

CULLIS ALFRED Rifleman 41667 Royal Irish Rifles 14th Bn. Formerly 7076, Bedford Regt.
Killed in action 16/08/1917 Panel 138 to 140 and 162 to 162A and 163A. TYNE COT MEMORIAL.
Born Hammersmith, lived Beckenham. Enlisted Poplar East.

CUNNINGTON WILLIAM JAMES Rifleman P/475 Rifle Brigade 12th Bn.
Died 17/08/1917 age 21 Panel 145 to 147. TYNE COT MEMORIAL.
Son of Mrs. A. Cunnington, of 53, Churchfields Rd., Beckenham, Kent, and the late Mr. W. B. Cunnington.

CURTIS HARRY W Private 240493 Queen's Own (Royal West Kent Regiment) 1st/5th Bn. Mesopotamian Expeditionary Force.
Died 08/07/1918 Grave XI. G. 6. BAGHDAD (NORTH GATE) WAR CEMETERY.
Born Penge, lived Beckenham. Enlisted Bromley.

CURWEN, HENRY STANLEY Second Lieutenant 15640 Norfolk Regiment 7th Bn.
Killed in action 13/10/1915 Panel 30 and 31. LOOS MEMORIAL.
Probate to brother Robert Curwen 21/1/1916. 1901 7, Westgate Road, Beckenham.

DALE-RICHARDSON H N Difficult to identify.

DALTON ALFRED THOMAS Sergeant L/10628 Queen's (Royal West Surrey Regiment) 2nd Bn.
Killed in action 7/11/1914 age 19 Panel 11-13, 14 YPRES MENIN GATE MEMORIAL.
Born abt 1895, son of Charles and Charlotte Dalton, 129 Churchfields Rd, Beckenham, enlisted Croydon.

DANDRIDGE ALFRED PERCY
Metal merchant, Alfred Dandridge, lived at Brooksleigh, 38 Albemarle Rd. His sons, Harold Charles, Alec Horton, William and Alfred Percy all assisted their father in his rag and metal business but joined the army when the war started. Their brother, William Alfred, had married Ellen and was living at 49 Engleheart Rd, Catford. Harold was a corporal in the Royal Garrison

Artillery, Alec was a captain in the 4th London Brigade Royal Artillery and Percy a lance corporal in the Kings Royal Rifle Corps 20th battalion. Percy wrote from the trenches in July 1916 speaking of his experiences in joining the army and finding himself out in the trenches all in the space of one week.

'The weight of the pack that has to be carried on all occasions when the Regiment moves leaves a lasting impression, consisting of a belt, pouches, valise, haversack, blanket and gas and shrapnel helmets. A long march on a hot day becomes a very poor pastime. Nearly all our time is taken up with cleaning and finding our equipment.

Ruin and desolation abounds, villages in a mass of ruins, churches desecrated, old trenches full of thick evil smelling mud and enough broken German implements to stock a museum. The best souvenir to take home is one's head.

It is not easy to get accustomed to the din and clatter of bursting bombs, popping machine guns, sizzling shrapnel, ping of rifle bullets and explosion of trench mortars. To see a company of soldiers rigged out in gas helmets is enough to boggle the imagination.

We have our cheery times with many a concert (Percy was well known in local music circles) *with songs, ballads, choruses and recitations. Pack up your troubles in your old kit bag goes very well until Fritz find the top of the dugout with his shell when one's smile changes to an anxious look of who can get out first before it all collapses. Life up near the line is of continual excitement, daily air attacks, artillery duels, attacks and counter attacks but overall there is a longing for peace, which our enemies must wish for even more than we do.'*

Sadly Percy died at Abbeville aged 29 on 6/8/1916 shortly after he wrote this letter and his grave is in the SOMME COMMUNAL CEMETERY.

DANDRIDGE WILLIAM ALFRED Rifleman 385104 in the 2nd/8th Bn. Post Office Rifles.
Died 20/9/1917, age 30 Panel 54 YPRES MENIN GATE MEMORIAL.
Both Percy and William are recorded on the St Paul's church memorial. Their brother Alec Horton Dandridge survived the war and married Jean Millar Grieve in a full choral service at St Paul's Beckenham 16/9/20.

DAVIES AND DAVIS
Of the 13 names we have only been able to trace 7.
DAVIES A died as a result of a flying accident 19/6/1917. He was an

accountant clerk for Beckenham Council, previously at Bermondsey, and joined the London Rifles in Aug 1914. In Dec 1915, he gained a commission in the S Staffords and went to the front, transferring to the RFC 55th squ in 1916. He was a fine athlete, cricketer and rugby player for London clubs. He has a memorial grave in the City of London Cemetery, Manor Park, 141.65650. BJ 7/7/1917.

DAVIES A E, DAVIES E and DAVIES F not found.

DAVIES, JOSEPH Private M2/078511 Army Service Corps Mechanical Transport attd. VII Corps Signal Coy Royal Engineers.
Died age 23 11/04/1917 Grave O. VIII. L. 9. ST. SEVER CEMETERY EXTENSION, ROUEN.
Born Bromley.

DAVIES W C H is possibly
DAVIES, WILLIAM Private 240313 Queen's Own (Royal West Kent Regiment) 10th Bn.
Died 15/07/1918 age 23 Grave XXVIII. D. 7A. LIJSSENTHOEK MILITARY CEMETERY.
Son of Charles and Mary Davies, of Eastbourne House, Sydenham Hill Rd., Sydenham.

DAVIS ALBERT Lance Corporal 42166 Middlesex Regiment C Co 4th Bn.
Died 26/8/1918 Panel 8-9 VIS EN ARTOIS MEMORIAL.
Husband of H E E Davis of 147 Victor Rd, leaves four children, youngest 6 months old. BJ 21/9/1918

DAVIS C W, DAVIS J not found.

DAVIS C T Is this Clifford Thomas Davies 2nd Lieutenant, age 22 RWK 10th Bn. died 7/6/1917 Panel 45 & 46 YPRES MENIN GATE MEMORIAL son of David and Clara, 26 Inchmery Rd, Catford.

DAVIS CHARLES T E, 69144, Private Royal West Surrey, 1st Bn.
Died 21/9/1918, age 19 Grave III.B.20. VILLERS HILL, BRITISH CEMETERY VILLERS-GUISLAIN.
Son of Mr and Mrs C Davis 27 St John's Rd, Penge.

DAVIS HENRY OSCAR, eldest son of Mr and Mrs H Davis of Paxwell, Lennard Rd, died of wounds 16/7/1916 in London Welsh in Rouen age 22. Old boy of the County School.

DAVIS THOMAS WILLIAM, Private, G/474 Royal West Kent Regiment.
Killed in action a 14/10/1915 age 21, Panel 95-97, LOOS MEMORIAL.
Eldest son of Mr and Mrs Thomas William and Emily Davis of 189 Ravenscroft Rd, Beckenham.

DAWSON THOMAS REGINALD 2nd Lieutenant, 19th (County of London) Bn. (St Pancras).
On 2/3/1916 age 20 at the Empire Hospital, Vincent Square, died of wounds received at Loos on 25/9/1915. Name is remembered on Bay 9 or 10 ARRAS MEMORIAL and at Westminster School.
Only son of Charles Reginald Dawson of Beckenham, a tea merchant and importer, and Eleanor Hannah, youngest daughter of William Spencer Mitchell of Cambridge.
Born 23/12/1895, admitted to Westminster as a King's Scholar on 23/9/1909, commissioned as a 2nd Lieutenant, 3/10/1914, he went to France on 17/6/1915. From The Times of 7/2/1916.

DEAN ALFRED GITTINGS Private TF203940 Duke of Cambridge's Own (Middlesex Regiment) 1st/7th Bn.
Killed in action age 33 16/9/1916 Pier and Face 12 D and 13 B. THIEPVAL MEMORIAL.
Son of Alfred Dean, born 1883.

DEDMAN THOMAS HENRY Acting Bombardier 324, RGA SR/334 disembarked Egypt 1/6/1915.
Killed in action 27/6/1916, aged 47, buried Mailly Wood Cemetery, Mailly-Maillet. On his way home from 15 months in the Dardanelles was transferred to France where he was killed within a few days. Brother of Mrs L R Porter of 370 Katherine Road, Forest Gate, London. Born Beckenham abt 1873, age at enlistment 41 when of 153 Parish Lane. His mother Susan was born in Lewisham; on the 1881 census her husband was Henry working as a bricklayer and living at Kelsey Cottages Beckenham.

DENNIS CHARLES WALTER Private G/4172 Queen's Own (Royal West Kent Regiment) 1st Bn.
Killed in action 5/5/1915 age 19 Panel 45 and 47. YPRES MENIN GATE MEMORIAL.
Son of Mrs. T. Dennis of 1 Sultan St. Beckenham. Enlisted Bromley.

DENNIS FRANK HERBERT Private 202879 Norfolk Regiment 1st/4th Bn.
Killed in action 11/12/1917 age 39 Grave D. 41. RAMLEH WAR CEMETERY Palestine.
Husband of Alice Mary Dennis, of 63, Crampton Rd., High St., Penge, London.
Enlisted Norwood, Surrey.

DENNIS WILLIAM JOHN Private 11819 Queen's Own (Royal West Kent Regiment). 8th Bn.
Died of wounds 30/3/1918 age 25 IX. A. 13. WIMEREUX COMMUNAL CEMETERY FRANCE.
Son of Thomas and Louisa Dennis of Beckenham, enlisted Anerley.

DENYER DAVID Private 12160 Hertfordshire Regiment.
Killed in action 18/10/1918 Grave IV.G.30 CAUDRY BRITISH CEMETERY France.
Born Beckenham, lived Sydenham, enlisted London.

DICKINSON ALBERT FREDERICK Private 27799 King's Shropshire Light Infantry. 7th Bn. Formerly 22065, T.R. Bn.
Died of wounds 16/7/1918 age 19, V. E. 46. PERNES BRITISH CEMETERY FRANCE.
Son of Henry William and Ann Harriet Dickinson of Beckenham. Born Clerkenwell, lived Beckenham, enlisted Bromley.

DILNOT HOWARD WILLIAM E
Son of William and Emma Dilnot 38 Parish Lane born 1898 Beckenham, died Bromley district 1st quarter 1919. Of the six Dilnot entries in the CWGC, there is not one with these initials.

DIVE HARRY EDMUND Lance Corporal 240400 "A" Coy. 1st/5th Bn. Queen's Own (Royal West Kent Regiment).

Drowned 14/9/1918 age 21 Panel 25 BASRA MEMORIAL Iraq.
Son of Thomas Edmund and Annie Kingsford Dive of 103, Blandford Rd., Beckenham.

DOGGETT FREDERICK SIDNEY Lance Corporal 2567 1st/16th Bn. London Regiment (Queen's Westminster Rifles).
Son of Frederick James and Catherine Doggett of 60 Clock House Rd. Beckenham, born abt 1894, stockbroker's clerk.

DOGGETT R Of the 36 Doggett records in the CWGC there is not a Doggett R.

D'OMBRAIN ROLAND MAUND 2nd Lieutenant I/5th Battalion, The Buffs (East Kent Regiment). attached., 53rd Sikhs (F.F.) as linguist.
Killed in action 8/3/1916 Mesopotamia Panel 43 and 65 BASRA MEMORIAL Iraq.
Husband of May D'Ombrain of Chilchester Lodge 67 Wickham Rd, Beckenham. Son of Henry, consulting engineer, and Edith D'Ombrain. Grandfather was the founder of the National Rose Society. Descendants of the Huguenot family d'Embruni. BJ 1/4/1916 p5.

DONE NEVILLE SAVAGE 2nd Lieutenant Royal Fusiliers 6th Bn. attd. 22nd Bn.
Died 10/3/1917 age 35. Pier and Face 8 C 9 A and 16 A THIEPVAL MEMORIAL.
Son of the Wesleyan Rev. William Done and Mrs. Maria Ellen Done of Hillcroft Groombridge Sussex; husband of Mrs. Hilda Doris Done (nee Woodward) of 14 Rednal Rd., King's Norton, Birmingham. Solicitors clerk. In 1914 lived at 22 Downs Rd., married 1911. In 1916 according to street directory lived at 32 Manor Road, Beckenham, Kent.

DONOHUE P F Two or three possible Patricks in the CWGC but no P F and no Beckenham connection.

DOUST CHARLES BOWDEN 2nd Lieutenant London Regiment 1st/5th Bn.
Killed in action 1/7/1916 Panel Pier and Face 9D THIEPVAL MEMORIAL.
Son of Mr and Mrs Charles H Doust of Inglehurst, Shortlands.

DOUST NORMAN SHELLIBEER 2nd Air mechanic Royal Flying Corps 21490.
Died 20/6/1918 at the Home Sanatorium 84 Southbourne Road, West Southbourne, Hampshire.
Born Lewisham abt 1890, age at enlistment 26, of Inglehurst Shortlands Kent.

DRAKE HENRY THOMAS Lance Sergeant S/2987 Rifle Brigade (The Prince Consort's Own) 9th Bn.
Killed in action 15/9/1916 age 19 THIEPVAL MEMORIAL.
Born Rotherhithe, lived Beckenham, 2 Cavendish Villas, Elmers End Rd, Elmers End.
Son of Henry Thomas and Alice Drake. Played football and cricket locally.

DRAPER ALFRED HERBERT (Herbert Alfred at birth) Lance Corporal G/1235 Queen's (Royal West Surrey Regiment) 10th Bn.
Killed in action 31/7/1917 YPRES MENIN GATE MEMORIAL.
Of 14 St Margaret's Rd, born Beckenham. Enlisted Croydon.

DRAWBRIDGE BERTRAM REGINALD Sergeant 115358 230th Siege Bty. Royal Garrison Artillery.
Died 2/8/1917 C. 6/8. PERTH CEMETERY (China Wall), Belgium Ieperwest-Vlaanderen II.
Born Greenwich 1894, son of Samuel stationmaster at New Beckenham Station in 1911 and Alice Mary Drawbridge.

DRAWBRIDGE LOUIS SPENCER Able Seaman H.M.S. Juno. Royal Navy J/3976.
Died 26/07/18 from disease aged 26, C.E. IX. I. 13. COLOMBO KANATTA GENERAL CEMETERY, Sri Lanka.
Brother of Bertram Reginald Drawbridge.

DRUGHORN WILLIAM FREDERICK Private STK/76 Royal Fusiliers 10th Bn.
Killed in action 15/7/1916 Grave III.H.13 POZIERES BRITISH CEMETERY OVILLERS-LA BOISSELLE.
Youngest son of Mr and Mrs J F Drughorn of Banavie, The Avenue, Abbey schoolboy, Kings College Canterbury. BJ 29/7/16.

DRUITT BERNARD DONALD Corporal, 1/12th London Regiment (The Rangers).
Killed in action 7/10/1916, age 22. Pier and Face 9C. THIEPVAL MEMORIAL.
Son of Emily and the late George Druitt, of 172, Birkbeck Rd., Beckenham.

DRYSDALE ALEXANDER ICELY Major, Royal Field Artillery A Bty, 87th Bde.
Killed in action 28/7/1916 aged 35 Pier and Face 1 A and 8 A. THIEPVAL MEMORIAL.

DRYSDALE HAMILTON DUNBAR Captain 26th Punjabi Indian.
Died 1/9/1915 aged 27 H9. CAMBRIN CHURCHYARD EXTENSION.
Born 12/5/1888 Exmouth.
Sons of Alexander Tovey and Louisa Drysdale (nee Icely) at one time of 2 Kingswood Rd, Beckenham, later of "The Links" West Drive Queen's Park Bournemouth.

DUNLOP R S Not found.

DURLING ROBERT STEPHEN 62179 Royal Fusiliers.
Died 19/3/1917 Grave III.M.191 FAUBERG D'AMIENS ARRAS.
Son of Thomas and Mary Ann of Beckenham. Robert Durling of Kelsey Cottage was one of the first group enlistments at East St on 20/11/1915.

DURRANT CHARLES rifleman 4606 Rifle Brigade (The Prince Consort's Own) 2nd Bn.
Killed in action 9/5/1915 PLOEGSTEERT MEMORIAL, Belgium, Comines-Warnetonhainaut.
Enlisted London, born Penge, in 1911 lived at 40 Kingswood Road, Penge.

DYBALL JAMES HENRY Private 35953 Loyal North Lancashire Regiment 1st Bn.
Killed in action 18/9/1918, panel 7 VIS-EN-ARTOIS MEMORIAL.
Born Carshalton, Surrey. 1911 115 Blandford Rd, Beckenham.

EARWICKER ROBERT P. Private, driver, L/9588, Queens 2nd Bn., overseas in Gibraltar 1911. Also described as drummer.
Died 14/1/1916.

Born Penge, enlisted Colchester 1914.

In 1901 lived 123 Penge Lane stepson of Charles Albert White, mother Alice Jane.

ECKETT CHARLES ARTHUR Private 41107 Royal Inniskilling Fusiliers 1st Bn.

Formerly 13428, Queens Royal West Surrey Regiment.

Killed in action 19/5/1917 Addenda panel ARRAS MEMORIAL.

Born abt 1881 Wimbledon, lived 97 Birkbeck Road, Beckenham, gardener.

EDWARDS, ARTHUR Private 8008 The Buffs (East Kent Regiment) 6th Bn.

Died 19/03/1918 age 37 Grave XIII. F. 34. COLOGNE SOUTHERN CEMETERY.

Son of Mr. W. T. Edwards, of 17, Clifford Grove, Penge, London.

EDWARDS FREDERICK CHARLES Lance Corporal 41734 Fusiliers (City of London Regiment) 1st.

Killed in action 4/11/1918 Grave I. H. 9. CROSS ROADS CEMETERY, FONTAINE-AU-BOIS.

Connection with Beckenham uncertain. Several with this name.

EDWARDS JOHN PERCIVAL Company Sergeant Major B/19418 Royal Fusiliers 26th Bn.

Died of wounds 7/10/1916 age 38 Grave Y2.7206 BECKENHAM CREMATORIUM & CEMETERY.

Husband of Florence Edwards of 32 Cromwell Rd, Beckenham. PASI Licentiate RIBA L C C Architects Dept. Military funeral with wreaths from LCC and Beckenham Tennis. BJ 14/10/1916 p3.

EDWARDS R Private 2150 24th County of London.

Died 26/5/1915 Panels 46/47 LE TOURET, FRANCE.

Son of Mr B Edwards Albemarle Rd. Of 11 pages in the CWGC, only one name belonged to the London Regiment 1st/24th.

EELY G H is in error and should be Charles Henry Eely born 1897 one of five sons of the builder Henry Eely born 1862 and his wife Elizabeth Ann of 4 Newlands Park. He was Private 9978 of the Royal Berks 2nd Bn. who died aged 18 on 29/5/1915 at Merviue, Grave

III.11.2. On the CWGC records he is Charles A and served as Flint.

EELY WILLIAM 303682 Canadian Field Artillery 10th Bde.
Died 5/11/1917 aged 29 Grave IX.C.2 VLAMERTINGHE.
Born 1889 was the brother of Charles Henry Eely.

ELLINOR WILLIAM ALFRED Sergeant 47437 Royal Horse Artillery and Royal Field Artillery 147th Bty.
Died of wounds and effects of gas 16/4/1918 on a home posting. Grave Y3.7574 at BECKENHAM CREMATORIUM & CEMETERY.
Born Norwood, enlisted New Cross, son of William Robert and Martha Ellinor of 41 Station Rd, Penge.

ELLIOTT ROBERT HENRY Lance Corporal G/6668 Queen's Own (Royal West Kent Regiment) 6th Bn.
Died 03/07/1916 Grave VII. T. 7. OVILLERS MILITARY CEMETERY.
Born abt 1892 son of Alice and Isaac Elliott of 61 Durban Road, Beckenham. Butcher Meat Market.

ELLIOTT WILLIAM GILBERT Private G/15907, later 72763 The Queen's (Royal West Surrey Regiment) 2nd Infantry Works Coy. transf. to (72763) 122nd Coy. Labour Corps.
Died 04/07/1918 age 26 Grave LXVII. F. 23. ETAPLES MILITARY CEMETERY.
Son of Mary Ann and the late Thos. H. Elliott, of 5, Richmond Park Rd., Kingston, Surrey.

EMBLEM WILLIAM Private Royal Fusiliers (City of London Regiment) Bn. Posted 2/2nd London 82867 Formerly 87367, 12th Middx. Regt.
Killed in action 24 /4/1918 Grave I.D.16 HANGARD WOOD BRITISH CEMETERY.

EMSON FRANCIS REGINALD, Assistant paymaster, RNR, on armed merchant cruiser HMS Clan McNaughton that foundered off Scotland on Wednesday 3/2/1915 with no survivors, Chatham Naval Memorial, panel 13. Husband of Catherine Dorothy of The Nook, 7 Oakfield Rd, Beckenham, son of Reginald Embleton Emson and Louise of Tulse Hill.

EVANS JANE Sister Queen Alexandra's Imperial Military Nursing Service.

Died 26/02/1918 HOLLYBROOK MEMORIAL, SOUTHAMPTON.
Daughter of Evan and Mary Rebecca Evans.

FABER VICTOR EDMUND Private M2/118983 Army Service Corps attd.
350th Elec. and Mechanical Coy Royal Engineers.
Killed in action 4/9/1918 Grave XII. C. 3. VILLERS STATION CEMETERY,
VILLERS-AU-BOIS France.
Born Brockley 1895, lived Beckenham, enlisted Coventry.

FAITHFULL DAVIES GILBERT VERE Lieutenant Royal Scots 13th Bn.
Died 23/04/1917 age 29 Panel Reference Bay 1 and 2. ARRAS MEMORIAL.
Son of the Rev. R. V. Faithfull Davies and E. H. S. Faithfull Davies, of 159,
Copers Cope, Beckenham.
Probate to REV RICHARD MERVYN FAITHFULL-DAVIES Brother.
1911 Ingoldesthorpe 15 Southend Road, Beckenham.

FAULKNER, GORDON HENRY Private 1658 Honourable Artillery
Company.
Died 18/02/1919 age 33 Grave U2. 296. BECKENHAM CREMATORIUM
AND CEMETERY.
Son of T. H. and Susie Faulkner, of "Willoughby", Rectory Rd., Beckenham.

FENNER, ALAN THOMAS Second Lieutenant North Staffordshire
Regiment 2nd/6th Bn.
Died 08/12/1917 age 18 Grave III. F. 8. ABBEVILLE COMMUNAL
CEMETERY EXTENSION.
Son of George Arthur and Ellen Fenner, of 75, Kent House Rd., Beckenham.

FERGUSON FRANK LOUIS Private G/75307 Royal Fusiliers 17th Bn.
Died 02/11/1918 age 19 Panel 3. Memorial VIS-EN-ARTOIS MEMORIAL.
Son of James and Caroline Ferguson, of 50, Mackenzie Rd., Beckenham,
Kent.

FERGUSON JOHN RALPH Private 63312 Royal Fusiliers 20th Bn.
Killed in action 07/11/1916 age 24 Grave III. K. 25. Cemetery A.I.F.
BURIAL GROUND, FLERS.
Brother of Frank Louis Ferguson. Of 50 Mackenzie Rd, Beckenham.
Member of St John's United Football Team who enlisted together in
November 1914. BJ 2/12/1916.

FIELD H. Just possible is from W Croydon 112 Wentworth Rd died 20/9/1917 from four pages of names on CWGC.

FIELD WILLIAM FREDERICK Lance Corporal, G/282 Queen's (Royal West Surrey Regiment) 8th Bn.
Killed in action 30/7/1917 II.B.10. CHESTER FARM CEMETERY France & Flanders.
Born and lived Beckenham, enlisted Croydon.

FINCH AUBREY MALCOLM CECIL Captain Seaforth Highlanders (Ross-shire Buffs, the Duke of Albany's) 4th Bn.
Killed in action 07/07/1919 age 22 Grave Mem. B40. ARCHANGEL ALLIED CEMETERY (buried Semenovka (Bereznik) Cem. Extension).
Son of William and Rona Amy Elizabeth Finch, of Beckenham, Kent; husband of Mabel Dorothy Owen (formerly Finch), of 133, Kent House Rd., Beckenham, Kent.

FINCH ERNEST WILFRED RUPERT Lieutenant Seaforth Highlanders "A" Coy. 4th Bn.
Died 07/08/1916 age 21 Grave III. A. 1. PUCHEVILLERS BRITISH CEMETERY.
Son of William and Rona Amy Elizabeth Finch, of Southdown House, West Wickham, Kent. Late of Beckenham.

FISHER F T A There was Frederick T A Fisher who died in the June quarter of 1919 age 27 so born in 1892 and a Frederick Fisher from 112 Arpley Rd, Penge, age 19 in 1911. He does not appear on the CWGC but the National Archives soldier's medal awards has Frederick T Albert G/1677 of the Royal West Kent Regiment 7th Bn.

FLEMING HAMILTON MAXWELL Captain Canadian Infantry 16th Bn.
Died 24/04/1915 age 39. Panel 24 - 26 - 28 - 30. YPRES (MENIN GATE) MEMORIAL.
Son of the late John Fleming, C.S.I., and Mary Fleming. Tower House, Bromley. Served in the South African Campaign. Born 1876 BJ p1 1/5/1915.

FLEMING JOHN ALLISTER Second Lieutenant Queen's Own (Royal West Kent Regiment) 1st Bn.
Died of wounds 22/07/1916 age 23 Pier and Face 11 C. THIEPVAL

MEMORIAL.
Son of the Revd. R. S. Fleming and Margaret L. Fleming, of 11, Elm Rd., Beckenham.

FOLLEY HENRY JAMES Private 6863 Royal Army Medical Corps H.M.H.S.
Death at sea 21/03/1917 "Asturias" Grave M. 6. 14548. TORQUAY CEMETERY AND EXTENSION.
Born Beckenham 1893, Birkbeck Rd in 1901.

FOORD GEORGE HOWARD Lieutenant Army Service Corps 176th Depot.
Died of wounds 13/10/1915 age 31 Grave A. 77. LANCASHIRE LANDING CEMETERY.
Son of Thomas Herbert Edward and Ida Foord of 42 Westmoreland Rd.
Husband of Gertrude F. Foord nee Marsland, of Hazelbury Cottage, Painswick, Glos. Solicitor and M.A. (Cambridge).

FORD JOHN BALLARD BERKLEY Captain Queen's Own Royal West Kent 2nd Bn. attd 7th Bn.
Died of wounds 16/2/1917 age 29 Grave V.B.25. DERNANCOURT COMMUNAL CEMETERY EXTENSION.
Son of Major General Sir Richard Ford and Lady Ford. Reference in BJ 3/3/1917.

FORSTER CHARLES EDWARD Private 1026 Australian Infantry, A.I.F. 22nd Bn.
Died 03/05/1917 VILLERS-BRETONNEUX MEMORIAL.

FORSTER JOHN Second Lieutenant King's Royal Rifle Corps 2nd Bn.
Killed in action 14/09/1914 age 21 LA FERTE-SOUS-JOUARRE MEMORIAL.
Son of Mr. H.W. Forster, M.P. and the Hon. Mrs Forster, of 41 Hans Place, London.
 Henry William Forster was MP for Sevenoaks until 1918 and then for Bromley followed by Governor General of Australia from 1920 to 1925. He married the Honourable Rachel Cecily Douglas-Scott-Montagu and both their sons were killed in WWI. Lieutenant Alfred Henry of the 2nd Dragoons, Royal Scots Greys died aged 21 on 10/3/1919 and is buried at

Exbury St Katherine, Hants so he is not on the Beckenham war memorial.

FOX WILLIAM JAMES Private 67412 Machine Gun Corps infantry 50th Bn.
Died 27/5/1918 SOISSONS MEMORIAL.
Wife 65 Churchfields rd, Beckenham. Had worked as clerk for 15 years to F Warne & Co, publishers.

FRASER, HUGH McNEILL Private 3132 London Regiment (London Scottish) 1st/14th Bn.
Died of wounds 03/02/1915 age 21 Grave I. A. 28. LE TOUQUET-PARIS PLAGE COMMUNAL
CEMETERY.
Son of John Alexander and Gertrude Loma McNeill Fraser, of Rutland House, Southend Rd., Beckenham.

FREEMAN Identification not possible with no forename.

FULLER A Of the 42 possibles in the CWGC, Alfred Mathew Fuller Private 40421 Middlesex Regiment 2nd Bn. formerly 12665 Royal Sussex, is likely.
Killed in action 23/10/1916 FONCQUEVILLERS MILITARY CEMETERY.
Born abt 1885 West Wickham, enlisted Maidstone. BJ18/8/1917 records Private A Fullex of the Middlesex Regiment killed 23/10/1916 of 30 Yew Tree Rd, Beckenham.

FULLER, CHARLES Private 400985 Essex Regiment 17th Bn. tranfr. to (460188) Labour Corps.
Died 01/11/1918 age 27 Grave 54. 527. NORWICH CEMETERY, NORFOLK.
Son of Mrs. F. E. Hickman, of 22, Croydon Rd., Elmers End, Beckenham, Kent.

FULLER, HENRY DALE Rifleman 32448 South Lancashire Regiment 1st/5th.
Died 09/04/1918 age 36 Panel 76 LOOS MEMORIAL.
Son of Henry and Emily Fuller, of 117, Lennard Rd., Beckenham.

FULLER JOHN HENRY MIDDLETON Captain 63rd Palamcottah Light Infantry attd. 83Rd Wallajahbad Light Infantry.
Died 04/11/1914 TANGA MEMORIAL.
Daughter Jean Violet Fuller born March 1915.

FULLER WILLIAM, 28327, North Hants Reg 7th Bn.
Died of wounds 15/5/1917 in hospital. Husband of Kathleen of the Kent House Rd PO, second son of Emily and Henry Fuller of Connemara, Lennard Rd. BJ 26/5/1917.

FULLOCKS A No trace.

FURZE CLAUDE Captain London Regiment (London Rifle Brigade) 1st/5th Bn.
Died of wounds 06/04/1918 age 27 Grave Plot 4. Row A. Grave 1. FORCEVILLE COMMUNAL CEMETERY AND EXTENSION.
Son of Mr. and Mrs. Frederic Furze, of 6, Welbeck House, London, W. I.

FURZE, FREDERIC Captain London Regiment (London Rifle Brigade) 5th Bn.
Killed in action 20/09/1917 age 36 Panel 52 and 54. YPRES (MENIN GATE) MEMORIAL.
Son of Frederic and Helen E. Furze, of 10, Chiswick Place, Eastbourne; husband of Alice Furze (nee Duthie). BROTHER OF CLAUDE FURZE In 1901, the family lived at The Coppice, 34 Southend Rd, Beckenham.

GALLIMORE WALTER ALBERT Rifleman 3988 London Regiment (Post Office Rifles) 1st/8th Bn.
Died 15/09/1916 Pier and Face 9 C and 9 D. THIEPVAL MEMORIAL.
From 21 Piquet Road, Anerley.

GARDINER, HENRY GEORGE Sergeant 26675 Royal Flying Corps.
Died 08/09/1917 age 38 Grave O. 592. SHORNCLIFFE MILITARY CEMETERY.
Husband of Caroline Frances Louisa Gardiner, of 13, Sheringham Rd., Anerley, London.

GARLICK, PERCY JAMES Private 9533 Oxford and Bucks Light Infantry 2nd Bn.

Killed in action 25/09/1915.
Birth Place Brittwell, Oxon. Enlisted Oxford. Husband of Mary Harman 1906. Lived Beckenham.

GARRARD PERCY DSO Major London Regiment (The Queens) 24th Bn. attd. 2nd/4th King's African Rifles.
  Died in German hands (as POW?) at Malawi 18/09/1918 Grave 44 MANGOCHI TOWN CEMETERY.
Married Doris Ponder in 1916 at Bromley.

GARWOOD, HARRY Rifleman S/27128 Rifle Brigade "C" Coy. 1st Bn.
Died 22/04/1918 age 20 Grave A. 15. LE VERTANNOY BRITISH CEMETERY, HINGES.
Son of Richard and Louisa Garwood, of 27, The Avenue, Beckenham. Born at Dedham, Essex about 1898.

GEE LEONARD FRANCIS Private G/15602 The Buffs (East Kent Regiment) 7th Bn.
Killed in action 30/09/1916 Pier and Face 5 D. THIEPVAL MEMORIAL.
Born Sydenham, 1911 2 Linden Grove Sydenham.

GIBBINS, ERNEST ARTHUR MM Private G/11077 Queen's Own (Royal West Kent Regiment) 1st. Bn.
Died 11/04/1917 age 25 Grave VIII. A. 174. BOULOGNE EASTERN.
Son of Fanny Turner (formerly Gibbins), of 10, Byne Rd., Sydenham, London, and the late Frederick Gibbins.

GIBLIN ERNEST Private G/11107 Queen's Own (Royal West Kent Regiment) 6th Bn.
Killed in action 03/07/1916. Grave VIII. A. 4. OVILLERS MILITARY CEMETERY.
Born Beckenham, Enlisted Bromley, Kent.

GIBSON, CECIL MERVYN Second Lieutenant York and Lancaster Regiment 1st/5th Bn.
Died 05/05/1917 age 23 Grave III. B. 20. PONT-DU-HEM MILITARY CEMETERY, LA GORGUE.
Son of Charles Mervyn Gibson and Charlotte Mary Gibson, of 55, Queen's Rd., Beckenham.

GIDDINGS GEORGE PRENTICE CHANDLER Gunner 113844 Royal Field Artillery 54th Bty.
Killed in action 30/07/1916 France. Grave IV. A. 2. QUARRY CEMETERY, MONTAUBAN.
Born West Croydon, Surrey Married Naomi Kemp 1914, Albert G born 1915.

GILLESPIE FRANCIS SYDNEY Captain Royal Sussex Regiment 13th Bn.
Died of wounds 18/06/1916 age 26 Grave VII. A. 19. MERVILLE COMMUNAL CEMETERY.
Son of John and Eleanor A. Gillespie, of 102, West Hill, Sydenham, London.

GILLINGHAM, SYDNEY JOHN Stoker 1st Class Royal Navy H.M.S. "Conquest." 311026
Died 28/03/1916 Grave WALTON-ON-THE-NAZE (OR WALTON-LE-SOKEN) (ALL SAINTS) CHURCHYARD EXTENSION.
(Served as John CASH). The ship's whaler was returning 38 of the crew from shore leave when it foundered in a snowstorm off Harwich, losing all the men.
Husband of Nellie Gillingham, 79, Ravenscroft Rd, Beckenham Road, Beckenham, son Sydney L H born 1912.

GLADWIN WALTER GEORGE Private 1946 London Regiment 1st/20th Bn.
Killed in action 25/09/1915 age 21. Panel 130 to 135. LOOS MEMORIAL.
Enlisted Blackheath. Address 1911 62 Bromley Road Catford.

GLAZEBROOK RICHARD CHARLES Private 30517 Essex Regiment 10th Bn.
Died of wounds 29/10/1916.Grave H. 4. LONGUEVAL Rd CEMETERY.
Born Beckenham, enlisted Bromley. 1911 10 Yewtree Rd.

GLEN, HARRY Private 8058 London Regiment (Royal Fusiliers) 1st Bn.
Killed in action 08/10/1916 Pier and Face 9 D and 16 B. THIEPVAL MEMORIAL.
Born Beckenham abt 1898, son of Thomas and Rebecca Glen of 22 Somerville Rd, Penge.

GOLDER ROBERT WILLIAM Private 104300 Machine Gun Corps (Infantry) 17th Coy. Formerly 48705, Royal Fusiliers.
Killed in action 25/08/1918 Grave II. F. 10. A.I.F. BURIAL GROUND, FLERS.
Enlisted Bromley.

GOLDSMITH FRANK Private 9121 The Queen's (Royal West Surrey Regiment) 2nd Bn.
Died of wounds 28/10/1914 age 23. Grave III. A. 19. Cemetery BOULOGNE EASTERN CEMETERY.
Son of David and Agnes Goldsmith, of Penge. Enlisted Guildford.

GOODIER ALBERT GEORGE Private G/3755 The Queen's (Royal West Surrey Regiment) 1st Bn.
Died 16/05/1916 age 40 Grave V. C. 73. BETHUNE TOWN CEMETERY.
Husband of second wife Kate Goodier, of 71, Crampton Rd., Penge, London and children Gilbert born 1913 and Leslie born 1915.

GOULD, RALPH BOHN Second Lieutenant South Wales Borderers 4th Bn.
Died 20/12/1916 age 26 Grave XXI. L. 1. AMARA WAR CEMETERY.
Son of Mr. A. K. and Mrs. A. M. Gould, of 25, Kingshall Rd., Beckenham. Eldest of three boys of Craven College.

GOVER WILLIAM ARTHUR Captain 7th Duke of Connaught's Own Rajputs 1st commission 20/1/1900. Awards Mentioned in Despatches.
Died Mesopotamia 03/03/1915 Panel 21. Column 1. TEHRAN MEMORIAL.
Born 29/1/1880. Of 15 Queen's Rd Beckenham. His father Gover, Alfred Greatbatch, matric. London Univ. July, 1863, practised before the High Court of Madras, a student of Gray's Inn 23/1/1865, called to the bar 18/11/1867.

GRAHAM HORACE WILLIAM Lance Corporal 562317 Royal Engineers.
Died 19/10/1918 age 26 Grave Q5. 7700. BECKENHAM CREMATORIUM AND CEMETERY.
Eldest son of John Albert and Rose C. Graham, of 97, Chaffinch Rd., Beckenham. Mobilised at the outbreak of war on coast duty until sent to

France August 1916, invalided home and discharged Aug 1917 but dying pneumonia.

GRANT HARRY T Private M2/031818 Royal Army Service Corps G.H.Q. Anti-Aircraft Gunnery School Died 13/02/1919 Grave II. C. 4. COLOGNE SOUTHERN CEMETERY.

GRANT HENRY TYLOR Private 201694 Royal Sussex Regiment "A" Coy. 4th Bn. British Expeditionary Force enlisted Bromley.
Died of wounds 16/01/1918 age 40 Grave IX. C. 20. MENDINGHEM MILITARY CEMETERY.
Son of Amos and Mary Grant, of Beckenham; husband of Emilie Ada Grant, of 26, Faversham Rd. A founder of the Beckenham Cycling Club and the swimming club before there were baths in Beckenham, Harry was a leading member of the Christ Church Choir, Institute and football team and captain of cricket.

GRANT, JOHN CARDROSS Captain Cameronians (Scottish Rifles) 10th Bn. Awards MC
Died 27/01/1916 age 23 Grave I. K. 24. NOEUX-LES-MINES COMMUNAL CEMETERY.
Son of Cardross and Sophia Hewitt Grant, of "Bruntsfield", 81, Albemarle Rd., Beckenham.

GRAVENEY, WILLIAM KILLEEN Sergeant 75004 Canadian Infantry 29th Bn.
Died 26/09/1916 age 28 Grave VII. E. 15. ADANAC MILITARY CEMETERY, MIRAUMONT.
Son of Elizabeth Green, of 12, Stodart Rd., Anerley, London and the late William Graveney. Born in Surrey, England. Enlisted at Vancouver, 1914.

GREGORY THOMAS FRANK Private 27391 Suffolk Regiment 2nd Bn., formerly G/16187, Middx. Regt.
Died 07/11/1917 Grave II. B. 12. FAVREUIL BRITISH CEMETERY.
Killed instantly due to a shell that burst behind him while on sentry duty.
Born Anerley, enlisted Croydon, Mrs T Gregory, his wife and seven children lived 16 Kimberley Rd. He had worked as a builder and decorator before volunteering at the outbreak of war.

HAINES, CHARLES FREDERICK Rifleman B/200410 Rifle Brigade "D" Coy. 11th Bn.
Died 10/02/1917 age 26 Pier and Face 16 B and 16 C. THIEPVAL MEMORIAL.
Son of Frederick and Elizabeth Haines, of 156, Victor Rd., Penge; husband of Kate Haines.

HAINES, FREDERICK ARTHUR Private 315561 Middlesex Regiment 1st Bn.
Died 27/09/1918 age 19 Grave VI. B. 32. VILLERS HILL BRITISH CEMETERY, VILLERS-GUISLAIN.
Brother of Charles Frederick.

HALFORD WILLIAM HENRY LOFFILL 2nd Lieutenant RAF ARRAS FLYING SERVICES.
Died 28/8/1918 on first day of Ypres offensive fighting aircraft six miles behind the lines. Son of Mr C H Halford of Woodlands, Beckenham.

HALL CHARLES 2nd Lieutenant The Buffs East Kent Regiment 8th Bn. Light Trench Mortar Bty.
Died attempting to throw out a live shell 28/3/1917 age 23 I.D.4. BULLY-GRENAY COMMUNAL CEMETERY British extension.
Son of Richard and Harriett of Quarrytea, Hayne Rd. Swimmer, boxer, footballer and runner he played water polo for the Beckenham Swimming Club and football for Clarke's College.

HALL E M
There is Edgar Montague of the Canadian Infantry from High Wycombe and E E M Hall from the London Regiment died 1918, both from the CWGC.

HALL SIDNEY 2nd Lieutenant RAF 4th sqdn.
Died 18/10/1918 and given a military funeral by the populace TOURCOING CEMETERY.
Son of Mr and Mrs R Hall of Quarryton, Hayne Rd, wife Ellen Hall.

HAMMOND HARRY 294 RWK 6th Bn.
Died 13/10/1915 Pas de Calais, grave IV, F. 15, BETHUNE TOWN CEMETERY, age 24.
Son of C and Alice Maud Hammond of Chancery Lane, Beckenham.

ORDINARY SEAMAN F.R.P. GERKINS
ROYAL NAVAL VOLUNTEER RESERVE   12.10.1918
ORDINARY SEAMAN W.GORDON
ROYAL NAVAL VOLUNTEER RESERVE   15:10.1918
RIFLEMAN H.A.HANCOCK
KING'S ROYAL RIFLE CORPS   30.6.1919
SAPPER C.H.HARRISON
ROYAL ENGINEERS   26.1.1918
ORDINARY SEAMAN T.B.INGLIS
ROYAL NAVAL VOLUNTEER RESERVE   29.3.1915
ORDINARY SEAMAN H.F.IVE
ROYAL NAVAL VOLUNTEER RESERVE   6.7.1918
WORKER A.E.JONES
QUEEN MARY'S ARMY AUXILIARY CORPS   21.11.1918
RIFLEMAN E.J.KNELL (SERVED AS) TOWN)
THE RIFLE BRIGADE   29.8.1916
CORPORAL C.L.MAXTED
ROYAL ARMY PAY CORPS   25.2.1919
ORDINARY SEAMAN J.G MURRAY
ROYAL NAVAL VOLUNTEER RESERVE   4.2.1915

The Screen Wall at Beckenham Cemetery showing one of the three Hancock brothers killed in WWI

HANCOCK ALBERT RICHARD Private M1/07456 Army Service Corps Mechanical Transport J Troops.
Died 23/8/1918 age 27. Grave 5 Plot 6 Row A MONTECCHIO PRECALCINO ITALY.
Son of Tom Beauchamp Jones and Margaret Hannah Hancock, 3 St Margaret's Villas, Elmers End. Brother of both Hugh Frederick George and Herbert Arthur.

HANCOCK HUGH FREDERICK GEORGE Private L/9447 R West Surrey Regiment 2nd Bn.
Died 30/10/1914 age 29 YPRES MENIN GATE MEMORIAL.

HANCOCK HERBERT ARTHUR Rifleman, C/7885, Kings Royal Rifle Corps.

Died 30/6/1919, age 24. Screen Wall X6.3.7972 BECKENHAM CEMETERY.

HARDING JOHN CHARLES Private 11884 Royal Welsh Fusiliers 8th Bn.
Died 7/8/1915 age 39, Grave IV.F.18 SHRAPNEL VALLEY CEMETERY. Husband of Florence Emily Harding 26 Clifton Terrace, Parish Lane, Penge.

HARDWICK H There are three possibles on the CWGC lists; a driver in the Royal Field Artillery died 2/8/1918, a Private in the RAMC died 19/7/1917 and Sergeant Henry of the Royal Irish Fusiliers died 24/6/1917.

HARPER M There are no likely Beckenham candidates for this name on the CWGC lists.

HARROD, GEORGE JOSEPH Private 240520 Queen's Own (Royal West Kent Regiment) 1st/5th Bn. Mesopotamian Expeditionary Force sent to relieve the siege of Kut. His brother Harry of the Oxford Regiment was also there but was exchanged and sent to India. George died 16/10/1916 of a pernicious fever while prisoner in the hands of the Turks. Grave XXI. Q. 13. BAGHDAD (NORTH GATE) WAR CEMETERY.
Born Beckenham, enlisted Bromley, 1911 46 Kimberley Rd when he was a golf caddy.

HARTNOLL, JAMES HENRY Private 41731 Worcestershire Regiment 14th Bn.
Died 16/04/1918 Panel 41. POZIERES MEMORIAL.
Birth place Winchester, Hants, lived Penge, enlisted Bromley, Kent. Married Lilian Pharo 1909. 1911 13 Thesiger Rd. Brother POW Charles W Hartnoll of 7 Franklin Rd, Penge.

HASTINGS THOMAS EMANUEL Private L/10478 Queen's Own (Royal West Kent Regiment) 7th Bn. Killed in action Trones Wood 13/07/1916 Pier and Face 11 C. THIEPVAL MEMORIAL.
Born Sydenham, lived 97 Churchfields Rd, Beckenham. Enlisted age 16 Bromley Aug 1914.
HATFIELD, HENRY JAMES Lance Corporal G/40656 Middlesex Regiment 12th Bn.

Died 03/05/1917 age 21 Bay 7. ARRAS MEMORIAL.
Son of Mr. and Mrs. H. A. Hatfield, of 11, Ravenscroft Rd., Beckenham.

HAWKER ALBERT JOHN butcher aboard Mercantile Marine HMHS Llandovery Castle. The pre-war ship of the Union Castle line was at first used as a troopship.
Died 27/6/1918 age 32 when the converted hospital ship was torpedoed by the German sub U86 off the coast of Ireland and lifeboats shelled killing 146 including 14 Canadian nurses. TOWER HILL MEMORIAL.
Son of the late George and Selina Hawker and husband of Matilda Agnes of 334 Blandford Rd.

HAWKINS G W Of the five in the CWGC with this surname and initials, one who died 27/11/1917 is possible.

HAWLEY, NELLIE Probationer Nurse 83/11/1057 Queen Alexandra's Imperial Military Nursing Service attd. H.M.S. "Osmanieh".
Died 31/12/1917 age 29 when the troopship hit a mine from the German sub UC 34 at the entrance to Alexandria harbour with 198 casualties including the Captain. Grave B. 46. ALEXANDRIA (HADRA) WAR MEMORIAL CEMETERY.
Daughter of Alfred Arthur and Stella Hawley, of 29, Kingshall Rd., Beckenham.

HEASMAN ARTHUR NEAL Bombardier 95408 Royal Field Artillery "D" Bty. 8 2nd Bde.
Died 04/11/1917 age 21 Panel 4 to 6 and 162. TYNE COT MEMORIAL.
Son of Mrs. A. C. Heasman, of 41, Stembridge Rd., Anerley, London.

HEDLEY FREDERICK WILLIAM ALBERT Private 40917 Suffolk Regiment 8th Bn.
Died 12/10/1917 age 37 Panel 40 to 41 and 162 to 162A. TYNE COT MEMORIAL.
Son of William James and Georgina Hedley of 61, Mackenzie Rd., Beckenham; husband of Edith Diana Hedley of 101, Birkbeck Rd., Beckenham, Kent.

HENDERSON WILLIAM HENRY Sergeant T4/038132 Army Service Corps attd. 79th Field Amb. Royal Army Medical Corps.

Died Balkans 17/10/1918 Grave VI. H. 26. DOIRAN MILITARY CEMETERY.
Born Greenwich, lived Penge, enlisted Bromley.

HENEKER, FREDERICK CHRISTIAN Lieutenant Colonel Leinster Regiment Commanding 21st (Tyneside Scottish) Bn. Northumberland Fusiliers.
Died 01/07/1916 age 43 Grave III. A. 1. OVILLERS MILITARY CEMETERY Hill G.
Son of the late Richard William and Elizabeth Tuson Heneker, of Sherbrooke, Quebec, Canada; husband of Constance Heneker, of Berily House, Southlands Grove, Bickley, Kent.

HERRMANN, ERIC GEORGE FREDERICK Private 6518 Royal Fusiliers 18th Bn.
Died 26/11/1915 age 20 Grave H. 2. CAMBRIN CHURCHYARD EXTENSION.
Son of E. Frederick Bertholt and Alice Herrmann, of 29, Beckenham Rd., Beckenham, Kent.
Born Upper Tooting, London.

HERRMANN WILLIAM JULIUS Leading Boatman (CG) (AB) 129891 Royal Navy.
Died 3/2/1915 The armed merchant cruiser HMS Clan Mcnaughton was mined with the loss of all 281 on board off coast of Ireland when on patrol in bad weather. Panel 7 PORTSMOUTH MEMORIAL.
Son of Ada M Herrmann, 4, Coastguard Cottages, Clacton-on-Sea, William born 1869.

HICKMAN W J There are five men with this name on the CWGC.

HICKS A 39 records on CWGC.

HIGGS ERIC STANLEY Lieutenant Royal Naval Volunteer Reserve HMS Newbury
Died at sea 15/2/1918 Grave R2.7171 BECKENHAM CEMETERY.
Born 1893.
HILL G 163 records on CWGC.

HILL JOHN R Rifleman 48081 Rifle Brigade posted to Post Office Rifles. Died of wounds in field ambulance 27/4/1918, age 18 Grave XIII.B.6 ST PIERRE AMIENS.
Son of the late William, hairdresser and Mrs Ada Hill of 52 Burnhill Rd, Beckenham.

HILLIER JOHN Private G/940 Queen's Own (Royal West Kent Regiment) 6th Bn.
Died of wounds received from a rifle grenade when on sentry duty 23/07/1915 age 22 Grave I. C. 98. BAILLEUL COMMUNAL CEMETERY EXTENSION, NORD.
Son of Henry and Annie Hillier, of 73, Churchfields Rd., Beckenham, member of Council outdoor staff.

HILLS W C Private Royal Inniskilling Fusiliers formerly Royal Berkshire Regiment and ANC.
Died 28/11/1917 age 25.
Son of Mr and Mrs J Hills of Post Office, Bromley Gardens, Shortlands, an Old Valley schoolboy and employee of Mr Ewens in Widmore Rd. BJ 12/1/1918. Not in CWGC.

HILLYER WILLIAM HAROLD Captain Royal Engineers 1st/4th (London) Field Coy. Awards MC.
Died 22/05/1916 age 35 Grave III. K. 14. BETHUNE TOWN CEMETERY.
Son of William John and Sarah Ann Hillyer, of 15, Shortlands Rd., Shortlands, Beckenham.

HINTON GEORGE Private L/7263 The Queen's (Royal West Surrey Regiment) 1st Bn.
Died 31/10/1914 Panel 11 - 13 and 14. YPRES (MENIN GATE) MEMORIAL.
Born abt 1885 Cirencester, Glos, enlisted Guildford. Son of Caroline Hinton of Beckenham of 54 Vineleigh Rd, Penge.

HOARE OSWALD JOSEPH Sapper 151734 Royal Engineers.
Died from heat stroke age 39 in the Persian Gulf. Grave X.D.5 BAGHDAD WAR CEMETERY.
Husband of Florence Bena Hoare with two children of 100 Durban Rd.

Was a senior sorting clerk in Beckenham Post Office. Several of his graphic letters have been published in the BJ.

HODGE, FREDERICK GEORGE Second Lieutenant London Regiment (First Surrey Rifles) 2nd/21st Bn.
Died 31/10/1917 age 20 Grave J. 74. Cemetery BEERSHEBA WAR CEMETERY.
Son of Frank Henry and Susie Hodge, of "Ellerslie", Venner Rd., Sydenham.

HODGSON FRANCIS FAITH Captain 84th Punjabis, attd 58th Vaughan's Rifles Frontier Force, Mohmand Campaign 1906, attached to Bareilly HQ as Brigade Machine Gun Officer.
Died from wounds received in night attack 17/5/1915. Grave XVII.B.46 CABARET-ROUGE, SOUCHEZ.
Educated Tonbridge and Sandhurst. Younger son of Mr and Mrs Henry Hodgson from Shortlands. Husband of Katherine Anna Hodgson of 3 Carlton Houses, Westgate on Sea.

HODGSON H H Private 152460 1st Canadian Mounted Rifles Bn.
Died 16/9/1918 grave I.D.36 VIS-EN-ARTOIS, HAUCOURT, FRANCE.
OR Hodgson Herbert H died at sea on HMS Actaeon TB 11 1916?

HORTON JAMES HENRY (DSO) Twice Mentioned in Despatches. Lieutenant Colonel. Indian Medical Service D.A.D.M.S. III Corps.
Died 23/07/1917 age 46 Grave XVI. A. 4. BAGHDAD (NORTH GATE) WAR CEMETERY.
Son of Major James Horton (late 4th Dragoon Guards), and Mary Horton, of 65, Copers Cope Rd., Beckenham. Served in the Somaliland Expedition, 1903-04. North-West Frontier Campaign, 1908. Balkan War, 1912-13. M.B. Long account in BJ 25/8/1917 p3.

HOTT S G No trace found in BMDs, census or CWGC.

HOUSDEN ARTHUR THOMAS Lance Corporal 762548 London Regiment (Artists' Rifles) "B" Coy. 1st/28th Bn. Died 30/10/1917 age 28 Panel 153. TYNE COT MEMORIAL.
Son of James Bunting Housden, of "Brooklyn", Cator Rd., Sydenham; husband of Mary Ann Eliza Rosina Housden.

HUGHES GORDON MacGREGOR Second Lieutenant Royal Berkshire Regiment 9th Bn. attd. 5th Bn.
Died 08/08/1916 age 21 Pier and Face 11 D. THIEPVAL MEMORIAL.
Son of Alfred MacGregor Hughes, of 34, Newlands Park, Sydenham, London, and the late Maria Hughes.

HUGHES, JOHN HENRY Second Lieutenant Queen's Own (Royal West Kent Regiment) 8th Bn.
Killed in action 03/07/1916 age 30 Grave IX. B. 1. OVILLERS MILITARY CEMETERY.
Probate 20/12/1916 to father, solicitor John Henry Hughes of 8 Park Hill Rd, Shortlands.

HUGHES, OWEN Second Lieutenant Royal Engineers 54th Field Coy.
Died 30/11/1915 age 25 Panel 4 and 5. LOOS MEMORIAL.
Son of the late Mr. and Mrs. G. H. Hughes; husband of Elsie L. Hughes, of 15, High St., Walton-on-the-Naze, Essex.

HUGHES, WILLIAM (MC) Second Lieutenant 76116 Bedfordshire Regiment 2nd Bn.
Died 14/09/1918 age 38 Grave North of Chancel. SHIRLEY (ST. JOHN) CHURCHYARD.
Son of Henry and Frances Hughes, of 7, Arthur St., King William St. Brother of John Henry Hughes.
Probate 12/12/1919 to father, solicitor John Henry Hughes.

HULL A 14 records on CWGC match the name.

HURRELL H J Possibly Henry died 18/10/1918 Delhi.

INGLIS JOHN ALFRED PIGOU (Jack) Lieutenant Royal Engineers.
Killed at Loos age 22, on 25/9/1915 Grave 11.D.8, FOSSE 7 MILITARY CEMETERY, QUALITY ST MAZINGARBE, PAS DE CALAIS.
Grandson of Brigadier Sir John Inglis of the siege of Luckow 1857, attended Rugby School and was a fine sportsman. His two sisters, Ernestine (Nesta) and Mildred, were boarders at Tudor Hall School, Chislehurst Common. Nesta saved the school from closure in the 1930s and became its much loved headmistress moving the school to Banbury in January 1946 where it remains highly successful to this day. The Chislehurst school was bought

by the KCC in 1946 and became the state school, Coopers. The Rev Rupert Inglis was killed 18/9/1916 forces chaplain age 53, youngest son of the above. BJ 30/9/1916 p3.

INGRAM HENRY JOHN Second Lieutenant Rifle Brigade16th Bn.
Died 22/09/1917 age 37 Grave IV. E. 25. RENINGHELST NEW MILITARY CEMETERY.
Son of Thomas and Matilda Jane Ingram. 1911 Southfield 42 the Avenue Beckenham.

INSKIPP DOUGLAS Second Lieutenant Machine Gun Corps (Infantry) 143rd Coy.
Died 16/04/1917 age 34 Grave B. 4. SAULCOURT CHURCHYARD EXTENSION, GUYENCOURT-SAULCOURT.
Son of Peter Inskipp; husband of Anne Cecilia Inskipp, of 44, Brailsford Rd., Tulse Hill, London.

ISTEAD THOMAS WILLIAM Stoker 1st Class K/26074 Royal Navy H.M. S/M. "E47."
Died 20/08/1917 age 21 Panel Reference 24. CHATHAM NAVAL MEMORIAL.
Son of Thomas Henry and Clara Louisa Istead, of 165, Churchfields Rd, Beckenham.

JACKSON MARTIN De CARLE Second Lieutenant Royal Field Artillery.
Died 05/11/1916 Pier and Face 1 A and 8 A. THIEPVAL MEMORIAL Killed in action.
Born abt 1886 Pollokshield, Lanarkshire Scotland. 1901 The Grange, Woldingham, Surrey. Lace warehouseman.

JANES HERBERT WILLIAM Private 78883 Royal Fusiliers 7th Bn.
Died 27/08/1918 age 18 Panel 3. VIS-EN-ARTOIS MEMORIAL.
Son of Mr. and Mrs. Janes, of 48, St. Margarets Rd., Elmers End, Beckenham.

JARVIS A 58 records match in CWGC.

JARVIS WALTER HENRY Acting Bombardier 40003 Royal Horse Artillery "Z" Bty. 5th Bde.
Died of wounds 08/11/1916 Grave X. 10. CARNOY MILITARY CEMETERY.

Born Penge, enlisted Woolwich.

JOHNSON A F ten records match the name in the CWGC.

JOHNSON GEORGE MOORE Surgeon on the armoured cruiser HMS Defence sunk during the Battle of Jutland with no survivors.
Killed in action 31/5/1916 age 37 Panel 10. PLYMOUTH NAVAL MEMORIAL.
Son of Mary Elizabeth Johnson and the late George William Moore Johnson of 27 Beckenham Grove.

JOHNSON, LEONARD C. Rifleman 321165 London Regiment (City of London Rifles) 1st/6th Bn.
Died 15/09/1916 age 19 Pier and Face 9 D. THIEPVAL MEMORIAL.
Son of William and Margaret Johnson, of 19, Tilson Rd., Tottenham, London.

JOHNSON WILLIAM ARTHUR Officer's steward 3rd class Royal Navy, L/5676, HMS Simoom was one of 18 destroyers and 6 light cruisers sent to engage a German force in the Flanders Bight. A torpedo from S50 exploded her magazine causing heavy casualties among the complement of 90.
Died 23/1/1917, Panel 25 CHATHAM NAVAL MEMORIAL.
Son of Robert Henry Johnson of 43 Durban Rd.

JOHNSTON DOUGLAS HERBERT 2496 / 5 Royal West Surrey Regiment (10th Bn.) Attestation 24/11/1915 Croydon age 20 Years 1 Month.
1911 31 Linden Grove Sydenham.

JOHNSTON RICHARD ALFRED Private 8776 North Staffordshire Regiment 2nd Bn.
Died 08/11/1918 Face 23. DELHI MEMORIAL (INDIA GATE) (Buried Nowshera Mil. Cem. L. 28.).
Born Penge, lived Anerley.

JOHNSTONE MAXWELL HARRY Private 62228 Royal Fusiliers 9th Bn.
Died 09/04/1917 age 20, Panel Bay 3. ARRAS MEMORIAL.

JONES KENNETH CHAMPION Second Lieutenant East Lancashire Regiment 1st Bn.
Died 01/07/1916 age 26 Pier and Face 6 C. THIEPVAL MEMORIAL.
Son of Frederick and Rose Jones, of 15, Orchard Rd., Bromley, Kent.

JONES LESLIE VICTOR Rifleman 554917 London Regiment (Queen's Westminster Rifles) "F" Coy.
Died 18/04/1917 home age 18 Grave G. 1050. LEWISHAM (LADYWELL) CEMETERY.
Enlisted Lewisham. Son of Walter James and Clara Florence Jones, of 25, Fernbrook Rd., Hither Green, London, born 1898 Lewisham.

JONES WALTER ERNEST Lance Corporal 20260 Northamptonshire Regiment 1st Bn.
Killed in action. 20/08/1916 Grave Sp. Mem. A. 15. BAZENTIN-LE-PETIT COMMUNAL CEMETERY EXTENSION.
Born Lewisham.

JORDAN HENRY JABEZ Sergeant 723288 London Regiment Bn. 24th.
Killed in action 22/8/1918 France & Flanders.
Birth place Leyton, residence 82 Craington Road Penge, enlisted Bromley.

JUNIPER ALFRED EDWARD Sapper 57395 Royal Engineers 91st Field Coy.
Killed in action 26/9/1915 Panel 4 and 5 LOOS MEMORIAL, PAS DE CALAIS.
Born 1883, Penge, lived 1911 83 Crampton Road Penge, enlisted Lambeth.

KEELER NORMAN JOHN Private 2374 RWK transferred to Labour Corps 126553.
Died age 21 7/2/1920 Grave W5.6031, BECKENHAM CREMATORIUM & CEMETERY.
Son of Spencer Keeler and Ellen Jane, 1911 86 Durban Rd.

KEMP ARTHUR ROWLAND officers' steward 2nd class HMS battle cruiser Queen Mary, age 21. The ship was one of two sunk at the Battle of Jutland 31/5/1916 when a shell detonated the magazine and split the ship in two. Only 20 of its 1,266 men were rescued.
Only son of Police Inspector Mervyn Roland Kemp, one time of Beckenham

Police Station and Harriette Evangeline of 149 Lower Kennington Lane. Reported BJ 17/6/1916.

FREDERICK ROBERT KILLICK Private G/3711 The Queen's (Royal West Surrey Regiment) 3/4th Bn.
Killed in action 29/07/1918 SOISSONS MEMORIAL.
Born abt 1895, lived 30 Ancaster Rd, Elmers End, enlisted Maidstone, Kent age19.

KILLICK MAURICE JOHN Chief PO 1st RN 157171 HMS Queen Mary.
Lost Jutland 31/5/1916.
Born 16/4/1875, Beckenham. Sister Millie 133, Beckenham Rd, Penge. Son of the late George, 28 years landlord of the Foresters Arms, Beckenham. Boy soloist in St George's choir. BJ p5 10/6/16.

KILLICK WILLIAM ALFRED Private 8191 East Surrey Reg 8th Bn.
Died 7/8/1918 age 29 Grave IV.E.15 VIGNACOURT BRITISH CEMETERY.
Son of William H. and Clara Maria Killick, of Islington, London.
AND
Three other Killick W in the CWGC records, possibly William Killick died 16/5/1915 Private Queen's Royal West Surrey 2nd Bn. William Killick born abt 1897 son of William and Emily of 13 Princes Rd, Penge.

KILMISTER EDWARD LEONARD CYRIL (sometimes KILMINSTER) Rifleman A/200174, 17th Bn. King's Royal Rifle Corps.
Died 16/9/1916 age 30 Grave D.28 MAILLY-MAILLET COMMUNAL CEMETERY EXTENSION.
Son of Edward George and Elizabeth Kilmister, of 38, St. James Avenue, born 1887.

KILMISTER HAROLD HOWARD LINSDELL MC Lieutenant Royal Fusiliers 9th Bn.
Killed in action 22/08/1918 age 27 Grave B. 37. MEAULTE MILITARY CEMETERY.
Brother of Edward Leonard Cyril, bp 1891.

KING GEORGE IVANHOE Private 201837 Northants Reg 7th Bn.

Died 8/4/1918 age 32 Grave IV.D.7 ROYE NEW BRITISH CEMETERY, FRANCE.
Husband of Rose Emily, eight children, youngest four months old, 20 Somerville Rd, Penge, house painter.

KINGSHOTT GEORGE Gunner 38995 Royal Horse Artillery and Royal Field Artillery C Bty 64th Bde.
Killed in action 10/10/1915 Panel 3 LOOS MEMORIAL.
Born Croydon, Surrey.

KINGSHOTT WILLIAM ERNEST Trooper 3171 Household Cavalry and Cavalry of the Line (incl. Yeomanry and Imperial Camel Corps) 2nd Life Guards "D" Sqdn.
Died 28/09/1917, age 20 Grave V. E. 20. LILLERS COMMUNAL CEMETERY.
Son of Mr. and Mrs. Kingshott, of Elmer Farm, Elmers End, Beckenham.
Born Croydon, enlisted Reading.

KNIGHT A H There are 21 in the National Archives.

KNIGHT GEORGE ALLEN SPRING Private 17669 East Surrey Regiment 9th Bn.
Died home 21/2/1919 Grave C 106 BROMLEY (ST. LUKE'S) CEMETERY.
Born Beckenham 1897, enlisted Maidstone, lived Downswood Stables, 80 The Avenue, Beckenham where father the coachman.

KNOWLES SIDNEY GILBERT Private 49533 Machine Gun Corps (Infantry) 160th Coy.
Died 18/01/1918 Grave O. 101. JERUSALEM WAR CEMETERY.
Born abt 1896 Norfolk, Snettisham age at enlistment 20.
Son of Mrs. Eliza Cooper (formerly Knowles), of 40, Albert Rd., Penge.

KNOX JOHN LAWRENCE Temp 2nd Lieutenant Royal Sussex Regiment 7th Bn.
Killed in action 20/11/1917 Panel 7 CAMBRAI MEMORIAL LOUVERVAL.
Son of John and Mary Jane Knox, 24 Sangley Road, South Norwood S E 1911 Baptised 4/4/1886.

WILLIAM ALLEN KOCH Private G/46380 Royal Fusiliers (City of London Regiment) 24th Bn.
Killed in action 1/6/1917 Grave II. B. 15. BOIS-CARRE BRITISH CEMETERY, THELUS.
Born and lived in Beckenham, husband of Harman Kate Goddard. Enlisted Bromley.

KREPPER OTTO WILLIAM Sergeant 5939 North Staffordshire Reg 1st Bn.
Died 21/05/1916 age 32 Grave II. A. 1. DRANOUTRE MILITARY CEMETERY.
Son of Josef and Emma Krepper, of 4, Crystal Palace Station Rd. 1901 Otto Krepper born 1885 is a musician at Shorncliffe Camp and a corporal.
There is no Krapper on the CWGC or the census. Emma Krepper is from Austria with her son William. The BJ of 3/6/1916 p1 shows band sergeant 1st North Staffs killed in action 21/5/1916 O W J Krepper, eldest son of Mrs E Krepper of 89 Ravenscroft Rd, Beckenham.

KYDD, JAMES PHILLIP Leading seaman, 215363, Royal Navy H.M.S. "Aboukir".
Leading seaman James Philip Kydd (Jim Smith) of 3 Mount Pleasant, Beckenham, aboard armoured cruiser HMS Aboukir when it was sunk

by a German submarine on 22/9/1914, also HMS Hogue and HMS Cessy when coming to the rescue, with loss of 62 officers and 1,397 ratings. Remembered on Chatham Naval Memorial.

Adopted son of Mr. S. and Mrs. Christina Smith, of 3, Mount Pleasant, Beckenham, Kent., born Beckenham 13/10/1883 Another local man lost on the Aboukir was Stoker HORACE CROKER who as a naval reservist had been working at the Shortlands pumping station.

LAGDEN PHILIP Private G/392 Queen's Own (Royal West Kent Regiment) 11th Bn. formerly 6th Bn.
Killed in action 31/7/1917 Panel 45 and 47. YPRES (MENIN GATE) MEMORIAL.
Born Beckenham, Kent, enlisted Bromley. Son of Emma Lagden, brother Alfred W. Lagden of 5, Champion Park, Lower Sydenham, London. 1911 Street Address 93 Ravenscroft Road, Beckenham.

LAKER CHARLES (ALFRED) Private 240378 Queen's Own (Royal West Kent Regiment) 2nd/5th Bn. attd. 8th Bn.
Died 02/09/1916 age 19 Pier and Face 11 C. THIEPVAL MEMORIAL.
Son of Mr. and Mrs. James Alfred Laker, of 39, Whateley Rd., Penge, London.

LAMBLE, THOMAS Rifleman S/3000 Rifle Brigade (The Prince Consort's Own) 11th Bn.
Killed in action 10/02/1917 Pier and Face 16 B and 16 C. THIEPVAL MEMORIAL.
Born Belfast, lived Holborn, enlisted London.

LANE MAURICE Captain Awards MC, MM London Regiment 2nd/20th Bn.
Died 29/12/1917 age 27 Grave U. 18. JERUSALEM WAR CEMETERY.
Son of Charles and Jessie Lane, of "Tugela", Copers Cope Rd., Beckenham.

LANE, MAURICE HUBERT Gunner 926360 Royal Field Artillery "B" Bty. 290th Bde.
Died 22/04/1917 age 20 Grave I. C. 30 ACHIET-LE-GRAND COMMUNAL CEMETERY EXTENSION.
Son of Alfred and Sarah Arm Lane, of 105, Marlow Rd., Anerley, London. 1911 census for 28 Dagnall Park South Norwood S E.

LANGFORD ARCHIBALD JAMES Private 21614 Highland Light Infantry 7th (Blythswood) Bn. Formerly 147130, R.F.A.
Killed in action, Egypt, 8/11/1917.
Born London, bp 20/8/1882, lived Beckenham, occupation pre-war shop assistant. Enlisted Streatham.
Married Gertrude Rhodes 1913.

LANGLEY A J Private 15371 Machine Gun Corps infantry 111th Coy.
Died 11/8/1916 III.D.3 HEILLY STATION CEMETERY MERICOURT-L'ABBE. Possible from CWGC.

LANGTON HUGH GORDON Second Lieutenant London Regiment (Royal Fusiliers) 4th Bn.
Died 26/10/1917 age 32 Grave Sp. Mem. 3. POELCAPELLE BRITISH CEMETERY.
Son of J. Gordon Langton and Emily Langton, of 9E, Hyde Park Mansions.
Husband of Una M. Langton, of "Glendura", 92, Hornsey Lane, London. A violin pupil of Professors Secvik (Prague), Wirth (Berlin), and Auer (Russia). First initiate of the Gordon Langton Lodge, No.3069. (Unusually, the personal inscription on his headstone consists of a piece of music.) Spent first winter of war in Kelsey Manor Barracks.

LARBY GEORGE WILLIAM HENRY Private TR10/193516 Training Reserve 24th Bn.
Died 22/10/1918 age 19 home Grave W5. 7674. BECKENHAM CREMATORIUM AND CEMETERY.
Son of John Larby, of 17, Acacia Rd., Croydon Rd., Beckenham. Enlisted Bordon, Hants.

LATTER GEORGE HENRY Private G/40438 Duke of Cambridge's Own Middlesex Regiment "A" Coy. 2nd Bn. Formerly G/12675, Royal Sussex Regt.
Killed in action age 33, 27/05/1918 SOISSONS MEMORIAL.
Son of William and Elizabeth Latter, husband of Louisa Latter, nee Jones, of 45A, Tremaine Rd., Anerley.

LAURENZI (LORENZI) DOMENICA (DONALD JAMES) Private 263025 Cheshire Regiment 23rd Bn.

Killed in action 31/08/1918 Grave I.J.2. OUTTERSTEENE COMMUNAL CEMETERY EXTENSION, BAILLEUL.
Born 1899 in Penge of Italian parents, lived Greenwich at 20 Fingal St in 1911, when there was only one family of that name in 'findmypast'. Enlisted Blackheath. Name was anglicised on CWGC.

LAW A H There are three with this name on the CWGC but not connected with Beckenham.

LAW J T There are three possibles from the CWGC: John Thomas died 5/9/1914 Royal Marine HMS Pathfinder, Rifleman James Thomas died 19/8/1917 from the London Regiment and J T Law died 7/12/1918 age 41 of RASC but wife in Hammersmith.

LAWRIE HUBERT AUGUSTUS Private 3321 London Regiment 1st/7th Bn.
Killed in action 25/09/1915, age 20. Grave VIII. S. 3/21.CABARET-ROUGE BRITISH CEMETERY, SOUCHEZ.
Lived in Beckenham. Born 1896. In 1911 303 Ivydale Rd. Son of Augustus William Charles and Julia Elizabeth Lawrie, of 8, Maclean Rd., Stondon Park, London.

LAWSON A
Alexander Lawson born abt 1900 is son of John and Alice Lawson of 35 Piquet Rd so brother of John Leighton Lawson.

LAWSON JOHN LEIGHTON Lance Corporal 10216 Seaforth Highlanders 1st Bn.
Died 10/03/1915 age 26 Panel 38 and 39 LE TOURET MEMORIAL.
Born at Barielly, India. Son of John and Alice Maude Brown Lawson, of 35, Piquet Rd., Anerley, London in 1911.

LEACH ARTHUR WILLIAM Private 89939 Machine Gun Corps (Infantry) 24th Bn.
Died 21/03/1918 age 20 Grave III. L. 8. ROISEL COMMUNAL CEMETERY EXTENSION.
Son of Arthur Ernest poultry farmer and Mary Ann Leach, of 103, Venner Rd., Sydenham. Born at Peckham.
1911 New Pond Cross in Hand, Uckfield.

LEACH CHARLES EDWARD Lance Corporal G/8752 Queens Own Royal West Kent B Coy, 10th Bn.
Died of wounds, 1/8/1917 age 29 Grave I.A.38 GODEWERSVELDE BRITISH CEMETERY, FRANCE.
Born Anerley, enlisted Bromley. Husband of Esther Sarah Leach of 27 Piquet Rd, Anerley.

LEAVENS ROBERT CHARLES WILLIAM Private 9492 Kings Shropshire Light Infantry 2nd Bn.
Died 13/4/1915 panel 47 & 49 YPRES MENIN GATE MEMORIAL.
Lived 29 Limes Rd, Beckenham. BJ 24/4/1915 p3.

LEMAY ALBERT Private S/392918 Army Service Corps from National Archives.

LEONARD ALBERT HENRY Private 253081 Canadian Infantry 28th Bn.
Died 01/10/1918 age 32 Grave II. A. 6. CANADA CEMETERY, TILLOY-LES-CAMBRAI.
Son of George and Emily Leonard, of 9, Blandford Rd., Beckenham, born abt 1885.
Residence Saskatchewan.

LEONARD DAVID Private 253079 Canadian Infantry 28th Bn.
Died 11/10/1918, age 35 Grave C.17, RAMILLIES BRITISH CEMETERY.
Born Bromley By Bow, abt 1883, lived 119 Carr Road and Forest Rd, Walthamstow but son of George and Emily Leonard of 9 Blandford Rd, Beckenham.
Occupation railway porter. Travelled to Canada April 1912 on Empress of Britain, leaving Liverpool and arriving St John.

LEVENS WILLIAM HENRY Sergeant 240620 Queens Own Royal West Kent 1st Bn.
Died 4/10/1917 Panel 106 to 108 TYNE COT MEMORIAL.
Son of auctioneer Herbert Levens and Lucy of 6 Manor Grove Beckenham in 1901 but he was born William Hannam Levens and CWGC has the name Henry.

LEWARNE FREDERICK DAVID Private 47202 Northumberland Fusiliers 22nd (Tyneside Scottish) Bn.

Died 16/04/1917 age 35 Grave IV. D. 25. BOULOGNE EASTERN CEMETERY.
Husband of Lily Lewarne, of 5, Chancery Lane, Beckenham, Kent.

LEWIS WILLIAM EDWARD Private 30105 Royal Inniskilling Fusiliers "C" Coy. 7th/8th Bn.
Died 16/08/1917, age 41 Panel 70 to 72. TYNE COT MEMORIAL.
Son of William and Sarah Lewis; husband of Mary Ann Lewis, of 27, Gowland Place, Beckenham.

LINDRIDGE, CYRIL Private S/13598 Gordon Highlanders 2nd Bn.
Killed in action, 21/07/1916 age 21 Pier and Face 15 B and 15 C. THIEPVAL MEMORIAL.
Son of William and Alice Lindridge, of 25, Linden Grove, Newlands Park, Sydenham.
Born abt 1895 Sydenham.

LINTON R Of the seven with this name on the CWGC, five are clearly from elsewhere leaving two with no relatives shown: R Linton died 22/10/1914 of the Cameron Highlanders and Royce Linton died 19/7/1915 from the York & Lancaster Regiment.

LOADER, SYDNEY THOMAS MM, Lance Corporal 703221 London Regiment 1st/23rd Bn.
Died 07/06/1917 Panels 52 to 54. YPRES (MENIN GATE) MEMORIAL.
Lived Anerley.

LOCK, THOMAS HENRY WILLIAM Gunner 119960 Royal Garrison Artillery 233rd Siege Bty.
Died 15/09/1917 age 31 Panel 6 to 7 and 162. TYNE COT MEMORIAL.
Son of Thomas and Jane Lock, of Worthing; husband of Ethel Lock, of 52, Marlow Rd., Anerley.

LONG CHARLES EDWARD Private 326601 Durham Light Infantry 29th Bn.
Died 22/08/1918 age 42 Grave XXV. G. 27A. LIJSSENTHOEK MILITARY CEMETERY.
Husband of Elizabeth Jane Long, of 153, Birkbeck Rd., Beckenham, Kent.

LONG WALTER VICTOR Private G/43957 Middlesex Regiment Duke of Cambridge Own 17th Bn.
Killed in action 01/12/1917 Panel 9. CAMBRAI MEMORIAL, LOUVERVAL.
Born Twickenham, occupation carman mineral water company, enlisted Ealing, lived Beckenham 34 Burnhill Road.

LONG CHARLES EDWARD Private 326601 Durham Light Infantry 29th Bn.
Died of wounds 22/8/1918, age 42, XXV.G.27A.LIJSSENTHOEK MILITARY CEMETERY.
Born abt 1876, husband of Elizabeth Jane of 153 Birkbeck Road, Beckenham, enlisted Bromley age 39.

LONGHURST, SEAWARD Second Lieutenant Sherwood Foresters (Notts and Derby Regiment) 11th Bn.
Died 01/07/1916 age 22. Grave Reference I. H. 56. MARTINSART BRITISH CEMETERY.
Son of Angelo and Frances Longhurst, of 118, Venner Rd., Sydenham, London.

LOVELL, ARTHUR L. Rifleman 2110 London Regiment (City of London Rifles) 1st/6th Bn.
Died 25/09/1915 age 25 Panel 130. LOOS MEMORIAL.
Son of William Frederick Lovell, of "Rothbury", 4, Brackley Rd., Beckenham. Gas company clerk.

LOVELL, HAROLD FREDERICK Air Mechanic 2nd Class 46047 Royal Air Force 37th Kite Balloon Sect. Died 05/09/1918 age 31 Grave II. C. 22. VIS-EN-ARTOIS BRITISH CEMETERY, HAUCOURT.
Son of William Frederick Lovell, of "Rothbury", 4, Brackley Rd., Beckenham. Jewellery shop assistant.

LOVELL JOHN BAWDEN Gunner 109458 ROYAL Garrison Artillery 119th Heavy Bty.
Died 21/8/1917 age 41 Grave VI.F. VLAMERTINGHE NEW MILITARY CEMETERY.
Born 1876, John was an ironmonger, 111 Beckenham High St, in the business of his parents John and Charlotte Lovell with his brother

William and sisters Charlotte and Alice.

LOVELOCK HENRY WILLIAM MM Lance Sergeant 350659 London Regiment 7th Bn.
Died 7/10/1916 age 26 Butte de Warlencount. Grave I.K.20 WARLENCOURT BRITISH CEMETERY.
Son of Mr William George, house builder, and Mrs Emily Lovelock of 54 Blandford Rd, Beckenham.
Enlisted August 1914, after six months training spent a year in France where he earned MM at Festubert, Loos, for saving his bombing section without loss. Old boy of the grammar school, cricketer for school and Christ Church, water polo for BSC and captain of St Matthews when they won the Darnell Life Saving Shield.
BJ 19/5/1917

LOVETT JOHN WILLIAM VICTOR Private 10526 Worcester Reg 2nd Bn.
Died 21/10/1914 Panel 34 YPRES MENIN GATE MEMORIAL.
Born 1887 Birmingham, married Emily Jarvis Bromley 1913.

LOWRY VYVYAN CHARLES Lieutenant East Surrey Regiment 5th Bn. (Territorial).
Killed in action 09/04/1918 Grave III. E. 5. CROIX-DU-BAC BRITISH CEMETERY, STEENWERCK, France.
Born Beckenham abt 1889, son of wine merchant Arthur and Clara Lowry of 43 Manor Rd, Beckenham.

LUSHINGTON, CECIL HENRY GOSSET Lieutenant Worcestershire Regiment "A" Coy. 10th Bn.
Died 03/07/1916 age 31 Pier and Face 5 A and 6 C. THIEPVAL MEMORIAL.
Son of Major and Mrs. Arthur James Lushington, of The Park, Sandling, Maidstone. Husband of Evelyn Marian Lushington. Born Peshawar, India.

LUSTED WILLIAM JOHN Lance Corporal G/1354 Queen's Own (Royal West Kent Regiment) 8th Bn.
Killed in action, 26/09/1915 Panel 95 to 97. LOOS MEMORIAL.
Born Burwash Common, Ticehurst, Sussex, lived Beckenham, Kent, enlisted Bromley.

LUSTED JAMES SIDNEY Private G/5512 Queens Own Royal West Kent 8th Bn.
Died 26/9/1915, Panel 95 to 97, LOOS MEMORIAL.
Born Heathfield, Sussex in 1891 and 1892, these brothers William and James served in the same battalion and were killed on the same day.

MACLEAN ALEC CLARKSON Lieutenant 296 Railway Company Royal Engineers
Died 9/4/1918 age 34, in France trying to prevent a field gun going into enemy hands. Grave E.19. HAVERSKERQUE BRITISH CEMETERY FRANCE.
Son of Major General H I Maclean and husband of Ruth N Davison Maclean of Hawthorns, 11 Sylvan Hill, Norwood.

MACLEAN HECTOR FORBES Sub Lieutenant midshipman on HMS Royal Sovereign volunteered for the motor torpedo boats attacking Russian ships in Krondstadt harbour and was killed in action on 18/8/1919. Naval memorial Plymouth. Second son of George Buchanan and Emily Matilda Maclean, of 11 Beckenham Rd from 1901.

MACLEAN IVAN CLARKSON DSO, MC and Bar, Captain Royal Army Medical Corps 2nd Bn. Rifle Brigade. Fearless, he would search shell holes well beyond the front for wounded men by torchlight.
Died 4/4/1918, age 36 Grave IV.B.33 PREMONT BRITISH CEMETERY, FRANCE.
Son of Major General H I Maclean and Frances Clarkson, brother of Alec Clarkson Maclean.

MADDOX CYRIL PERCY 2nd Lieutenant Yorkshire Reg 2nd/4th Kings Own Yorkshire Light Infantry.
Died 20/11/1917 Grave II.D.22 HERMIES HILL BRITISH CEMETERY, FRANCE. Born Southgate 1896 son of Percy and Emmeline Maddox.

MALLETT ERIC SYDNEY 2nd Lieutenant East Lancashire Regiment 1st Bn.
Killed in action at Beaumont Hamel 1/7/1916 Pier and Face 6C THIEPVAL MEMORIAL.
Lived Sylvanhurst Blakeney Road, Beckenham. Probate London 6/2/1917 to Henry Stanley Mallett.

MANGER ERIC 2nd Lieutenant Machine Gun Corps 2nd Bn.
Killed in action age 19, 10/7/1917 Grave VI.E.4, RAMSCAPPELLE RD MILITARY CEMETERY.
Born abt 1898, lived 18 Beckenham Road, son of Charles Ernest and Gertrude Annie Manger.
Enlisted in Hon Artillery Co in April 1916.

MANN JAMES EMIL HUBERT Sergeant 9054 3rd Coy 2nd Honourable Artillery Company.
Died of wounds 17/5/1917 age 31 IV. D. 4. FLESQUIERES HILL BRITISH CEMETERY.
Husband of Claire Hampton Johnson (formerly Mann nee Wallis) of 1 Palmeira Place, Hove, Sussex.

MARCHANT CHARLES Private 56213 2nd Bn. Royal Welsh Fusiliers. Formerly Private, 35007, Royal Fusiliers (City of London Regiment).
Died of wounds 13/9/1918 age 27 II. B. 7. GOUZEAUCOURT NEW BRITISH CEMETERY.
Charles was numbered amongst the ten other ranks who died on Friday 13/9/1918.
Son of George and Kesia Marchant of Brook Farm, Four Elms, Edenbridge; husband of Mabel Marchant of Bough Beech Edenbridge Kent. II. B. 7.

MARKS JOHN JAMES Private 5597 Prince of Wales's Leinster Regiment (Royal Canadians) Formerly 13426, Sussex Regiment 7th Bn.
Killed in action 1/2/1917 POND FARM CEMETERY Belgium Heuvelland West-Vlaanderen.
Born Bloomsbury abt 1880, lived Beckenham, enlisted London. Husband of Mrs. E. S. Marks of 17 Langley Rd. Elmers End, Beckenham.

MARSH WALTER Corporal CH/16716 H.M.S. Cyclops. Royal Marine Light Infantry.
Died Sunday, 30/6/1918 age 27. Naval. 28.1466, GILLINGHAM (WOODLANDS) CEMETERY.
Son of Henry and Louisa Marsh of 116 Blandford Rd. Born Beckenham, abt 1892, husband of Gertrude Harris (formerly Marsh) of 60 Medway Rd. Gillingham.

MARSLAND FRED Staff Sergeant 164812 Royal Engineers.
Died 27/9/1917 age 40 SALONIKA LEMBET Rd military cemetery.
Born abt 1877 Wandsworth, son of the late John and Kate Marsland.
Husband of Ethel M Marsland of 15 Bromley Rd, Beckenham, builder.
Member Beckenham Hockey Club and Elm Rd. Baptist church.

MARTIN A J Second Lieutenant East Surrey Regiment 7th Bn. attd. 10th Bn.
Died 02/08/1916 age 20 V. C. 38. WARLOY-BAILLON COMMUNAL CEMETERY EXTENSION.
Son of John R. and M. Jessie Martin, of The Ridge, St. Botolphs Rd., Sevenoaks.

MARTIN CHARLES Corporal S/6581Rifle Brigade 9th Bn.
Died 25/09/1915 age 26 Panel 46 - 48 YPRES (MENIN GATE) MEMORIAL.
Son of Mary Martin, of 3, Watlington Grove, Lower Sydenham, London.

MARTIN CUTHBERT CHARLES WOODHAM Rifleman 7517 London Regiment (Queen Victoria's Rifles) 1st/9th Bn. Formerly 4883, 8th London Regt.
Killed in action 25/09/1916 Pier and Face 9 C. THIEPVAL MEMORIAL.
Grandson of John, bricklayer, and Nancy of 17 Blandford Ave, Beckenham, born abt 1897, Penge. Enlisted London. Second employee of Beckenham Post Office to be killed.

MARTIN SYDNEY ROBERT Lance Corporal 7084 East Surrey Regiment 9th Bn.
Killed in action 13/6/1917 age 21 Panel 34 YPRES (MENIN GATE) MEMORIAL.
Enlisted Kingston-on-Thames, Surrey. Son of Henry and Kate Martin of 38 Westbourne Rd, Forest Hill.

MASON CECIL SIDNEY Rifleman 2064 (County of London) (Queen Victoria's Rifles) 1st/9th Bn.
Killed in action 4/9/1915 age 21 Carnoy Military Cemetery France & Flanders.
Enlisted London, born South Norwood, lived 50 Elmers End Rd, Anerley.

MASON J C possible family from Belvedere, gunner James Charles 147010 d 1/2/18 Greece.

MAUNTON ALBERT Corporal G/934 Queen's Own (Royal West Kent Regiment) 6th Bn.
Killed in action, age 31, 3/7/1916 THIEPVAL MEMORIAL France & Flanders.
Born Bromley, Kent. Husband of Caroline Henrietta Maunton married 1906.
At 3.15am on 3 July, the third day of the Battle of the Somme, 6/RWK attacked a salient in the German lines near the village of Ovillers. Although many were killed before reaching their objective a significant number entered the German front line and held out there for much of the day, until forced to fall back.
Remembered on the Sydenham South Suburban Gas Works war memorial.

MAUNTON WALTER CHARLES Private G/4805 Queen's Own (Royal West Kent Regiment) 2nd Bn.
Died 27/7/1917 Mesopotamian Expeditionary Force.
Born Bromley, 1887, son of Alfred J and Annie E Maunton of 18 Gowlands Place. Enlisted Bromley. Husband of Mary Maunton, married 1909.

MAW GEORGE OLIVER M.R.C.S L.R.C.P Temporary Captain Royal Army Medical Corps attd 13th Bn. Rifle Brigade on active service administration in H M Army.
Died of wounds at or near Albert in France 10/7/1916, I.B.24. ALBERT COMMUNAL CEMETERY EXTENSION.
Son of the late Dr George Maw and Beatrice Eva of Coningsby, Beckenham Grove, Shortlands.

MAY GEORGE HENRY Gunner 97091 Royal Garrison Artillery 278th Siege Bty.
Died 30/07/1917 age 39 Grave I. C. 5. DICKEBUSCH NEW MILITARY CEMETERY EXTENSION.
Son of Mr. May, of London; husband of C. M. May, of 20, Phoenix Rd., Penge.

MAYOR SPENCER GEORGE Corporal 1798 Royal Fusiliers (City of London Regiment) 18th Bn.

Died from meningitis caught in France 26/11/1915 Grave IV. G. 11. BETHUNE TOWN CEMETERY.
Born Loughton, Essex abt 1873. Probate London 12/2/1916, to his brother Francis Maitland Mayor.
Organist Holy Trinity church, Beckenham.

McBROWN R C Not traced.

McKAY CHARLES HENRY Corporal 3369 RAF SE Area Flying Inst School.
Died at Steyning age 22 1/11/1918 Grave V6 7723 BECKENHAM CEMETERY.

MEARS FREDERICK Private 201409 Queen's Own (Royal West Kent Regiment) 2nd/4th Bn.
Died 07/11/17 aged 30 BEERSHEBA WAR CEMETERY Israel.
Son of Mrs. M. Mears, of 7, Burrell Row, Beckenham, occupation greengrocer's assistant.

MEARS WILLIAM TURNER Private 29198 Prince Albert's Somerset Light Infantry 1st Bn. Formerly G/21614, Royal Fusiliers.
Killed in action 30/08/1918 age 40 Grave A 10 ETERPIGNY BRITISH CEMETERY.
Husband of Lucy Mears, of 105, Parish Lane, Penge. Enlisted Maidstone.

MILES LEONARD PERCY 2nd Lieutenant Royal Fusiliers 6th Bn. attd. 8th Bn.
Killed in action 07/10/1916 Grave III. A. 18. BEAULENCOURT BRITISH CEMETERY, LIGNY-THILLOY.
Of Netherfield, Scotts Lane, Shortlands, Kent. Probate 18/8/1917 to Arthur Miles auctioneer and surveyor.

MILLER HENRY GEORGE ERNEST Private 8648 Lincolnshire Regiment 2nd Bn.
Died of wounds 7/7/1915 Grave II. A. 10. ABBEYVILLE COMMUNAL CEMETERY FRANCE.
Born Brixton, Surrey. Enlisted London.

MILLER JOSEPH EVAN Rifleman S/36204 Rifle Brigade (The Prince

Consort's Own) 3rd Bn.
Killed in action 27 /3/1918 age 36 Panel 81 to 84. POZIERES MEMORIAL France.
Enlisted Lambeth, born Sydenham, lived Stockwell.

MINTER C J
Charles John Minter lived 77 Parish Lane, son of stonemason John Fagg and Sarah Ann Minter born Beckenham abt 1894, a gardener. Not on CWGC. Possibly C Minter, Private in London Regiment died 1916.

MITCHELL A E There are 13 records of this name in the CWGC.

MOCKRIDGE ROBERT EDWARD DVR 54183 Royal Horse Artillery and Royal Field Artillery.
Killed in action 2/9/1918 age 38 Grave IV.A.4 GOMIECOURT SOUTH CEMETERY.
Lived 84 Bromley Gardens, Shortlands, Kent, occupation milk roundsman. Son of the late Thomas Edward and Elizabeth Mockridge; husband of Grace Kezia Mockridge of 7 Waldo Rd, Bromley.

MONK LEONARD JAMES Private 41113 Queen's Own (Royal West Kent Regiment). 7th Bn.
Died from pneumonia in France, 9/11/1918 age 24 L. A. 6. ETAPLES MILITARY CEMETERY.
Son of John Philip, gardener, and Louisa Esther Monk of 6 Acacia Rd, Beckenham Kent. Enlisted Maidstone, occupation shop assistant.

MOODY F There are 31 matches in the CWGC.

MORGAN ARCHIBALD ONSLOW Private G/40414 Duke of Cambridge's Own Middlesex Regiment 2nd Bn. Formerly G/12733, Royal Sussex Regt.
Killed in action 23/10/1916 age 38 Pier and Face 12 D and 13 B. THIEPVAL MEMORIAL.
Son of Daniel and Sarah Morgan of 76 Ravenscroft Rd. Beckenham.
Born Kenley, Surrey, lived Beckenham, enlisted Maidstone.

MORPHEW FREDERICK THOMAS Private 2646 Australian Infantry A.I.F.
Died 29/7/1916 B.37.3 ST SEVER CEMETERY ROUEN.

Son of William Henry, house painter and Ruth Morphew of Blandford Rd, Beckenham, butcher's shop assistant, born 1892.

MORRIS SYDNEY JAMES Private F/225 Duke of Cambridge's Own Middlesex Regiment "A" Coy. 17th Bn.
Killed in action 08/08/1916 age 26 Pier and Face 12 D and 13 B. THIEPVAL MEMORIAL.
Son of Mrs. S. Morris, of "Rosetta", Acacia Rd., Beckenham, Kent. Born Beckenham, enlisted Kingsway, Middlesex.

MORTLOCK ALBERT GEORGE Private G/939 Queen's Own (Royal West Kent Regiment) 6th Bn.
Killed in action 7/10/1916 Pier and Face 11 C. THIEPVAL MEMORIAL.
Born Penge abt 1895 son of William and Ruth Mortlock. 1911 23 Churchfields Road, Beckenham. Occupation van boy. Enlisted Bromley.

MOSS A There are 66 matches for this name in the CWGC.

MOSS ARTHUR STANLEY Private 67509 Royal Fusiliers posted to 2nd/2nd Bn. London Regiment (Royal Fusiliers). Formerly Tr/10/57197, 103Rd T.R. Bn.
Killed in action 24 Dec 1917 age 19, Panel 28 to 30 and 162 to 162A and 163A. TYNE COT MEMORIAL, Belgium.
Son of Arthur and Jane B. Moss of 38 St. Margaret's Rd. Elmers End Beckenham. Enlisted Bromley.

MOSS MARK JOHN T Rifleman 3868 London Regiment (Queen's Westminster Rifles) 16th Bn.
Died 18/9/1916 age 22 Grave XXV.H. 7 DELVILLE WOOD CEMETERY, LONGUEVAL.
Son of John and Frances Moss of 229 Minard Rd, Catford. 1911, Blandford Rd, Beckenham.

MOTT SYDNEY GEORGE Rifleman 42825 Royal Irish Rifles 12th Bn. Formerly T4/236545, R.A.S.C.
Died of wounds 17/8/1917 age 35 III. F. 17. MENDINGHEM MILITARY CEMETERY, Belgium.
Born Sydenham, enlisted Bromley, 1911 lived 10 Holmshaw Road, Lower Sydenham.

MUGGRIDGE HUBERT GEORGE CECIL Corporal, G/24488 Queens Own Royal West Kent.
Killed in action 3/5/1917 age 29, Bay 7 ARRAS MEMORIAL.
Younger son of the late Joseph and Mrs Emily Muggridge of 18 Manor Rd, Beckenham, later of Bexhill.
A keen tennis player and member of the Catford lacrosse club, he trained at the Hythe School of Musketry.

MURPHY DENNIS Private M2/221748 784th M.T.Coy. Army Service Corps.
Died 30/7/1917 Mesopotamia age 38 Grave XI. K. 13 also remembered on the grave of his widow, Ellen, of 63 Thayers Farm Road, Beckenham, Chislehurst Cemetery.
Born Clayton, Co. Cork abt 1881, lived Beckenham. Enlisted Bromley.

NAVES RICHARD Private 4986 Coldstream Guards.
Died 29/10/1914 age 31 Panel 11, YPRES MENIN GATE Belgium.
Born Purfleet, Essex, enlisted Woolwich, 1914 directory 27 Alexandra Cots, Albert Rd, Penge. Husband of Lily May Naves of 6 Stanstead Rd, Forest Hill.

NEAL GEORGE WILLIAM Lance Corporal 8078 Norfolk Regiment 2nd Bn.
Killed in action 7 /1/1916 Mesopotamia. age 22 Panel 10 BASRA MEMORIAL.
Born Beckenham about 1892, enlisted London lived 10 Clifton Terrace, Parish Lane, Penge. Son of George William and Florence Frances Neal of 28 Thesiger Rd, Penge.

NEAT REGINALD HARRY Private G/25382 Queen's Own (Royal West Kent Regiment) 11th Bn.
Killed in action, age 19, 15/12/1917 Plot 1. Row F. Grave 7. GIAVERA BRITISH CEMETERY ARCADE, Italy.
Enlisted Camberwell, son of Mr Harry W and Margaret Neat of Beckenham in 1911 in 157 Ravenscroft Rd.

NEISH RONALD IRVIN Rifleman 48936 Rifleman Rifle Brigade.
Died 20/07/1918 age 19 Grave III. A. 2. PERNOIS British Cemetery (Halloy les Pernois) (Somme France).

Born abt 1900, 1911 27 Cromwell Road, Beckenham.

NEWMAN GEORGE SIDNEY Rifleman 6767 (County of London) (1st Surrey Rifles) 21st Bn. Formerly 2661, 5th East Surrey Regt.
Killed in action 8/10/1916 Pier and Face 13C. THIEPVAL MEMORIAL.
Born Dulwich abt 1897, lived Beckenham in 1911 at 179 Birkbeck Rd, occupation chemist messenger boy, enlisted Wimbledon. Son of N C and Emma Newman.

NEWSAM HARRY PLIMSOLL Corporal 120150 Royal Garrison Artillery, 317th Siege Bty.
Killed in action 20/3/1918, age at enlistment 40. Plot 2, row D, grave 5. GIAVERA BRITISH CEMETERY ARCADE.
Lived 65 Kent House Rd, Beckenham, born Beckenham, enlisted Bromley, occupation company secretary. Son of William and Caroline Mary Newsam of Beckenham.

NORRIS WILLIAM JAMES Lance Corporal G/20548 Queen's Own (Royal West Kent Regiment) 7th Bn.
Died of wounds, 23/11/1918 age 19. East part of MALONNE COMMUNAL CEMETERY.
Born Sydenham, lived Beckenham, enlisted Bromley. Son of William and Ellen Norris, of 238, Blandford Rd., Beckenham. In 1911, 8 Clifton Terrace, Parish Lane, Penge.

NORTH ALBERT FREDERICK Private 2110 London Reg (London Scottish) 1st/14th Bn.
Died 9/11/1914, III.C.11 BOULOGNE EASTERN CEMETERY.
Born West Ham 1893, he was a boarder at 62 Kimberley Rd in 1911, a milk carrier, and married Alice K Bates in 1913, Bromley. An Albert North is living in 18 Fairfied Rd in 1914 directory.

NORTHCOTE DOUGLAS HORACE GILBERT Lieutenant 3rd Battalion East Kent Regiment (Buffs) attached to the 1st Battalion Wiltshire Regiment.
Killed in action aged 21, 12/3/1916 Panels 12 to 14 MENIN GATE MEMORIAL.
Born 9/4/1893, son of the late Horace Northcote, merchant of Park Rd, Beckenham, and Stella Louisa (nee Reynolds) of 11, Playfair Mansions, Queen's Club Gardens, Kensington, London W14. Educated Abbey School

and King's School Canterbury 1907 to 1912 with a junior scholarship in December 1908. Keen tennis player and won the final of the school doubles competition of 1911 partnered by R.J.N. Norris. Won school Geography (Members) Prize, the Stanley Prize for history for 1910/11 and was Hon Secretary of the Canturian from September 1911. Probate 4/5/1916 to Stella Louisa Northcote.

Was articled to J.H. Welfare, solicitors of 60 Coleman Street London EC. 2nd Lieutenant in the 3rd (Reserve) Battalion East Kent Regiment August 1914, promoted to lieutenant in 1915 and attached to the 1st Battalion Wiltshire Regiment. At 2.45am on the morning of the 12/3/1915 the 1st Battalion Wiltshire Regiment left Locre and marched via Kemmel to the trenches known as "F" in front of Spanbroek Molen. Arrived about 5.30am and occupied four lines of trenches on the reverse side of the hill. The morning was dull and misty so that the artillery barrage which was meant to precede the attack was delayed. The morning remained misty and as a result apart from occasional sniping and shell fire things were quiet. At 1pm the mist began to lift and by 2.30pm the air was clear and the artillery barrage began, firing shrapnel to cut the enemy wire and large quantities of high explosive to damage their trenches. This continued with a slight pause until 4.10pm when the infantry assault was launched from the trench known as F2, about 25 yards in front of the first line trench. The first line was crossed by A Company using "Flying Bridges" which had been placed over the first line trench and passed through gaps in the British wire. The men moved forward across the 200 yards of no man's land under heavy rifle and machine gun fire. A few managed to get up to the German wire where they were pinned down. B Company tried to crawl forward, but were forced back after 50 yards and the survivors fell back to the trench F2. The survivors of A Company withdrew under cover of darkness. Douglas Northcote was one of four officers killed with three others being wounded. There were 29 other ranks killed, 45 wounded and 12 missing. He was mentioned in despatches.

NYE JOHN BOX Private G/7834 Queen's Own Royal West Kent 6th Bn. Died 3/5/1917 age 38, Bay 7 ARRAS MEMORIAL.
In 1914, a carpenter, he lived at 65 Parish Lane, Penge with his wife Gertrude and four children.

OAKES ALFRED HENRY ROYAL Private 7722 Army Pay Corps, Army Pay Office Warley.

Died 23/2/1917 age 37 Grave A.170. BROMLEY ST LUKES CEMETERY. Son of Alfred William Davison and Marian Leontine Oakes of Knockwood, Shortlands.

OAKES GEORGE FREDERICK THOMAS Captain Royal Engineers. Died 15/7/1916 age 33 Grave I.B.38 HEILLY STATION CEMETERY MERICOURT L'ABBE.
Brother of Alfred Henry Royal Oakes; husband of Nellie Oakes of Briar Bank Farnaby Rd, Bromley. Accomplished valuable surveys in the Abor expedition 1911-1912.

OBEE GEORGE H Private 201721 Seaforth Highlanders (Ross-shire Buffs, the Duke of Albany's) 4th Bn.
Born Beckenham, Kent Died of wounds, home, 11 /5/1917 Grave W1. 5079. BECKENHAM CREMATORIUM AND CEMETERY.
Enlisted Beckenham, lived Beckenham.

OLDING J Possibly John Olding of the Black Watch died 1918 but Beckenham connection not found.

OLIVER FRANCIS EDWARD Corporal 2839 London Regiment 20th Bn. Died 18/09/1916 age 20 Grave II. H. 47.Cemetery HEILLY STATION CEMETERY, MERICOURT-L'ABBE.
Son of Francis Higby Oliver and Rebecca Oliver, of 124, Lennard Rd., Beckenham. His brother John Campbell Oliver also fell.

OLIVER, JOHN CAMPBELL Private 2918 London Regiment 1st/20th Bn. Died 26/09/1915 age 23 Panel Reference Panel 130 to 135. LOOS MEMORIAL.
Brother of Francis Edward Oliver.

OLIVER THOMAS KENNETH GRAHAM Lieutenant Royal Air Force 73rd Sqdn.
Died 05/09/1918 age 19 Grave G. 13. CHAPEL CORNER CEMETERY, SAUCHY-LESTREE.
Only son of the late Thomas Alexander and Agnes Henrietta Challacombe Oliver (nee Galbraith). Born at Valparaiso, Chile. 1901 census Queens Road, Buckhurst Hill.

ORAM THOMAS HENRY Private G/40444 Duke of Cambridge's Own (Middlesex Regiment) 2nd Bn. Formerly G/12581, Royal Sussex Regt. Killed in action 23/10/1916 Pier and Face 12D and 13B. THIEPVAL MEMORIAL.
Born Ditchling, Sussex. Enlisted Bromley. 1911 lived South Norwood.

OUZMAN, ROBERT ALFRED JOHN Company Sergeant Major 593131 London Regiment (London Irish Rifles) 2nd/18th Bn. 11/5/15 became 141st Bde. 47th Div.
Died 23/12/1917 Grave T. 47. JERUSALEM WAR CEMETERY.
Lived Beckenham, enlisted London.

PACKHAM CONROY Lieutenant RAF, died in an aero accident in Egypt 17/10/1918 age 27, eldest son of Mrs A Packham of Beckenham Rd and husband of Ethel Brenda Packham.

PADBURY CYRIL ROBERT Private M2/224213 Army Service Corps 565th Mechanical Transport Coy attd VIth Corps Heavy Artillery.
Died 24/8/1918 Grave III.E.7 BAC DU SUD BRITISH CEMETERY BAILLEUVAL.
Son of William Richard, coachbuilder, and the late Emily Gray Padbury of 22 Wickham Rd, Beckenham, born 1899.

PAINE CHARLES WILLIAM Private L/11195 Queen's Own (Royal West Kent Regiment) 7th Bn.
Killed in action 13/07/1916 age 17 Pier and Face 11 C. THIEPVAL MEMORIAL.
Son of Frederick and Martha Paine, of 4, Acacia Rd., Beckenham, Kent. Born Farnham, lived Beckenham.

PARFITT S None of this name on CWGC.

PARKINSON F One record on CWGC but no Beckenham reference. Died 13/10/1918 Duke of Wellington's.

PARKINSON No initial given on memorial but could 2nd Lieutenant James H Parkinson of 15 Barnmead Rd, Beckenham killed 2/7/1916 be a possibility? He was the son of Mr Walter H and Mrs Ada Wellesley Parkinson late of Cedars Rd, Beckenham and brother of the Walter

Wellesley Parkinson headmaster of Freeman's School, Brixton. BJ 22/7/1916.

PARSONS EDWIN ERNEST Private 24957 Suffolk Regiment 3rd Bn.
Died 28/05/1917 age 21 Grave C. 93. FELIXSTOWE NEW CEMETERY.
Son of George and Eliza Parsons, of 72, Crampton Rd., Penge, London.
Enlisted Bromley, born Beckenham.

PARSONS F C J Record on CWGC and Soldiers died in Great War for Parsons Frederick Charles Private G/60324. Middx Reg 1st/8th Bn.
Died of wounds 25/6/1918 Grave IV.J.4. AUBIGNY COMMUNAL CEMETERY EXTENSION.
From Beckenham.

PARTRIDGE G A Three records on CWGC. Possibly George Arthur driver in NZ Field Artillery age 44 with wife in NZ but parents George and Mary in Ewhurst.

PASSIFUL EDWARD ARTHUR (ALSO PASSIFULL) Private 3/10255 Suffolk Regiment.
Husband of Emily with sons Frederick and Leslie living in 1911 with wife's parents Frederick, market gardener, and Hannah Aviss at 17 St Margaret's Rd, Elmers End. Born Suffolk 1874, roadman.
Died Bromley early in 1917. Registered in National Archives but not in CWGC.

PATERSON JOHN HERBERT Lieutenant 19th Lancers (Fane's Horse) and 21st Sqdn. Royal Air Force.
Died 21/06/1918 age 25 Grave O. 197.CAIRO WAR MEMORIAL CEMETERY.
Son of John and Freda Rosa Paterson, of "Shalimar", 56, Foxgrove Rd., Beckenham.

PAVIER WILLIAM JOHN Private G/945 Queen's Own Royal West Kent Regiment 6th Bn.
Died 14/10/1915 age 25 panel 95 to 97 LOOS MEMORIAL.
Son of Eliza Pavier of 20 Kangley Bridge Rd, Lower Sydenham.

PEACOCK LEONARD FLANDERS Private 10242 Royal Fusiliers 20th Bn.

Died 30/07/1916 age 30. Pier and Face 8 C 9 A and 16 A. THIEPVAL MEMORIAL.
Son of the late William John and Sarah Peacock, of "Nervion", 16 Beckenham Grove, Shortlands.

PEACOCK GERALD FERGUSON Private T/202773 The Buffs (East Kent Regiment) 6th Bn.
Killed in action 09/08/1917 Bay 2. ARRAS MEMORIAL.
Born East Finchley, Middx. Enlisted Lincoln's Inn, Middx. 1911 lived 8 Bromley Grove, Shortlands, Kent, son of William, accountant and Constance Mary Peacock.

PEARCE DUDLEY GEORGE Captain The Buffs (East Kent Regiment) 8th Bn.
Died 03/09/1916 age 25 Grave XXVII. A. 5. SERRE ROAD CEMETERY No.2.
Son of George and Stella Pearce, of "Brabourne Lees", Bournemouth. Born Mill Hill, Middlesex.
1911 34 Foxgrove Road, Beckenham.

PEEL The Rev Hon MAURICE BERKELEY MC and bar, Chaplain 4th class, Army Chaplain's department.
Died serving the wounded and dying, 14/5/1917 Grave V.A.31. QUEANT ROAD CEMETERY BUISSY.
Son of 1st Viscount Arthur Wellesley Peel, husband of the late Emily Peel, vicar St Paul's church, Brackley Rd 1909 to 1915.

PEEL ROBERT Captain Cheshire Regiment formerly 3rd Manchester Regiment, eldest son of the late Captain Robert Moore Peel 6th Inniskilling Dragoons.
Died age 51 7/12/1917 Anerley.
Born Edgebaston Birmingham 1867, living with his sister, Linda Corbin, at 7 Beckenham Rd in 1911, married Mildred O Barker 1912. Family in 1891 lived at 2 Overbury Ave, Beckenham.

PERCIVAL HAROLD HEYWOOD A/Corporal 400402 Essex Regiment 1st Bn. Formerly 31107, Suffolk Regt.
Died of wounds 11/10/1918 Grave I.B.10, BEAULENCOURT BRITISH CEMETERY LIGNY-THILLOY.

Born Bermondsey, son of Edward and Sarah Percival; husband of Mabel Percival of 61 Royston Rd, Penge, lived 1911, 12 Lucas Road, Penge.

PETLEY, WALTER HORACE JOHN Rifleman 2021 London Regiment (London Rifle Brigade) 1st/5th Bn.
Killed in action 10/09/1916 age 23 Pier and Face 9 D. THIEPVAL MEMORIAL.
Son of Mrs. Amy F. Petley and the late Horace James Petley, of "Ormesby", 8 Langley Rd., Beckenham. Enlisted London.

PHARO JOHN WILLIAM Private 2844 Queen's Royal West Surrey Regiment D Coy 2nd/4th Bn.
Killed 12/9/15 age 39 Grave I.C.2. AZMAK CEMETERY SUVLA TURKEY.
Son of John William Pharo, husband of Alice Caroline Pharo nee Curtis of 25 Whateley Rd, Penge.

PHILLIPS E A Ten matches in CWGC.

PICKUP ALFRED JAMES 2nd Lieutenant Yorkshire Regiment 2nd Bn.
Died 26/9/1915 age 27 Panel 44 & 45 LOOS MEMORIAL.
Younger son of Mr and Mrs J Pickup of Beechcroft, Beckenham.

PLAYFAIR VICTOR HAMILTON Lance Corporal 390209 London Regiment (Queen Victoria's Rifles) 9th Bn.
Died home 26/02/1917 Grave M3. 7311. BECKENHAM CREMATORIUM AND CEMETERY.

POOLE AMOS Private 213444 Middlesex Regiment 302nd Reserve Labour Coy. transf. to 743rd Area Employment Coy. Labour Corps.
Killed in action 25/08/1917 age36 Grave III. B. 28. COXYDE MILITARY CEMETERY.
Husband of Amelia Poole, of 78, Kimberly Rd., Beckenham. Born Slough, enlisted Bromley.

POOLE LEONARD FRANCIS Private G/5374 Queen's Own (Royal West Kent Regiment) 8th Bn.
Killed in action 26/09/1915 Panel 95 to 97. LOOS MEMORIAL.
Born Kentish Town, lived Beckenham.

POPLETT JOHN HENRY Private 31030 East Surrey 1st Bn.
Died 8/5/1917 Bay 6 ARRAS MEMORIAL.
Son of Mrs Elizabeth Poplett of 77 Ravenscroft and husband of Emily of 115 Avenue Rd, Beckenham.

POPLETT JAMES CARPENTER Private G/3170 Queen's Royal West Surrey 1st Bn.
Killed instantly by a bomb 12/8/1916 Pier and Faces 5D and 6D THIEPVAL MEMORIAL.
Brother of John Henry Poplett.

PORTER, HUGH GORDON Second Lieutenant Royal Garrison Artillery155th Cheshire Heavy Bty.
Killed in action 06/11/1916 age 23 Pier and Face 8 A. THIEPVAL MEMORIAL.
Son of Hugh Gordon Porter and Harriet Elizabeth Porter, of "Homefield", 48 Foxgrove Rd., Beckenham.

POWELL WALTER EDMUND Private 66632 Royal Army Medical Corps 101st Field Amb. Formerly an Old West Kent Territorial with Hedley Thornton and the Beckenham St John's Ambulance.
Died staying with a wounded man who he had covered with his coat 12/8/1916 age 24 Grave I.B.35 FLATIRON COPSE CEMETERY MAMETZ FRANCE.
Elder son of Mr and Mrs Walter Powell of Didcott, Berks; married E Powell nee Veale of 50 Bowden Hill, Newton Abbot when there selling books before joining up. BJ 2/9/1916 p3.

PRATT ARTHUR FREDERICK 515490 London Regiment London Scottish 1st/14th Bn.
Died 24/11/1917 Panel 11&12 CAMBRAI MEMORIAL LOUVERAL.
Son of William and Rose Pratt, 152 Parish Lane, Penge, born abt 1898.

PRESTON ALFRED 205780 1st driver 12th Coy Tanks D Bn.
Killed in action 22/8/1917 age 21 Panel 159 to160 TYNE COT MEMORIAL.
Eldest son of Ernest and Minnie Preston of 88 Birchanger Rd, South Norwood, formerly 26 Bromley Rd, Beckenham.

PRESTON CHARLES T Private 79424 Durham Light Infantry 1st/6th Bn., previously four years with Kent Cyclist Bn. Territorials.
Died 31/5/1918 age 26 SOISSONS MEMORIAL FRANCE.
Son of Mr and Mrs C T Preston of 38 Durban Rd; husband of D E Preston. Employed eight years by Army & Navy Stores, London. BJ 12/7/1919.

PRICE ERNEST ROBERT Lance Sergeant G/1441 The Queen's (Royal West Surrey Regiment) 7th Bn.
Died 02/07/1916 age 30 Grave I. B. 10. HEILLY STATION CEMETERY, MERICOURT-L'ABBE.
Son of Robert and Caroline Rachael Price, of "Oakdale", 2, Maberley Rd., Elmers End, Beckenham. His brother Walter Charles Price also fell.

PRICE WALTER CHARLES Private 6912 The Queen's (Royal West Surrey Regiment) 10th Bn.
Died 20/05/1918 age 35 Grave IX. E. 17. YPRES RESERVOIR CEMETERY.
Son of Robert and Caroline Price, of "Oakdale", Maberley Rd., Elmers End, Beckenham, husband of Emily Alice Price. His brother Ernest Robert Price also fell. 1911 Oakdale, Maberley Road, Elmers End.

PRICE JAMES THIRKELL MC, twice mentioned in despatches, Captain Royal Field Artillery 77th Bde.
Died 21/4/16 age 21 II.H.21 VERMELLES BRITISH CEMETERY.
Son of the late E A and Mrs Price of Montclair, Beckenham; husband of Mariquita Price of Lyme Regis, Dorset.

PRIDDY SIDNEY RANDALL Bombardier 14215 Royal Field Artillery D Bty 93rd Bde.
Died 18/3/1916 age 21 Plot 2. Row B. Grave 1 FERME-OLIVIER CEMETERY, BELGIUM.
Son of Robert Edward and Margaret Annie Priddy of 39 Lennard Rd, Beckenham. Telephonist and signaller, he was out mending a shelled wire when he was killed.

PROVIS ERNEST SNELL Second Lieutenant Royal Munster Fusiliers 4th Bn. attd. 8th Bn.
Killed in action 16/06/1916 age 38 Grave I. F. 2. MAZINGARBE COMMUNAL CEMETERY EXTENSION.

Son of John and E. E. Provis, of 8, Queen's Rd., Beckenham. Born Tunbridge Wells. Lived 54 Barnmead Road, Beckenham.

PRYOR J Two of this name in CWGC: fireman Mercantile marine died 23/2/1916 and corporal in Royal Engineers died 28/4/1916.

PURDUE CHARLES Sergeant B/2986 Rifle Brigade 3rd Bn.
Died 1/9/1916 age 20 I.B.50 DANTZIG ALLEY BRITISH CEMETERY MAMETZ FRANCE.
Son of Charles storekeeper and Emily Isabel Purdue from Bournemouth but of 92 Bromley Rd in 1911.

PURNELL ARTHUR CHANNING Captain Middlesex 16th Bn.
Killed in command of a bombing party on 1/7/1916, age 34 Pier and Face 12D & 13B, THIEPVAL MEMORIAL.
Son of Emily Blandford Purnell. Record holder with R E Houston of the Thames double skulls.

PURVIS T R Sergeant 575 Royal West Kent 8th Bn.
Although missing from the battle of Loos was not officially notified as dead until 17/6/1916. See BJ. Known as Tom, he was a local footballer and a great leader in battle. Son of Mrs Purvis 18 Sultan St, Beckenham.

RAND GEORGE A Private 9993 Royal Fusiliers 1st Bn., reservist called up at outbreak of war.
Died 27/7/1917 III.G.4 DICKEBUSCH NEW MILITARY CEMETERY EXTENSION BELGIUM.
Husband of M Rand of 83 Crompton Rd Penge and son of the greengrocer in Station Rd.

RAND JAMES H Company Sergeant Major, L/8221 Queen's Royal West Surrey Regiment 7th Bn.
Died 10/8/1917 age 31 Panel 11-13, 14 YPRES MENIN GATE MEMORIAL.
Husband of Adelia Gertrude Aimee Rand of White Horse Lane, South Norwood. 1901 lived Penge, 1911 in Gibraltar with army.

RANGER FRED SAMUEL Private G/24760 Middlesex Regiment 21st Bn.

Killed in action 23/3/1918 age 20 Bay 7 ARRAS MEMORIAL.
Son of Mrs Ranger of 80 Station Rd, Penge. Born Penge, enlisted Maidstone.

RANSON REGINALD GEORGE Rifleman 2569 London Regiment (Queen's Westminster Rifles) 16th Bn.
Died 29/3/1915 Grave III.B.3. HOUPLINES COMMUNAL CEMETERY EXTENSION.
Son of the late George Henry and Frances Sarah Ranson of The Furze, 58 Wiverton Rd, Sydenham.

RAY JACK Rifleman 302210 London Regiment (London Rifle Brigade) "B" Coy. 1st/5th Bn.
Killed in action 08/10/1916 age 23, Pier and Face 9 D. THIEPVAL MEMORIAL.
Son of Mrs. Jane Elizabeth Ray, of "St. Piers", Nutfield Rd., South Merstham, Surrey.
Born Anerley, lived Beckenham, enlisted London .

RAYNER JAMES Private L/6786 The Queen's (Royal West Surrey Regiment) 1st Bn.
Died of wounds, 07/10/1914, age 33 Grave A. 6. (Sp. Mem.). BRAINE COMMUNAL CEMETERY.
Son of James Rayner, of Beckenham, Kent; husband of Mrs. C. A. Gaffney of 31, Creeland Grove, Catford,
Born Chelsea, Middx, lived Penge.

RAYNHAM CECIL HAROLD Private 29983 East Yorkshire Regiment 1st Bn. Formerly G/13068, R. West Kent Regt.
Killed in action, 25/04/1918 age 28 Grave XIV. A. 7. HARLEBEKE NEW BRITISH CEMETERY.
Son of Charles Richard and Rebecca Raynham of 55 Martins Road, Shortlands, Bromley; husband of Winifred Raynham, of 8, Yewtree Rd., Beckenham, Kent.

READ FRANK VICTOR Pioneer, Royal Engineers.
Drowned 4/5/1917 when on way to Egypt as ship the HMT Transylvania was torpedoed although was seen launching a life raft. As the troops were being rescued, a second torpedo had been released from the U-boat U63 and the ship sunk immediately with the loss of 421 men. Most were buried

at the SAVONA cemetery. Youngest son of Mr and Mrs Read of 18 Green Lane, Penge, an old County School boy, he joined the Civil Service as a GPO engineer, was a brilliant pianist and a member of the Beckenham Swimming Club.

READING HAROLD LESLIE 2nd Lieutenant Horse Artillery and Royal Field Artillery "D" Bty. 108th Army Bde.
Killed in action 05/11/1917 age 19 Grave III. F. 18. CANADA FARM CEMETERY.
Son of Mr. and Mrs. W. A. Reading, of Douglas House, Beckenham, Kent.
Probate to William Alfred Reading. 1911 54 Wickham Road, Beckenham.

REDFORD F W Not found in CWGC but Frederick William Redford died Maidstone in 1920 age 37 and a married able seaman was serving on the ship Pegasus in 1911 aged 28 with a marriage in 1906 in Bromley of a man of the same name!

REID GERALD MORTIMER Lieutenant London Regiment (Finsbury Rifles) 11th Bn.
Killed in action 09/05/1918 age 32 Grave II. N. 14. BOUZINCOURT RIDGE CEMETERY, ALBERT.
Son of Mrs. J. A. Reid, of The Hydro Hotel, Eastbourne. Born at Beckenham, bpt 16/10/1886.

REID H C T Not found in CWGC, but a possibility is Henry Charles T Reid born St Helena 1894 in the army births and Henry C in the Herts Reg who died in 1917 in the deaths.

REIDY HAROLD ST JOHN REIDY, Captain, Army Service Corps.
Died 19/10/1918 Grave IV. H. 21. ABBEVILLE COMMUNAL CEMETERY EXTENSION.
Probate to Richard James Reidy of Elmslea, Beckenham, Adm London 18/11/1920.
Born in Brazil abt 1889.

REYNOLDS EDWARD HEWETSON Rifleman 41198 Royal Irish Rifles 1st Bn. Formerly 14304, 10th Res. Cav. Regt.
Died 13/02/1917 age 32 Grave Div. 3. F. 18. STE. MARIE CEMETERY, LE HAVRE.

Son of Hewetson Russell Reynolds and Jane Elizabeth Reynolds, of Catford. Born Catford, lived Beckenham, enlisted London.

REYNOLDS FRANK DANIEL MC Lieutenant The Queen's (Royal West Surrey Regiment) 8th Bn.
Died 09/09/1917 age 23 Grave M3.3389. BECKENHAM CREMATORIUM AND CEMETERY.
Son of Mr. and Mrs. D. Reynolds, of Burleigh Lodge, Mill Lane, Herne Bay. Born at Camberwell, London.

RICHARDS D L Lance Corporal 8756 2nd Dragoon Guards Queen's Bays.
Died 25/11/1917 Grave II.E.17 ROCQUIGNY-EQUANCOURT RD BRITISH CEMETERY FRANCE.

RICHARDSON ARTHUR Private 43425 Middx Regiment 1st Bn.
Died 26/9/1917 age 34 Panel 113 to 115 TYNE COT MEMORIAL.
Husband of Constance Richardson BJ p3 6/7/1918 and CWGC.

RIDDLES FRANCIS HENRY Private G/8415 Queen's Own (Royal West Kent Regiment) 11th Bn.
Died 15/09/1916 age 22 Panel Pier and Face 11 C. THIEPVAL MEMORIAL.
Son of Francis James and Elizabeth Riddles, of 36, Tennyson Rd., Penge. Born Greenwich abt 1895, enlisted Lewisham, lived Penge.

RIDOUT WILLIAM Private G/6652 Duke of Cambridge's Own Middlesex Regiment 21st Bn.
Killed in action 23/03/1918 Panel Bay 7. ARRAS MEMORIAL.
Born abt 1891 Beckenham, enlisted Maidstone, Kent. 1911 72 Station Rd, Penge.

RIGGS WILLIAM JOHN Private 275408 Prince Albert's Somerset Light Infantry "D" Coy. 1st Garrison Bn. Formerly 241120, Royal West Kent Regiment.
Died 01/08/1918 age 33 KARACHI 1914-1918 WAR MEMORIAL.
Son of Henry Ralph and Sarah Riggs. Born abt 1886 Canning Town, Essex, lived Beckenham, enlisted Bromley. 1911 354 Albert Rd, North Woolwich.

ROBERTS ARTHUR WILLIAM Private G/14293 The Buffs (East Kent Regiment) 7th Bn.

Killed in action 18/09/1918 Panel 3. VIS-EN-ARTOIS MEMORIAL.
Born abt 1900 Trinity, Newington, lived Beckenham, enlisted Bromley.

ROBERTS ALBERT CECIL Lance Corporal 703606 London Regiment 1st/23rd Bn. Formerly 2462, 3rd London Regt.
Killed in action 16/09/1916 Pier and Face 9 D 9 C 13 C and 12 C. THIEPVAL MEMORIAL.
Son of Benjamin Roberts headmaster Bromley Rd School.

ROBERTS HARRY LESLIE 2nd Lieutenant Royal Horse Artillery and Royal Field Artillery 189th Bde.
Died of wounds 10/09/1916 age 20 C. 19. MILLENCOURT COMMUNAL CEMETERY EXTENSION.
Son of Mr. B. A. and Mrs. E. E. Roberts, of 6, Shaftesbury Rd., Beckenham.
Born abt 1897.
1911 11 Whitmore Rd, Beckenham.

ROE D Not found in CWGC.

ROSE EDWARD Sergeant 9597 East Surrey Regiment C Company 2nd Bn.
Died Hill 60 24/5/1915 age 26 Grave V.H.27. SANCTUARY WOOD CEMETERY, BELGIUM.
Son of the late George and Louisa Rose of 40 Kimberley Rd, Beckenham.

ROSE E not known.

ROSS NORMAN DOUGLAS Rifleman 2835 London Regiment (The Rangers) 1st/12th Bn.
Killed in action 25/04/1915 Panel 54. YPRES (MENIN GATE) MEMORIAL.
Lived Beckenham.

ROUTEN HENRY Private 38732 Suffolk Regiment Depot 1st reserve garrison.
Died home 28/01/1919 age 43 Grave W5. 7830. BECKENHAM CREMATORIUM AND CEMETERY.
Husband of Madeline Routen, of 74, Station Rd., Penge, London. Born Penge, enlisted Bromley.

ROWDEN PERCY GEORGE Private 53161 Royal Fusiliers (City of London Regiment) 2nd Bn.
Died of wounds 10/09/1917 age 31 Grave VI. B. 16. DOZINGHEM MILITARY CEMETERY.
Son of Jane Rowden, of 40, Anerley Hill, Upper Norwood, London, and the late William Thomas Rowden.
Born Cambridge Rd, Anerley abt 1886. 1911 40 Anerley Road, Upper Norwood.

RULE ALFRED Private T/976 Queen's Own (Royal West Kent Regiment) 1st/5th Bn. attd. 2nd Bn.
Died 13/01/1916 age 29 Grave J. 10. KUT WAR CEMETERY.
Son of George and Elizabeth Ann Rule of 12, Shaftesbury Rd., Beckenham.

RUMENS WILLIAM ERNEST Private G/9786 Queen's Own (Royal West Kent Regiment) "B" Coy. 8th Bn.
Killed in action 03/09/1916 age 34 Pier and Face 11 C. THIEPVAL MEMORIAL.
Son of Mrs. E. Rumens, of 63, Churchfields Rd., Beckenham. Enlisted Bromley, born abt 1882, Beckenham.

RUSSELL ALFRED JOHN Private 43711 Royal Inniskilling Fusiliers 9th Bn.
Killed in action 31/07/1918 Grave III. G. 7. BAILLEUL COMMUNAL CEMETERY EXTENSION, NORD.
Born Penge, enlisted Blackheath.

RUSSELL RICHARD REGINALD WILLIAM Private SE/9460 Army Veterinary Corps 14th Vet. Hosp.
Died 01/04/1917 age 45 Grave II. D. 25. ABBEVILLE COMMUNAL CEMETERY EXTENSION.
Son of Richard and Julia Catherine Russell, of Otford Castle, Sevenoaks, husband of Constance L. W. Russell, of 68, Marlow Rd., Anerley. Born Otford, enlisted Woolwich.

RUST PHILIP Private 2617 London Regiment 1st/13th Kensington Bn.
Died 25/5/1915 age 22 VIII.D.44. BOULOGNE EASTERN CEMETERY.
Son of Philip and Minnie Rust of 203 Beckenham Rd, Beckenham.

SALES FREDERICK CHARLES Private G/13057 Royal Sussex Regiment 7th Bn.
Killed in action 08/05/1917 age 40 Bay 6. ARRAS MEMORIAL.
Son of Samuel and Ruth Sales, 89, Brunswick St., Reading; husband of Edith Mary Sales, of 63, Arrol Rd., Beckenham. Born Tunbridge Wells, enlisted St Swithins Lane.

SALES JOHN WILLIAM Private 9215 Machine Gun Corps (Infantry) 61st Coy. Formerly G/19090, R. Fus.
Killed in action 04/09/1916 Pier and Face 5 C and 12 C. THIEPVAL MEMORIAL.
Born abt 1896 Beckenham, lived Beckenham, enlisted Finsbury. 1911 41 Burnhill Road, Beckenham.
Son of John and Agnes Sales.

SAMPSON WILLIAM FREDERICK Private 8356 Household Cavalry and Cavalry of the Line (incl. Yeomanry and Imperial Camel Corps) Bn. 6th Dragoon. Guards (Carabineers).
Killed in action 1/4/1918 II.A.10. CAYEUX MILITARY CEMETERY, France.
Born Battersea, lived Beckenham, enlisted London. 1911 133 Ravenscroft Road Beckenham.

SANDERCOMBE PERCIVAL EDGAR Private 6319 Australian Infantry, A.I.F. 9th Bn.
Died 27 Feb 1917 Grave H.2. BAZENTIN-LE-PETIT MILITARY CEMETERY.
Son of Frederick Samuel Sandercombe and Happy Turner, 1901 104, Arpley Road, Penge. Left Beckenham age 21 for Australia where he volunteered for the Imperial Forces. BJ p3 24/3/1917.

SAUNDERS Ambrose James
Cycle and motor engineer born Byfleet 1882, married Kezia Elizabeth Wells 1903, lived at 2 Belmont Rd, Beckenham. Four possible A J Saunders CWGC.

SAUNDERS CLEMENT STANLEY Private 242816 The Buffs East Kent Regiment 6039 1st/5th Bn.
Died 24/2/1917 XXIX.B.105/116 AMARA WAR CEMETERY, IRAQ.

Only son of Clement and Emily Saunders of 1 Kendall Rd, Beckenham.

SAXTON GEORGE H Private 242369 Sherwood Foresters Notts & Derby Reg 11th Bn.
Died 9/10/1918 age 38 Panel 7 VIS-EN-ARTOIS MEMORIAL.
Born Bermondsey abt 1880, lived West Wickham, a gardener in 1911.

SCAWEN LEWIS MILFORD Lance Corporal 5457 Leinster Regiment.
Died 5/8/1917 III.B.5 BRANDHOER NEW MILITARY CEMETERY.
Son of Henry and Ellen Lewis of 5 Monivea Rd, Beckenham. Partner in firm of Scawen & Dart builders in Beckenham High St.

SCHWARZ G Rifleman 678160 London Regiment 1st Surrey Rifles 21st Bn.
Died 24/8/1918 I.B.14, BRAY HILL BRITISH CEMETERY BRAY-SUR-SOMME.
Of 18 Blandford Ave, Beckenham.

SCRIVEN WILLIAM Private G/5371 Queen's Own Royal West Kent Regiment 8th Bn.
Died 26/9/1915 age 22 Panel 95 to 97 LOOS MEMORIAL.
Husband of Kate Dorothy Lidbetter formerly Scriven of 26 Chancery Lane, Beckenham. Lived 30 Whateley Rd, Penge, enlisted 3/1/1915, employed by dairyman Mr Dyer, three bros in forces, RE, RFC, RE in India. BJ 24/3/1917.

SEALE SIDNEY Private L/9989 British Expeditionary Force Royal Sussex Regiment 2nd Bn.
Killed in action 30/10/1914 Panel 20. YPRES (MENIN GATE) MEMORIAL.
Born Beckenham abt 1890, enlisted Croydon, 1911 148 Blandford Road, Beckenham.
Son of Phillip and Mary Ann Seale, apprentice printer machine minder.

SEDGWICK NORMAN LESLIE Gunner 85286 23 Royal Field Artillery X3rd Trench Mortar Bty.
Died 04/11/1918 age 23 Grave IV. B. 10. ROMERIES COMMUNAL CEMETERY EXTENSION.
Son of Joseph and Mary Ann Sedgwick, of 6, Kelsey Square, Beckenham, Kent. Born Beckenham abt 1896.

SELLER S None of this name in CWGC records.

SEMARK FRED Private TF/2590 Queen's Own Royal West Kent Regiment 2nd/4th Bn.
Died 14/8/1915 age 17, Panel 155 HELLES MEMORIAL, Gallipoli.
Third son of Harry and Alice Semark of 15 Seward Rd killed by a sniper at the battle of the Dardanelles. Enlisted at The Triangle, Penge.

SEMARK S Not found in CWGC.

SEMARK WILLIAM Private G/3918 Queen's Own Royal West Kent 7th Bn.
Died 19/11/1916 Pier and Face 11C. THIEPVAL MEMORIAL.
Husband of Beatrice Semark of 45 Blandford Rd, Beckenham with three daughters and one son, William Dudley.

SHARPE G B Not Found in CWGC.

SHARPE ARTHUR G/4171 Queens Own RWK 6th Bn.
Killed in action 8/10/1915 Panel 95 to 97 LOOS MEMORIAL.
Son of Mr and Mrs W Sharpe of 135 Ravenscroft Rd, Beckenham.

SHARPE P W Percy William Sharpe on CWGC in RN died 22/8/1916 with no apparent Beckenham connection.

SHARPE PERCY G Private 47739 The Queen's (Royal West Surrey Regiment) 16th Bn. transf. to (74222) 124th Coy. Labour Corps.
Died 06/08/1917 age 19 Grave III. A. 10A. MONT HUON MILITARY CEMETERY, LE TREPORT.
Son of William and Clara Eliz. Flora Sharpe, of 135 Ravenscroft Road Beckenham. Born Beckenham abt 1898.

SHEARING ALFRED JETHRO AB 134678 HM TRAWLER Loch Naver RN.
Died 13/5/1918 age 48, PORTSMOUTH WAR MEMORIAL.
Son of James and Mary Ann Shearing of 19 Heathfield Rd, Bromley; husband of Edith Annie Shearing of 23 Raymond Rd, Beckenham.

SHEPHERD G F Private 477832 Royal Canadian Regiment.

Died 15/09/1916 VIMY MEMORIAL.

SHERLEY-PRICE WALLIS Private M/204572 Army Service Corps.
Died 29/1/1918 XXI.F.11A. ETAPLES MILITARY CEMETERY.
Son of Henry and Jane Sherley-Price of Pettistree, Beckenham; husband of
G Sherley-Price of 3 Kirby St, Ipswich.

SHERLOCK JESSE (JACK) Private 802448 Canadian Infantry 18th Bn.
Reported shot by an officer 8/8/1918 age 44 after capture at Amiens by
Germans XVI.F.4 VILLERS BRETONNEUX MILITARY CEMETERY.
His brother James Sherlock had a grocer's store at 54 Beckenham Rd.

SHEWARDS ERNEST WILLIAM W Private 34981 Essex Regiment 1st
Bn.
Killed in action 31/1/1918 age 31 Grave V.G.9 OXFORD ROAD
CEMETERY, BELGIUM.
Joined up June 1916; previous to starting his own grocery business, he
worked at the Home & Colonial Stores in the High St, Beckenham. Leaves
Mrs Laura Shewards of 113 Northcote Rd, West Croydon and two little
girls, one Bessie age 9. Son of William and Mary Shewards from Stourport,
Worcs.
Appears in CWGC and Findmypast under Sheward.

SHUTER CHARLES Private T/202509 Buffs (East Kent Regiment) 1st
Bn.
Died of wounds age 30, 8/6/1917 Q. 11. PHILOSOPHE BRITISH
CEMETERY, MAZINGARBE.
Born Farningham, Kent, lived Worthing, also 37 Burnhill Rd, Beckenham.
BJ 30/6/1917. Son of the late Edward Charles Shuter; husband of Jessie
Shuter nee Pearce, 1911 12 Shortlands Gardens Bromley.

SIMMS B A
Name not found in any of the sources including CWGC. There is a Bertie
Charles Alfred Simms from Oxon.

SIMMONS P F Although as spelled here the name is not on the CWGC,
there is PERCY FREDERICK SIMMONDS, Private 2796 Otago Regiment
NZEF 2nd Bn.
Died 16/11/1918 age 30 XIII.B.12 ROCQUIGNY EQUANCOURT RD

BRITISH CEMETERY.
Husband of Carrie Agnes Simmonds of 7a Worbeck Rd, Anerley.

SIMPSON ERNEST HERBERT (or Henry) Lieutenant Royal Garrison Artillery G Anti Aircraft Bty. Anzac Sect.
Killed in action 2/10/1917 age 41. IV. E. 21. LONGUENESSE St OMER SOUVENIR CEMETERY.
Second son of F H Simpson of Thornbury, Beckenham; husband of Violet nee Bishop of North Dene, Beckenham, now Violet Gerry of 3 Belle Vue, Sunderland.

SIMPSON GEORGE KENNETH MC Lieutenant RFC 14th Kite Balloon section, 4th Balloon Wing.
Died in an accident 7/3/1917 when he waited for his air mechanic to clear the balloon before he jumped and was overcome by the flaming balloon on the way down. II.B.18. BRAY MILITARY CEMETERY.
Youngest son of Mrs Emily Simpson and the late Henry John of Lymington, Hants, he was educated at Dulwich College and returned from Vancouver to enlist in the RGA in March 1915.

SKINNER DOUGLAS HILTON Captain Queen's Own Royal West Kent.
Died age 24 from spinal paralysis after hit by a sniper 16/7/1916, I.B.12. DAOURS COMMUNAL CEMETERY EXTENSION.
Elder son of Hilton and Emily Catharine Skinner of Ash Lodge, Hayes, educated Eastbourne & Charterhouse, 4th year medical student Oxford, enlisted Sept 1914, France July 1915.

SMALLMAN ARTHUR FREDERICK STRONG 2nd Lieutenant Hon Artillery Co 1st Bn.
Died 14/11/1916 aged 25 VII.E.5. ANCRE BRITISH CEMETERY BEAUMONT-HAMEL.
Son of the late Sir Henry George Smallman and Lady Louisa of 30 Leigham Court Rd, London.

SMALLMAN CHARLES STRONG Private 1284 Hon Artillery C Co.
Died 12/12/1914 age 20 YPRES MENIN GATE MEMORIAL.
Son of the late Sir Henry George Smallman and Lady Louisa of Eliot Lodge, Beckenham.

SMART CHARLES Sergeant G/227 Queen's (Royal West Surrey Regiment) 6th Bn.
Killed in action 1/4/1917 age 32 Grave H.24. STE CATHERINE BRITISH CEMETERY.
Husband of May A Smart of 16 Oak Grove, Anerley.

SMITH A, SMITH A J, SMITH C W have not been possible to identify.

SMITH CHARLES ALBERT Private Royal Marine Light Infantry on HMS Louvain.
Died 20/1/1918 when the troop transport armed boarding steamer was torpedoed by the German sub U22 in the Kelos Strait, Aegean Sea with the loss of 224 lives.
Born 9/6/1899, South Norwood. Son of Mr George Vinall and Mrs Florence Helen Smith, 11, Seward Road, Beckenham. 1911 384 Blandford Road Beckenham.

SMITH E Driver T4/059291 Army Service Corps H T attd 39th Field Amb.
Died 8/6/1916 Mesopotamia Grave XIV.E.28 AMARA WAR CEMETERY IRAQ.
Son of John Smith 16 Burnhill Rd, Beckenham.

SMITH GEOFFREY WATKINS. Could this be Smith G H? Captain Rifle Brigade 13th Bn.
Killed in action 10/7/1916 age 34 Grave III.J. 27. POZIERES BRITISH CEMETERY OVILLERS LA BOISSELLE.
Son of Horace and Susan Eleanor Penelope Smith of Ivybank, Beckenham. Fellow and tutor New College Oxford, zoology specialist. Reported BJ 29/7/1916.

SMITH WILLIAM GEORGE Private RAMC British 27th Field Ambulance.
Killed in action 18/7/1916 age 26 II.H.17. PERONNE ROAD CEMETERY MARICOURT.
Son of Edward and Sarah Ann Smith, formerly of Ravenscroft Rd, Beckenham lately of 49a Lewis St, Toronto, Canada, now New Bedford, Mass, USA. BJ 2/9/1916.

SMITHERS ROBERT INDIGO RAPLEY Corporal 10820 Welsh Regiment 2nd Bn.

Killed in action 24/08/1916 age 21 Grave 5.H.21. LONDON CEMETERY AND EXTENSION, LONGUEVAL.
Son of James and Martha Smithers, of 8, Brook Place, High St Beckenham.
Born Beckenham, 1911 at 1 Gowland Place, enlisted London.

SMYTH GEORGE CHARLES Private 61152 Machine Gun Corps Infantry 186th Coy.
Died 11/10/1918. Grave IV.C.13. TEHRAN WAR CEMETERY.
Son of George Daniel and Agnes of 165 Birkbeck Rd, Beckenham, born abt 1897, Clapham.

SMYTH EDWIN PERCIVAL Lieutenant Queen's Own Royal West Kent 7th Bn.
Died 28/6/1918 Plot 3 row E grave 8. TANNAY BRITISH CEMETERY THIENNES.
Beckenham Scoutmaster, son of Edwin and Alice Emma Smyth.
BJ 13/7/1918 and CWGC as Smyth not Smythe.

SNELL A
Of 16 names on the CWGC, Alfred James Snell is possible, died 9/5/15 age 20 from Peckham.

SPALL BERNARD H. A. Sergeant 54706 Sapper Corps of Royal Engineers 295th Railway Coy.
Killed in action 21/03/1918 age 32 Grave I. K. 15. DRANOUTRE MILITARY CEMETERY.
Son of Henry Richard and Emma Spall, of 91, Oakfield Rd., Anerley, London.
Born Beccles, Suffolk Enlisted London. 1911 22 Birkbeck Road Beckenham.

SPARKES FRANK EVANS Lance Corporal 8380 London Regiment 5th Bn. (City of London) (London Rifle Brigade).
Killed in action 13/5/1915 Panel 52 and 54. YPRES (MENIN GATE) MEMORIAL.
Born Harlesden 1885, living 54 Croydon Road, Beckenham 1911, enlisted London. Son of Francis John and Sarah Jane Sparks.

SPENCER ALFRED Sto 1st RN HMS Formidable 277613.
Died 1/1/1915 as one of 512 men out of 780 lost when the battleship was

hit by two torpedoes off Portland. The captain's dog is buried in a marked grave in Abbotsbury Gardens, Dorset. Born 5/12/1874, Peckham. Husband of Alice Louisa, 9 Lea Road, Beckenham, 1911 2 Fire Station Cottages Station Road Shortlands.

SPEYER CECIL ARTHUR Second Lieutenant London Regiment (Royal Fusiliers) "C" Coy. 4th Bn. Went to France with the 1st Bn. Hon. Artillery Company, Sept 1914.
Killed in action 16/08/1917 age 22 Panel 52. YPRES (MENIN GATE) MEMORIAL.
Son of Arthur A. and Julia M. Speyer, of The Red Cottage, Magpie Hall Lane, Bickley, Kent.
Born 1896 Shortlands, school Tonbridge.

SPOONER FRANK PERCIVAL Private 8011 Scots Guards1st Bn.
Died 28/09/1915 age 23 Panel 8 and 9. LOOS MEMORIAL.
Son of William Henry and Mary Anne Spooner, of 10a, Felmingham Rd., Anerley.
Bp 16/10/1892 Lambeth, 1911 24, Whitestile Road, Old Brentford.

SPRINGALL GEORGE EDWARD Corporal 9343 The Loyal North Lancashire Regiment 1st Bn.
Died 14/9/1914 Grave 6.B.12 CHAUNY COMMUNAL CEMETERY BRITISH EXTENSION.

SQUIRRELL PERCY HAYWARD Driver 31953 Royal Field Artillery a Bty 68th Bde.
Died 31/12/1918 age 26 Grave V6. 7798 BECKENHAM CREMATORIUM AND CEMETERY.
Son of the late Arthur Hayward and Mrs Julia Squirrell of 66 Kingswood Rd, Penge.

STAGG JOHN REGINALD DCM Second Lieutenant P/S 1159 Middlesex Regiment 16th Bn.
Killed in Action 18/9/1916 age 37 I. F. 43. EUSTON ROAD CEMETERY, COLINCAMPS.
{LONDON GAZETTE 20/6/1916. For the award of the Distinguished Conduct Medal. P/S 1159 Sgt. J. R. Stagg 16th Battalion Middlesex Regiment. "For conspicuous gallantry when in charge of a patrol after

completing his work in a very skilful manner under fire, he carried a man back to safety under very heavy rifle fire."} Son of Rowland and Helen Annie Stagg, of 46 the Avenue Beckenham, Kent. Writer and journalist under name John Barnet. Played rugby for Kent.

STAGG HAROLD WILLIAM Second Lieutenant Machine Gun Corps (Infantry) 15th Bn.
Died 28/03/1918 Bay 10. ARRAS MEMORIAL.
Bp 17/5/1882 Brother of John Reginald Stagg.

STANDRICK JOHN HAROLD MC 2nd Lieutenant London Regiment (London Irish Rifles) 2/18th Bn. from Inns of Court OTC 1915 and A/ Captain 1917.
Died on 21/2/1918, aged 25. JERUSALEM WAR CEMETERY, Israel.
His MC was gazetted on 15/2/1918 and the citation published on 16/7/1918 was for conspicuous gallantry and devotion to duty; his ability and skill as a leader resulted in the success of the operations against the main enemy defence line. His task was one of great responsibility, as his company was the directing pivot of the movement forward for the final assault. Throughout the day he showed exceptional skill in handling his company and a complete indifference to danger. He is buried in Jerusalem War Cemetery, Israel and remembered on the war memorial at the Private Banks Cricket and Athletic Club, Catford.
Son of Alfred and Naomi Jane Standrick of 8A, Oxford Avenue, Merton Park, born in Shepton Mallet, Somerset. He was employed by Coutts & Co.
Contributed by Andy Pepper

STEEDMAN THOMAS GEORGE Private 56139 Welsh Regiment 9th Bn.
Formerly 2711, 2/1St Hunts Cyclists Bn.
Killed in action 23/3/1918 Bay 6 ARRAS MEMORIAL.
Born 1881 Curragh, Co. Kildare, lived Penge, 188 Maple Road in 1901.
Enlisted Bromley. Son of James Steedman attendant at Crystal Palace.

STEER WILLIAM Private G/2953 Queen's Own (Royal West Kent Regiment) 1st Bn.
Killed in action 27/08/1916 age 38 Pier and Face 11 C. THIEPVAL MEMORIAL.
Son of Mrs. Emma Steer, of 31, Albert Rd., Penge, London. Born Penge, Kent. Enlisted Bromley.

STEMBRIDGE HENRY CHARLES Lance Corporal 302914 London Regiment (London Rifle Bde 1st/5th Bn.
Died 16/8/1917 age 40 Panel 52 & 54 YPRES MENINE GATE MEMORIAL.
Son of Samuel Eastman and Emily Catherine Stembridge of Home Cottage, 102 Beckenham Rd, Beckenham.

STEMBRIDGE OSCAR SAMUEL (PICKLES) Private 1488 Honourable Artillery Company.
Died 2/5/1915 age 24 Grave XIV. L.1. VOORMEZEELE ENCLOSURE NO 3, Belgium.
Brother of Henry Charles Stembridge.

STENNING N J STENNING. No records found but the following applies to William James.
WILLIAM JAMES Private263129 Gordon Highlanders 5th Bn.
Died 28/07/1918 age 18 SOISSONS MEMORIAL.
Son of police constable William James Stenning, of 199, Blandford Rd., Beckenham, Kent.

STEWART G H Not found.

STEWART GEORGE JAMES Lance Sergeant A/20108 Canadian Infantry16th Bn.
Died 07/08/1916 age 37 Grave IV. G. 10. LARCH WOOD (RAILWAY CUTTING) CEMETERY.
Son of John and Agnes Stewart, of South Queensferry, West Lothian; husband of Eveline Alice Stewart, of 41, Clock House Rd., Beckenham, Kent.

STEWART JOSEPH driver 48520 Royal Field Artillery 66th Bty, Mesopotamia.
Died 5/11/1917 Panel 7 JERUSALEM MEMORIAL, ISRAEL.
Grandson Mrs J Stewart of 151 Ravenscroft Rd, member Anerley Swifts football club.
BJ 27/7/1918 and CWGC.

STILWELL WALTER FREDERICK Lance Corporal 51 East Surrey Regiment 7th Bn.
Died 13/10/1915 age 19 Panel 65 to 67 LOOS MEMORIAL.

Son of Eli and Emma Stilwell 1901 of 30 Gowland Place and 1911 of Eden Park Farm, Upper Elmers End Rd, Beckenham.

STOCKS DAVID de BEAUVOIR DSO and Chevalier Legion D'honneur, Commander RN HM Submarine K 4.
Died 31/1/1918 age 34 in a collision off the coast of Fife, Panel 28 PORTSMOUTH NAVAL MEMORIAL.
Only son of John Wallace Stocks (retired Bengal planter) 1911 of 29 Wickham Way, Beckenham; husband of Cheridah A Stocks of Westcombe, Evercreech, Somerset who was the 2nd woman to gain the Royal Aero Club Aviator's Certificate in 1911.

STOCKWELL FRANK GEORGE Corporal 28351 Essex Regiment 13th Bn.
Died 3/12/1918 age 29 II.C.6. BERLIN SOUTH-WESTERN CEMETERY, GERMANY.
Born abt 1890 Penge, lived Penge, enlisted Bromley. 1911 3 Clarina Road Penge. Husband of Maud Allen formerly Stockwell of Glenwood Rd, Catford.

STONE ERNEST GEORGE Rifleman 301263 London Regiment (City of London) (London Rifle Brigade) 5th Bn.
Killed in action 1/7/1916, III.B.25 GOMMECOURT BRITISH CEMETERY No 2 HEBUTERNE.
1911 Lived 15 Linden Grove, Sydenham, 1901 57, Wordsworth Road, Penge, enlisted London.

STUBBERSFIELD JOHN HENRY Private 611841 Labour Corps Formerly 5924 Welsh Regiment. (Found only in National Archives not in CWGC).
Born abt 1884, boot repairer from 57 Croydon Rd, Elmers End, husband of Winnifred Maud married 1909.
Died Marylebone 1920 2nd qu. (No war details found.)

SULLIVAN WILLIAM ROBERT Sapper Deal /5415S Royal Engineers Naval Division.
Died of wounds 9/8/1916 I.C.16 BARLIN COMMUNAL CEMETERY EXTENSION.
Son of Mr William and Mrs Elizabeth Ann Sullivan of 107 Croydon Rd, Anerley, formerly of Blandford Rd.

Occupation telegraphist at Greenwich PO. BJ 26/8/1916

SWAIN THOMAS ARTHUR Private 10112 Seaforth Highlanders (Ross-shire Buffs, the Duke of Albany's) 2nd Bn. Formerly 96131, R.F.A.
Killed in action 23/10/1916 age 26 Grave VI. U. 8. GUARDS' CEMETERY, LESBOEUFS.
Son of Thomas and Jane Swain, of 48, Redvers Rd., Brighton. Native of Beckenham, Kent. Enlisted Bromley.

SWALES ROBERT JOHN Corporal G/1665 Queen's Own (Royal West Kent Regiment) 7th Bn.
Killed in action 12/10/1917 Panel 106 to 108, TYNE COT MEMORIAL.
Born abt 1894 Portsmouth, Hants, lived 18 Franklin Road 1911, son of William Henry and Alice Maud Swales.

TALLENTIRE A F
Of three in the CWGC list of ten with the initial A, the nearest is Arthur Tom of the RFC died in a flying accident 20/10/1915 age 27 from Cator Rd. BJ 30/10/1915 p1.

TARRING LEONARD WALTER Corporal TF/240734 Queen's Own Royal West Kent 1st Bn.
Died 26/10/1917 XI.C.12. HOOGE CRATER CEMETERY BELGIUM.
Born 1898 West Ham. 1911 lived 38 Bromley Gardens, Shortlands, son of Frederick and Ada Tarring.

TAYLOR ALBERT CHARLES Private G/2445 Queen's Own Royal West Kent 7th Bn.
Killed in action 29/9/1916 age 24 X.G.7. CONNAUGHT CEMETERY THIEPVAL.
Son of Albert John and Mary Ann Taylor of 18 Burrell Row, Beckenham.

TAYLOR GEORGE HENRY Private 9610 C Co Royal Sussex Regiment.
Died 3/5/1917 age 26 Bay 6 ARRAS MEMORIAL.
Son of Mr. and Mrs. George Taylor, of 13, Burnhill Rd., Beckenham, husband of Amy Agnes Friend married 1912 E Grinstead.
The BJ 27/10/1917 describes George Henry Taylor as the brother of William Taylor sons of George and Jane Taylor. Also BJ 17/8/1918.

TAYLOR WILLIAM JOHN GEORGE Private 31785 Northumberland Fusiliers 11th Bn. Previously Royal West Kents.
Died 14/03/1917 age 26. Grave VIII. A. 186. BOULOGNE EASTERN CEMETERY.
Son of William and Sarah Taylor; husband of Ada Alice Taylor, of 1, Eden Rd., Elmers End, Beckenham. 1911 46 St Margaret's Road Elmers End.

TAYLOR WILLIAM JOSEPH Corporal 27535 Hampshire Regiment 15th Bn.
Killed in action 20/09/1917 age 21 Panel 88 to 90 and 162. TYNE COT MEMORIAL.
Younger son of Mr. and Mrs. George Taylor, of 13, Burnhill Rd., Beckenham, Kent; husband of Bessie Violet Mary Taylor (nee Gurd 1915), of 10, St. James's St., Shaftesbury, Dorset.

TAYLOR W 806 matches in CWGC.

TEGG CECIL JOHN AB J/6885 RN HMS Princess Irene.
Died 27/5/1915 age 22 when the ship, which had been requisitioned as a mine layer, exploded while being loaded with mines in the Medway off Sheerness, Kent with the loss of 352 lives.
Panel 8 PORTSMOUTH NAVAL MEMORIAL.
Son of John and Emma Reade Tegg of 2 St Margaret's Rd, Beckenham.

THORNTON HEDLEY THOMAS Second Lieutenant Queen's Own (Royal West Kent Regiment) 5th Bn.
Died 25/01/1916 age 34 Grave Reference near east end of church. BECKENHAM (ST. GEORGE) CHURCHYARD.
Son of Tom William and Clara Thornton, of 42, High St., Beckenham.

THORNTON STANLEY Private 4857 Honourable Artillery Company 2nd Bn.
Killed in action 3/5/1917 Bay 1 ARRAS MEMORIAL.
Enlisted Armoury House. 1911 42 High Street Beckenham, son of Tom William and Clara Thornton.

THORP LESLIE Second Lieutenant Royal Fusiliers 10th Bn.
Died 16/11/1916 age 21 Pier and Face 8 C 9 A and 16 A. THIEPVAL MEMORIAL.

Son of Walter Edward, produce merchant, and Agnes Thorp, of 6, Hayne Rd., Beckenham, Kent.

THRIFT ARCHIBALD RICHARD 33172 Private Alexandra, Princess of Wales's Own (Yorkshire Regiment) 10th Bn. Formerly 12735, R. West Kent.
Died of wounds 25/4/1917 home Grave V3.7358 BECKENHAM CEMETERY & CREMATORIUM.
Born Beckenham, lived 1911 51 Croydon Road Beckenham, enlisted Bromley.
Son of Samuel, grocer, and Emma Thrift.

TOMEI CONSTANTINE JOHN Private 10844 Queen's Own Royal West Kent Regiment 11th Bn.
Died 19/9/1916 age 18 Grave Sp. Mem. 18 HEILLY STATION CEMETERY MERICOURT-L'ABBE.
Son of Raffaillo and Settima Tomei of 2 Phoenix Rd, Penge.

TOMEI PHILIP Private 52140 Lincolnshire Regiment 7th Bn.
Died 25/8/1918 age 19 Grave Q.III.I. 19. ST.SEVER CEMETERY EXTENSION ROUEN.
Brother of Constantine John.

TONG EDWIN WILLIAM Lance Corporal G/24494 Middlesex Regiment 2nd Bn.
Killed in action 6/5/1917 Pier and Face 12D & 13B THIEPVAL MEMORIAL.
Born Beckenham, enlisted Chiswick.

TOOMEY GEORGE T Private G/12952 Royal West Kent Regiment.
Killed in action 7/10/1916 Pier and Face 11C THIEPVAL MEMORIAL.
Born Beckenham 1891, son of widow Mary at 21 Tennyson Rd in 1901 with two older brothers, was working as an assistant to Mr Kelly wine seller at 17 Green Lane Penge in 1911. Husband of Mrs Toomey of Whateley Rd, Penge with young baby. BJ 4/11/1916.

TOVEY GEOFFREY THOMAS Rifleman 385052 London Regiment (Post Office Rifles) 2nd/8th Bn.
Died 20/9/1917 Panel 54 YPRES MENIN GATE MEMORIAL.

Son of Thomas and Ellen Tovey of 22 Westbourne Rd, Sydenham.

TOVEY JACK OWEN Rifleman 551912 London Regiment (Queen's Westminster Rifles) C Coy.
Died 20/8/1918 age 22 Grave V.F.7 BEACON CEMETERY SAILLY-LAURETTE.
Son Mrs E Tovey of 22 Westbourne Rd, Sydenham, brother of Geoffrey.

TOWSE CLIFFORD HENRY Captain Queen's Own Royal West Kent Regiment B Coy 6th Bn. Served in S African Campaign.
Killed during shelling of the trenches 8/11/1915 age 45 Panel 95 to 97 LOOS MEMORIAL.
Son of William Beckwith Towse and Rosetta; husband of Mary Rowse of 9 Westmoreland Rd, Bromley. Recruiting officer for Beckenham at beginning of the war.

TREMBATH ALAN (ALLAN) EDWARD DCM Captain London Regiment (Prince of Wales' Own Civil Service Rifles) 15th Bn.
Died 26/05/1915 Grave I. D. 17. BROWN'S ROAD MILITARY CEMETERY, FESTUBERT.
Son of Henry Gough, husband of Lucy Mabel nee Gront married 1911 in Isleworth.
Born 1879, lived 19 Westfield Rd, Beckenham.

TUCKER LIONEL EDWARD Sapper 454755 Royal Engineers 20th T.F. Depot R E.
Died home 09/04/1918 age 27 Grave W5. 7566.BECKENHAM CREMATORIUM AND CEMETERY.
Son of John, gas fitter, and Emily Tucker; husband of Florence May Tucker, of 11, Phoenix Rd., Penge, born Thornton Heath, lived 20 Palace Road Penge, enlisted Bromley.

TULL G Two matches in CWGC: Rifleman S/35962 Rifle Brigade 2nd Bn. died 28/5/1918 Grave 1829 RETHEL FRENCH NATIOJNAL CEMETERY or Able Seaman London Z/3018 RNVR Howe Bn. RN div Grave III.F.25. POINT DU JOUR MILITARY CEMETERY ATHENS.

TURNER J 387 matches in CWGC.

TURNER S 93 matches in CWGC.

TURVEY ALBERT EDWARD Lance Corporal 17634 Dorsetshire Regiment 1st Bn.
Killed in action 3/9/1916 age 37 Panel 76 LOOS MEMORIAL.
Husband of Minnie of 23 Yew Tree Rd, Beckenham.

TWEEN FREDERICK CHARLES Private 2933 Queen's Own Royal West Kent Regiment 6th Bn.
Died of wounds 14/3/1916 Grave V.B.29. BETHUNE TOWN CEMETERY.
Lived 75 Ravenscroft Rd and employed at Sherlock's in Beckenham Rd for three years before the war.

TWEEN JOHN (JACK) Private 4264 Queen's Own Royal West Kent 8th Bn.
Died from gas poisoning 4/9/1916 age 18 IV.B.61. HEILLY STATION CEMETERY MERICOURT-L'ABBE.
Brother of Fred, they were both employed at Mr Sherlock's Stores in Beckenham Rd and lived at 75 Ravenscroft Rd according to report in BJ of Jack's death. Jack was Austin John in 1911 census when their address was 88 Churchfields Rd.

TYSON T E Lance Corporal 10229 Welsh Regiment 2nd Bn.
Died 7/11/1914 Grave 2.17. LES GONARDS CEMETERY VERSAILLES.

UMNEY CECIL FRANCIS Second Lieutenant Dorsetshire Regiment 7th Bn. attd. 5th Bn.
Killed in action 26/09/1916 age 20 Grave VIII. E. 5.C REGINA TRENCH CEMETERY, GRANDCOURT.
Son of William Francis, Doctor of medicine, and Beatrice Ethel Umney of Lawrie Park Rd., Sydenham.

UNDERWOOD WALTER OLIVER Rifleman 10902 King's Royal Rifle Corps 4th Bn.
Killed in action 24/04/1915 Panel 51 and 53. YPRES (MENIN GATE) MEMORIAL.
Son of Walter and Mary Underwood 42 Beckenham Rd, husband of Lily Camelia Underwood, of 27 Thayer's Farm Rd., Beckenham. Born Brixton, lived Beckenham, enlisted London, 1911 123 Mackenzie Road Beckenham.

UPTON PERCY Private 18663 Princess Charlotte of Wales's Royal Berkshire Regiment 8th Bn.
Died of wounds 24/03/1916 age 28 Grave V. B. 8. LILLERS COMMUNAL CEMETERY.
Son of Joseph and Charlotte Sarah Upton, of 47, Kent House Rd., Beckenham. Born Holloway, enlisted Reading.

VOLCKMAN KENNETH PERKS Private 26702 Grenadier Guards No. 4 Coy. 2nd Bn.
Died of wounds 03/10/1918 age 27 Grave XVI. E. 4. GREVILLERS BRITISH CEMETERY.
Born Dulwich, occupation draper, enlisted Newcastle. Son of Charles and Elizabeth Volckman.

WADE JOHN ETHER Service not found.
Son of George Ether and Rose of 37 St Margaret's Rd, Elmers End, Beckenham.
Born 1895 Camberwell, brother to William.

WADE WILLIAM Private G/1680 The Buffs East Kent Regiment 7th Bn.
Killed in action 1/7/1916 age 23 Pier and Face 5D THIEPVAL MEMORIAL.
Eldest son of Mr George Ether and Rose Wade of 37 St Margaret's Rd, Elmers End, an old boy of St James's Schools and member of St James's Men's Social Club. Report BJ 29/7/1916.

WAKEFIELD WILLIAM H Gunner RGA
Enlisted 7/ 10/ 1916 age 31, Beckenham postman, elder son of Mr W Wakefield of 8 Thayers Farm Rd.
BJ 8/9/1917.

WAKENELL GEORGE EDWARD Private 240157 Queen's Own (Royal West Kent Regiment) 1st/5th Bn.
Died 29/10/1916 age 21 Grave XXI. N. 44. BAGHDAD (NORTH GATE) WAR CEMETERY.
Son of Arthur (horse keeper) and Priscilla Wakenell, of 126, Croydon Road (1901) Beckenham. Born Forest Hill, enlisted Beckenham.

WALKER C M Rifleman A/201566 King's Royal Rifle Corps 20th Bn.
Died 26/9/1917 age 20 Grave G.1. WESTOUTRE BRITISH CEMETERY.

Son of Frederick Charles and Alice Maud Mary Walker of Mayfield 4 Barnmead Rd, Beckenham.

WALL EDWARD WILLIAM Private 25158 The Loyal North Lancashire Regiment 9th Bn.
Died 07/07/1916 age 22 Pier and Face 11 A. Memorial THIEPVAL MEMORIAL.
Son of Edward, boot repairer, and Ellen Jane Wall, of 28, Station Rd., Penge, London.

WALSH WILLIAM E Private 81864 Royal Defence Corps 168th Protection Coy.
Died 29/1/1919 Grave S7. 7825 BECKENHAM CREMATORIUM & CEMETERY.
Was permanently unwell after being gassed and contracted influenza while working at the docks in Grimsby.
Of 132 Blandford Rd. BJ 1/3/1919.

WARD CHARLES Private 41951 Bedford Regiment C Coy 4th Bn.
Killed in action 10/5/1918 age 18 Grave I.F.2. ENGLEBELMER COMMUNAL CEMETERY FRANCE.
Son of Mr and Mrs C G Ward of Tennyson Rd, Penge. Was employed at Abbey School, Beckenham.
BJ 1/6/1918

WARD REGINALD Private 15556 Duke of Cornwall's Light Infantry 1st Bn.
Died of wounds 07/11/1917 age 20 Grave XXI. GG. 15A. LIJSSENTHOEK MILITARY CEMETERY.
Son of Eliza Potter (formerly Ward), of 28, Crampton Rd., Penge, London, and the late William Ward. Born Peckham, enlisted Lewisham. Also served in Salonika and previously wounded at Armentieres.

WARMAN CECIL NELSON Private 350430 London Regiment 7th Bn.
Killed in action 07/10/1916 age 21 Grave I. K. 21. WARLENCOURT BRITISH CEMETERY.
Son of Albert Henry (compositor) and Mary A. E. Warman, of 29, St. John's Rd., Penge. Enlisted Sun St.

WARREN W 82 records in CWGC.

WATKINS HARRY Private 39332 Essex Regiment 1st Bn.
Died 5/4/1918 age 35 Bay 7 ARRAS MEMORIAL.
Son of the late Mr F G and Mrs M Watkins of Caterham; husband of
Florence Ethel Marian Watkins of 70, Durban Rd, Beckenham.

WATTS T S There are two possibles in the CWGC. Thomas Samuel of
Royal Sussex Reg 2nd Bn. died 21/11/1915 Loos and Thomas Sidney of
Royal West Surrey 6th Bn. died age 19 29/2/1916 Bethune son of Walter
Wordsworth and Elizabeth E Watts of Camberwell.

WEATHERILL ARTHUR FREDERICK Private G/5451 Queen's Own
Royal West Kent Regiment 8th Bn.
Died 26/9/1915 Panel 95 to 97 LOOS MEMORIAL.
Son of Frederick and Lucy Weatherill of 2 Railway View, Crampton Rd,
Penge.

WEATHERILL F J Not in CWGC.

WEATHERILL F W Possibly is Lance Corporal Frederick W 8416 of the
Border Reg and 99952 Corporal of the Liverpool Reg from the National
Archives. Not in the CWGC. ERNEST WEATHERILL was killed on
15/2/1917 age 20, Private in the Buffs 1st/5th Bn. and is remembered grave
XXI.M.1 AMARA WAR CEMETERY, IRAQ. He is reported in the BJ
1917 as the son of Ernest and Rose Weatherill of 15 Tennyson Rd with four
other sons, Frederick, John, Sidney, Charley and son-in-law in the army.
Frederick in the 1911 census is described as a soldier born 1890. Is he
either Weatherill F J or F W?

WEBB ALBERT EDWARD Gunner 95163 Royal Field Artillery 63rd Bde.
Died 30/07/1916 age 22 Screen Wall X5. 3. 7145. BECKENHAM
CREMATORIUM AND CEMETERY.
Son of Robert and Rosina Webb, of 39, Parish Lane, Penge, London.

WEBB FREDERICK GEORGE Private G/1032 Queen's Own Royal West
Kent Regiment 8th Bn.
Died 21/3/1918 age 22 Panel 58 & 59 POZIERES MEMORIAL.
Son of Robert T E and Rosina Webb of 39 Parish Lane, Penge.

WELLS C R Lance Corporal 13385 Yorkshire Regiment 8th Bn.
Died 3/8/1916 Grave A.1.ORPINGTON ALL SAINTS CHURCHYARD
EXTENSION.

WENDT GEORGE NORMAN Private 6290 London Regiment (P.W.O.
Civil Service Rifles) (County of London) 15th Bn. Formerly 4765, 28th
London Regt.
Killed in action 26/9/1916 Pier and Face 9D, 9C, 12C. THIEPVAL
MEMORIAL.
Lived Wimbledon, enlisted Dukes Rd, born Beckenham abt 1897.1901 18,
Manor Road, Beckenham. Son of Annie Wendt.

WEST, ALFRED GEORGE Gunner 203122 Royal Horse Artillery and
Royal Field Artillery "D" Bty. 123rd Bde.
Killed in action 24/08/1918 age 30 Grave XIX. F. 6.BIENVILLERS
MILITARY CEMETERY.
Husband of Gertrude West, of 172, Mackenzie Rd., Beckenham.

WEST T There are at least 30 possibilities on CWGC.

WEST W W Five possibles on CWGC.

WESTCOTT WILLIAM ERNEST Second Lieutenant 6689 Royal Air
Force 8th Training Sqdn.
Died 28/04/1918 age 19 Grave S2. BECKENHAM CREMATORIUM
AND CEMETERY.
Son of Francis Henry and Elizabeth Westcott, of 11, Barnmead Rd.,
Beckenham.

WESTLAKE H Out of eight on CWGC one born Croydon.

WESTON STANLEY VALENTINE MM 2nd Lieutenant Machine Gun
Corps Infantry.
Died 18/2/1919 S7.7859 BECKENHAM CREMATORIUM &
CEMETERY.
Son of Charles and Alice of 7 Wiverton Rd, Penge.

WHEELER HARRY LLOYD 2nd Lieutenant The Buffs (East Kent
Regiment) 9th Bn.

Died 26/12/1915 age 20 Grave II. L. 6. BETHUNE TOWN CEMETERY. Son of Richard Lloyd Wheeler and Susan Elizabeth Wheeler, of Radford House, 100, Lennard Rd., Beckenham.

WHEELER LEONARD CARTWRIGHT Sergeant 703324 London Regiment 1st/23rd Bn.
Died7/6/1917 age 27 Panels 52 to 54 YPRES MENIN GATE MEMORIAL.
Brother of Harry Lloyd Wheeler.

WHITE ALFRED W Private 509 A Co Royal West Kent. 7th Bn.
Killed in action 3/5/1917 Bay 7 ARRAS MEMORIAL.
Husband of Mrs White of 70 Kimberley Rd, Beckenham. BJ 26/5/1917

WHITE GEORGE WILLIAM Private G/12297 The Buffs East Kent Regiment 1st Bn. transferred to 437851 434th Agricultural Coy Labour Corps.
Died 23/2/1918 home Screen Wall X5. 2. 7506 BECKENHAM CREMATORIUM AND CEMETERY.
Born Burgess Hill, Sussex Lived Beckenham. Enlisted Bromley. Son of George William Baptist Minister and Sophia Nelson White.

WHITE WILLIAM THOMAS Private T/205185 Queen's Royal West Surrey Regiment 8th Bn.
Died 31/7/1917 age 36 Panel 11-13 and 14. YPRES MENIN GATE MEMORIAL.
Son of the late Thomas and Clara White of Balfour Rd, Bromley Common; husband of Ethel Elizabeth White of 16 Faversham Rd, Beckenham. BJ 2/8/1919

WHITTAKER H 37 records in CWGC.

WILD BENJAMIN THOMAS GEORGE Private 241641 East Surrey Regiment 1/6th Bn.
Killed in action 5/1/1918 Aden Plot 3.7. MAALA CEMETERY.
Lived 1911 5 Kelsey Square, Beckenham. Enlisted Bromley. Husband of Maud Mary Weatherley married 1908.

WILD HERMANN CAESAR Private 9867 Honourable Artillery Company.
Died 16/5/1917 age 32 A.12B. BOISGUILLAUME COMMUNAL

CEMETERY EXTENSION.
Son of dealer in precious stones, Gustav and Ida Wild of 9 Cator Rd, Beckenham.

WILLIAMS H 444 records in CWGC.

WILLIAMS J 823 records.

WILLIAMS N F No matches in CWGC.

WILLIS A H Six possibilities in CWGC.

WILLIS JOHN Private S/469 Queen's Own (Royal West Kent Regiment) 1st Bn.
Died 30/07/1916 age 35 Pier and Face 11 C.THIEPVAL MEMORIAL.
Husband of Harriet Willis, of 16, Sultan St, Beckenham, married 1905. Son of William and Mary Jane Willis born 1881.

WILLIS THOMAS Driver T4/084457 Royal Army Service Corps.
Died 14/4/1919 age 48 Grave Screen Wall X6.2.7927 BECKENHAM CREMATORIUM & CEMETERY. Husband of Esther Willis of 36 Churchfields Rd. Son of William and Mary Jane Willis, brother of John Willis.

WILLS FRANK GORDON Lance Corporal 290752 Bedfordshire Regiment 1st Bn.
Died 30/09/1918 age 31 Grave XII. D. 14. GREVILLERS BRITISH CEMETERY.
Son of Mr. and Mrs. James Wills; husband of Ellen Wills, of 35, Ravenscroft Rd., Beckenham. Born at Dartford.

WILSON O C Four records in CWGC. Possible is Private M2/266969 RASC 820th Coy.
Died 10/12/1918 Grave 1574 KIKRA BRITISH CEMETERY KALAMARIA, GREECE.

WIMBLE HERBERT REGINALD Corporal London Regiment (London Rifle Brigade) 1st/5th Bn.
Died 03/05/1915 age 29 Panel 52 and 54.YPRES (MENIN GATE)

MEMORIAL.
Son of Charles and Clara Jane Wimble, of The Royal Victoria Hotel, St. Leonards-on-Sea, Sussex. 1911 Thirlmere 25 Southend Road, Beckenham. Enlisted, Aug. 1914. Born Beckenham 1886. Broker's clerk.

WINCH WILLIAM HAFFENDEN Lieutenant The Buffs A Coy 1st/5th Bn. Died of wounds 13/1/1916 age 21 Grave V.L.12 BASRA WAR CEMETERY. Son of William Francis and Jane Swinford Winch, educated The Abbey, Beckenham and Repton, enlisted four days after outbreak of war, left for India November 1914 and in December 1915 to Mesopotamia. BJ 12/2/1916.

WINN J 18 records on CWGC.

WINTERTON WILLIAM Gunner 275381 Royal Garrison Artillery 1st Lowland Heavy Bty.
Died 23/9/1918 age 36 Grave G.14. SUN QUARRY CEMETERY CHERISY.
Son of Thomas and Sarah born abt 1980, lived Alexandra Cottages, Penge.

WIST W W No men of this name in CWGC, census or BMDs. The nearest is George W Wist born 1884, a footman at Queens Gate.

WITHERS GEORGE FREDERICK Lance Corporal R/16616 King's Royal Rifle Corps 7th Bn.
Killed in action 06/12/1917 age 38 Panel 115 to 119 and 162A and 163A. TYNE COT MEMORIAL.
Husband of Nina E. Withers, of "Kiaora", Addington Grove, Sydenham, London. Born Birkenhead. Lived Sydenham, enlisted Finsbury Barracks, Middx. 1901 79, Kingshall Road, Beckenham.

WODE W none on CWGC.

WOOD WILLIAM Corporal 2560 Middx Regiment 4th Bn., previously from 1899 RWK 2nd Bn. in China, India and Boer War 1901/2.
Died 12/8/1918. Grave V.B.11. ST AMAND BRITISH CEMETERY.
Elder son of the late Mr W and Mrs Wood of Sultan St, Beckenham and husband of A H Wood of 16 Thesiger Rd, Penge, with four small boys. BJ 31/8/1918.

WOOLWARD WALTER Sergeant 24142 East Surrey Regiment7th Bn.
Died of wounds 10/08/1917 age 40 Grave VI. B. 28. DUISANS BRITISH
CEMETERY, ETRUN.
Son of William and Mary Ann Woolward, of Lodge 2, Friars Ford, Goring.
Born Penge abt 1878, enlisted Rotherhithe, attestation date 13/9/1898.

WORSLEY HENRY Private 203516 Queen's Own (Royal West Kent
Regiment) 2nd/4th Bn.
Died 15/05/1917 age 18 Grave D. 127. ALEXANDRIA (HADRA) WAR
MEMORIAL CEMETERY.
Son of Joseph and Lucy Worsley, lived Beckenham.

WRIGHT REGINALD A possibly 4910 Rifleman London Irish Rifles.
Died 15/9/1916 XVI.F.6 CATERPILLAR VALLEY CEMETERY
LONGUEVAL.
From CWGC.

YATES EDWARD HENRY Private 11315 Irish Guards 1st Bn.
Died of wounds 15/04/1917 Grave N. 174214. BROMPTON CEMETERY.
Husband of Amy Yates, of 75, Streatham Hill, Brixton, London. 1901 41,
High Street, Beckenham. Son of Henry and Amelia Yates of 12 Bevington
Rd, Beckenham. BJ p3 23/3/1917 in French hospital.

YOUELS HARRY ALBERT Private 1149 Royal Fusiliers 22nd Bn.
Killed in action 24/05/1916 age 28 Grave II. A. 4. ZOUAVE VALLEY
CEMETERY, SOUCHEZ.
Son of George Thomas and Elizabeth Youels of 22, Oakhill Rd., Beckenham.
Born Limehouse lived Beckenham. Enlisted Shepherd's Bush.

YOUNG THOMAS HUNTINGTON Sergeant R/4300 King's Royal Rifle
Corps 13th Bn. Served in the South African War. 22 years' service.
Died 14/07/1916 age 43 Pier and Face 13 A and 13 B. THIEPVAL
MEMORIAL.
Son of Thomas Anthony Young, of 73, Queen's Rd., Beckenham, Kent;
husband of Sarah Ann Young, of 53, Limerston St., King's Rd., Chelsea,
London.

Chapter Thirteen: Alfred Jethro Shearing and other Beckenham families

Alfred Jethro Shearing was born in Leatherhead in 1870 and married Edith Annie Edser, also from Leatherhead, in Wandsworth in 1903. Their sons Alfred James and Frederick Charles were born in Knightsbridge and Clapham in 1904 and 1906 respectively but Winifred Edith, Frank Edwin and Arthur William were born in Beckenham in 1908, 1911 and 1914 when they were living at 32 St George's Rd. Alfred was a council fireman for 13 years and was subsequently housed at 8 Church Rd.

The memorial board in St George's church, Beckenham

The fire station was originally developed by Peter Hoare of Kelsey Manor in 1869 at the corner of Kelsey Square to take a horse-drawn fire engine in charge of Captain Charles Purvis. He was a tenant of Foxgrove farm where the firemen practised but in 1882 the local authority took over and adapted the stables of the manor house as a fire station. The firemen used the houses either of Church Rd or St George's Rd until 1929 when council houses were built at the back of the fire station. Beckenham's Fire Brigade was the most efficient in the whole London area. By 1913 it was using motorised fire engines but things were to change for Alfred Shearing when he, as a member of the RNVR, volunteered at the beginning of the war in 1914.

The trawler H.M. Loch Naver launched in Aberdeen in 1906 was requisitioned in February 1915 as a minesweeper in the RN. Alfred became an able seaman in the RNVR and transferred to the RN where he became a PO on the Loch Naver and responsible for mine laying throughout the war. It was hard for his children who attended Bromley Rd School because they were bullied over the fact that their father was not serving at the front and was still alive. However at about 2pm on 13 May 1918, the Alexandria lighthouse keeper off Mindisi Point in the Aegean Sea reported the disappearance of a trawler in a cloud of smoke. The Loch Naver had been destroyed by a torpedo from the German submarine UC74 and all 13 hands were lost.

He is remembered on the Portsmouth naval memorial described as the son of James and Mary Ann Shearing of 19 Heathfield Rd, Bromley and husband of Edith Annie Shearing of 23 Raymond Rd, Beckenham. Among Edith's treasures were many cards sent from abroad during Alfred's time at sea when he could not get home to his family.

Alfred was Mary Hardcastle's grandfather and Winifred Edith her mother who married John Moutrie Hardcastle in 1936. Mary was a Beckenham schoolteacher and headmistress of Worsley Bridge Rd Primary School from 1989 to 1997. She believes that there was a memorial board to Alfred in the Beckenham Town Hall which is now at the Bromley Museum but certainly his name is on the memorial behind the lectern in St George's parish church. Alfred was the great-grandfather of another relative, Jim Shearing. Jim is a pilot in South Africa but is Mary's first cousin once removed since he is the son of Frederick Charles's son, Anthony Michael.

Four of the five children of Alfred were educated by the Admiralty. The two eldest attended the Royal Naval College, Greenwich and Mary's mother Winifred won a scholarship to the Beckenham County School for Girls where she was one of the first intake of 153 girls at the age of 10 in 1919.

Frank missed out as the Admiralty's generosity stopped at child three but restarted in time for Arthur to benefit at the Beckenham & Penge Grammar School for Boys, which was hard for Frank. However he proved his ability with his work at the displays of the Festival of Britain in 1951. Mary followed her mother at the County School in 1948.

Beckenham Fire Brigade about 1900 IM

The Family of Vernon Finch

On the left-hand side of the St George and the dragon memorial board there are two members of the family of William Finch born 1859 Clerkenwell and Rona Amy Elizabeth Scott from Totnes, Devon born 1863. They were living at 8 Fairfield Rd in 1911 when they had been married for 26 years and had had 12 children, 8 still living.

They all had the most wonderful names, the three girls, Beatrice Frances Violet Helen Finch born Camberwell 1897, Gladys Edith Ruthen Finch and Constance Jessie Muriel Finch born last of the family in Beckenham. They became the Aunts Beat, Gladys and Muriel.

The five boys from Camberwell were Arthur William Bernard b 1870, Cyril Gemullas Finch b 1891, Leonard Basil Ary b 1893, Vernon's father, Ernest Wilfred Rupert b 1895 and Aubrey Malcolm Cecil born 1897 but Cyril died at the age of 18 in 1910 leaving just four boys. Arthur was a solicitor's clerk, Leonard was employed as a clerk on the Beckenham council and Ernest was a clerk in marine insurance. Their father, William, was a civil servant working in the overseas department of the general post office.

Arthur joined the Royal Sussex as a 2nd Lt and moved to the 3rd London

Rifles entering the war in France in September 1916. He was taken prisoner and did not return from captivity until March 1919 when all the local POWs were entertained to dinner at the public hall.

All their names were inscribed on a souvenir programme. On Saturday April 12 1919 he married Lily Hall in St George's church where he had been a chorister. Lily's sister Violet was the bridesmaid.

Leonard enlisted in the army on 21 June 1915 as a clerk in the labour corps of the Royal West Kents. He married Maud Lilian Wright in the summer of 1917 and they had three sons. Malcom Leonard was born in June 1919 and emigrated to Canada where he died in Toronto in 1970. Kenneth Rupert born in 1921 served in WWII as a warrant officer in the RAF and gained the DFM. He died in Worthing in 2006. Vernon is the youngest of the family and after attending the Beckenham & Penge Grammar School for Boys with his brothers he became a teacher at both Marian Vian and Pickhurst before moving to Bearsted. There he became a successful and much loved headmaster not only of the village school but also the larger Rosacre Junior School with 400 pupils.

Two of Vernon's uncles did not survive the war. They were both in the Seaforth Highlanders. Ernest Wilfred Rupert Finch died at the age of 21 on 7 August 1916 as Lt in the A Company of the 4th battalion and is buried at Puchevilier's British Cemetery. He had enlisted shortly after the outbreak of war and quickly promoted to company quartermaster sergeant from where he soon obtained his commission and was acting captain for several

months after returning to the front in July 1915. After a year of trench warfare and recent severe fighting he fell mortally wounded by a bursting shell. He died on 7 August 1916 in a casualty station. He was well known locally as a footballer and cricketer and would be widely missed in Beckenham.

Aubrey Malcolm Cecil Finch was a captain serving in Russia when he was murdered at Archangel at the age of 22 in 7 July 1919 and was buried in the Archangel cemetery at Semenovka. He had not long been married to Mabel Dorothy Glover living at 133 Kent House Rd. His parents had just left Beckenham to move to South

Aubrey Malcolm Cecil Finch VF

Down House in West Wickham, eventually Hawes Lane where Vernon remembers visiting as a small boy.

Victor Watts 1896 to 1899 – the Centurion Pictures CW

Victor Lindley Watts was born in 35 Barnmead Road, Beckenham on 21 February 1896. Later his parents and two older brothers moved to a nine roomed house called 'Camelot' at 5 Kings Hall Road from where Victor went to St Dunstan's College for Boys in Catford.

Victor left St Dunstan's, age 16, in 1912. Two years later at the outbreak of WW1, he joined 'G' Company of the 2nd Battalion of the then 20th London Regiment. For two years he served in France with the British Expeditionary Force. Promoted to a sergeant, Victor returned to England in June 1917 and was commissioned into the Essex Regiment.

Three months later he joined the Royal Flying Corps and completed his pilot's course in August 1918. He transferred to 13 Squadron in the newly-formed Royal Air Force and was soon patrolling the front line in France in his single engine RE.8 biplane.

Only 13 days before the end of war, Pilot-officer Watts was shot down by German fighters over no man's land. His observer was killed outright and when the plane crashed both Victor's legs were severely damaged. Despite his injuries he managed to struggle out of the wreckage but fell back against the engine sustaining multiple burns.

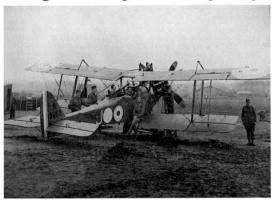

It was some time before he was picked up because a rescue party had assumed that neither of the two men could have survived. As a result, Victor spent many months in various hospitals. His right leg was amputated but this did stop him playing golf nor working as a civil servant with the Inspectorate of Armaments at Woolwich Arsenal. He retired to Eastbourne where he celebrated his centenary in 1996. He died three years later.

The photo below shows Victor's medals. In addition to **Pip, Squeak and Wilfred** i.e. the 1914-15 Star, the British War Medal and Victory Medal, on the right is the Knight medal of the French *Légion d'honneur* awarded in 1998 to all surviving veterans of the First World War from any allied country who had fought on French soil, as part of the commemoration of the 80th anniversary of the war's end.

This account comes from Colin Watts and Cliff Watkins of Beckenham.

Denis Manger's Tale of his family in WWI

Denis's grandfather, Herbert Edward Manger, born 1871 and father, Leslie Manger born 1896 both served in WWI and survived the carnage. The family lived at 18 Westfield Rd in Beckenham and consisted of Herbert with his wife Kathleen born 1870 and their three children all born in Beckenham, Emmie in 1893, Leslie in 1896 and Jack in 1905.

Herbert's parents, Henry and Selina Manger, had moved into Beckenham by the 1881 census when they settled in Gloucester Villas, later to become 30 St George's Rd. Their children were Emily, George and Charles Ernest all born near Sandwich, Herbert Edward born at Margate and William,

From L to R, Jack, Emmie, Herbert, Kathleen, and Leslie in 1914 DM

Eleanor and Mary born in Beckenham.

Herbert was a rate collector who had formerly served in the 2nd Volunteer Battalion of the Queen's Own Royal West Kent Regiment and so when he enlisted in the 10th battalion on 27 September 1914 he was appointed corporal followed by sergeant on the 1 December as in the above photograph. By May 1915 he had been promoted to regimental quartermaster sergeant. He did not serve abroad until in the BEF on 3 May 1916, serving in Etaples, Cayeux and Ecavet in 1917. In March 1919 he was transferred to the Reserve and demobbed, receiving the Meritorious Service Medal in recognition of his services in France and Flanders. This was announced in the London Gazette 3 June 1919 by which time he was approaching the age of 50.

Regimental Sergeant Major Herbert Edward Manger in 1915 DM

Leslie and Dorothy DM

Leslie was a bank clerk with the London City and Midland Bank in their Bromley branch. He joined the HAC (Honorary Artillery Company) on 4 October 1915 spending 261 days in France where he received back injuries in November 1916 that made him unsuitable for service abroad. He was finally discharged in January 1919 and returned to his work at the bank. He married in 1929 at Christ Church and he and his wife Dorothy Kate Harmer had three children, Geoffrey who lives in Australia, Valerie in Leicestershire and Denis who still lives in Beckenham. Their mother Dorothy lived until she was 101!

Herbert's brother, Charles Ernest, and his wife Gertrude Annie from Rowden Rd in Beckenham both worked for the council as relieving officers and Register of Births and Deaths. They had two sons, Eric and Guy born in 1898 and 1900. Like his cousin Jack, Guy missed active service but Eric was not so lucky. He followed Leslie into the HAC in April 1916 and became a 2nd lieutenant in the 2nd Machine Gun Corps but this was a very risky appointment. He was killed in Belgium on 10 July 1917, aged only 19. His grave is in the Ramscapella Rd Military Cemetery.

Rev the Hon Maurice Berkeley Peel, MC, 1873-1917

Sir Robert Peel the younger

The Rev Maurice Peel lived at the vicarage, Eyeworth House, 17 Park Rd, Beckenham with his wife Emily when he was the vicar of St Paul's church, Brackley Rd from 1909 – 1915. They had a baby boy called David Arthur born in Beckenham on 4 October 1910. They also had a daughter in March 1912 but Emily died five days later. Her life is commemorated in the beautiful font white marble angel at the back of the church where my three sons were baptised. The girl was baptised Mary Emily in the church on 23.5.1912.

The name Peel has grand origins because Maurice's father was Arthur Wellesley Peel,

The Tamworth pig

one-time speaker of the House of Commons and fifth son of Sir Robert Peel, 1788-1850, the immensely wealthy Tory and anti-Catholic, twice prime minister. As Home Secretary he had organised the London policemen as Peelers. Sir Robert was thrown from his horse on 29 June 1850 while riding up Constitution Hill and died as a result.

From St Paul's, the Rev Maurice transferred to Tamworth, Staffs in 1915, after he had been badly wounded when acting as chaplain to the 1st Royal Welsh Fusiliers at the Battle of Festubert in France. This battle took place between 15 and 25 May 1915 and was unsuccessful because the BEF lacked the heavy artillery with high-explosive shells that could destroy the enemy trenches. When this fact reached the newspapers it resulted in the downfall of the Asquith Liberal government. His father had grown up in Tamworth where the Peels had developed the Tamworth breed of pigs.

The Rev Maurice was awarded the MC from the King at Buckingham Palace on Monday August 30th 1915 as a most respected forces chaplain but he was killed in France on 15 May 1917 at Bullecourt, Pas de Calais, searching for the wounded at the front. His practice was to live with the men and in action to go over with the third wave, so that he might tend all those who had fallen earlier.

The Rev Maurice Peel from St Paul's archives

He would appear like a guardian angel to give succour to the wounded and prayers for the dying scattered among the ruins. He had bled to death after being shot through the stomach and his body was left in front of the church.

There is a statue of St George outside the Glascote parish church dedicated to his memory and his name also appears on the Beckenham war memorial. TW Thornton's published 'A Hero Saint', a memoir of the Rev Peel, by Gerald Sampson, vicar of St Paul's, & Maurice Berkeley Peel C F. M C. in 1917. A copy of this book exists in the St Paul's archives. There is more information on The Honourable Rev. Maurice Berkeley Peel MC in Jonathan Walker's book; 'Blood Tub: General Gough And The Battle Of Bullecourt, 1917'.

His son, David Arthur, was educated at Oxford and married the daughter of another well-known Tory, the Hon Sara Carola Vanneck, 1913-2001, on 14 April 1936. They had three sons and one daughter; Jonathan Sidney 1937, Charles David 1940, Robert Alexander 1943 and Julia Victoria Mary 1939. Their father, also MC, died bravely on 12 September 1944 as officer commanding no 1 squadron armoured battalion of the Irish Guards.

David's sister, Mary Emily, had committed suicide on 18.9.1934 by shooting herself with her brother's rifle. The Mercury of 22.9.1934 described the tragedy. Earlier on the same day she had been a bridesmaid at a friend's society wedding. David and Mary had been raised by their uncle, Col Sidney Peel after they were so cruelly orphaned.

The font, thought to be in the image of Emily Peel, in St Paul's church, Brackley Rd, Beckenham

Sgt Charles Albert Victor Lyford

Born in Hackney in 1882, Charles was fostered by a couple in Churchfields Rd when he was eight where he lived thereafter. His father had died of TB and his mother needed him cared for while she worked. He was happily married by 1916 with his wife Elizabeth and three children, Alice aged 8, John aged 4 and Clara 6 months but as a member of the Royal West Kents Regiment, he was on his way to India.

There were 5,000 from 34 regiments waiting for the Cunard troopship Coronia to sail from Devonport, Plymouth over Christmas 1916. Setting off down Plymouth Sound on 5 January 1917 they joined a convoy of six other troopships and one passenger ship, the Corinthic, bound for Australia. The other troopships were Empress of Britain, Walmer Castle, Nesta, Pakhea and Tyndarius escorted by the cruiser Shannon and nine destroyers travelling round the Cape of Good Hope to avoid the danger of submarines. It took a month to reach Cape Town. In his diary, Charles describes the awfulness of living aboard a coal-burning ship with filthy coal dust everywhere especially when refuelling at Free Town, Sierra Leone and the disgraceful food, consisting of boiled sausage, sour bread, rank margarine and hard peas except for the rare occasion when they had bully beef straight from the fridge. Leaving Cape Town on 15 February with the Empress of Britain and the escort Orkoma they called in at Durban and arrived in India on 3 March.

One man and three women are levelling the flints by hand before the steamroller flattens the road. The building in the background is one of the barracks where the soldiers lived. Most of their time in India was spent helping to lay roads.

Charles' son John was the father of Helen (Lyford) Oliver who lives in Beckenham and supplied us with the story of her grandfather. She possesses his diary and several photographs, commenting on his beautiful handwriting in the labelling on the backs.

Chapter Fourteen: Timeline

Date	Activity
06/28/14	Assassination of Francis Ferdinand at Sarajevo
07/05/14	Kaiser William II promised to support Austria v. Serbia
07/28/14	Austria declared war on Serbia
08/01/14	Germany declared war on Russia
08/03/14	Germany declared war on France and invaded Belgium
08/04/14	Britain declared war on Germany
08/06/14	Kitchener's call to arms for a one million strong land force to be called the New Army
08/13/14	B E F in France
08/23/14	B E F retreat from Mons
08/26/14	Russia defeated at Tannenberg
09/06/14	Start of battle of Marne
10/13/14	The VAD Red Cross Hospitals of Kent receive message to be ready
10/18/14	First battle of Ypres
10/29/14	Trench warfare begins to dominate and Turkey joins Germany in war
01/19/15	First Zeppelin raid on Britain
02/19/15	Britain bombarded Turkish forts in Dardanelles
04/25/15	Allied troops landed on Gallipoli. Australians commemorate landing with Anzac Day
05/07/15	Lusitania sank in 18 mins by U-boat, 1,915 died, 761 saved
05/23/15	Italy declared war on Germany and Austria
08/05/15	Germany captured Warsaw from Russia
09/25/15	Start of battle of Loos
10/13/15	Zeppelins bomb South London but hit housing although

	forbidden by the Kaiser
12/08/15	The four main Allies meet to decide future strategy. Haig replaces John French
12/19/15	Allies evacuate Gallipoli
01/27/16	CONSCRIPTION begins in Britain. Joffre proposes Spring offensive
02/21/16	Start of battle of Verdun. July 1st agreed for attack on the Somme
04/29/16	Britain surrenders to Turks in Mespotamia
05/31/16	Battle of Jutland
06/04/16	Start of Brusilov offensive
06/05/16	Lord Horatio Herbert Kitchener died when HMS Hampshire sunk by a mine
07/01/16	Start of battle of Somme with 60,000 casualties, many Pals
08/10/16	End of Brusilov offensive
09/15/16	Massive use of tanks at the Somme
12/07/16	Lloyd George becomes PM
02/01/17	Unrestricted submarine warfare by Germany
04/06/17	U S A declares war on Germany
04/16/17	France unsuccessful offensive on Western Front
07/31/17	Start of 3rd battle of Ypres
10/24/17	Italy heavily defeated at Caparetto
11/06/17	Britain 's major offensive on Western Front
11/20/17	Britain's tanks win at Cambrai
12/05/17	Armistice between Russia and Germany
12/09/17	Britain captured Jerusalem from Turks
01/01/18	Food rationing started in Britain with sugar
03/03/18	Treaty of Brest-Litovsk between Russia and Germany
03/21/18	Germany broke through on the Somme in operation Michael
03/29/18	Allied Commander on Western Front is Marshall Foch
04/09/18	German offensive in Flanders
04/30/18	Meat, cheese, butter, margarine rationed

07/15/18	2nd battle of Marne starts collapse of Germany
08/08/18	Allied advances until 2nd Battle of Somme defeats Germany in 100 days offensive
09/19/18	Collapse of Turks
10/04/18	Germany requests armistice
10/29/18	Mutiny of Germany's navy
10/30/18	Turkey made peace
11/03/18	Austria made peace
11/09/18	Kaiser William II abdicated
11/11/18	Germany signed armistice with Allies. Official end to the war
01/04/19	Peace conference in Paris
06/21/19	Surrendered German fleet scuttled at Scapa Flow
06/28/19	Treaty of Versailles
07/26/19	Beckenham's Peace Day held in Kelsey Park
07/24/21	Beckenham War Memorial unveiled by Bert Hanscombe

INDEX

INDEX

INDEX

INDEX

INDEX